THE
DERVISH WARS

THE
DERVISH WARS

Gordon and Kitchener in
the Sudan
1880–1898

ROBIN NEILLANDS

JOHN MURRAY
Albemarle Street, London

First published in 1996
by John Murray (Publishers) Ltd.,
50 Albemarle Street, London W1X 4BD

A catalogue record for this book is
available from the British Library

ISBN 0-7195-5631-7

Typeset in Linotron Baskerville by
Rowland Phototypesetting Ltd.,
Bury St Edmunds, Suffolk

Printed and bound in Great Britain by
The University Press, Cambridge

This one is for
Penny Visman
who knows and loves the Sudan

Contents

Illustrations

The author and publishers would like to thank the following for their permission to reproduce illustrations: The National Army Museum: Nos. 1, 10, 13, 15, 17, 22, 23, 26, 27, 29, 30, 33, 34, 36, 37; The Anne S. K. Brown Military Collection: 2, 3, 4, 5, 6, 7, 8, 9, 16, 18, 19, 21, 24, 25, 28, 31, 32; *The Illustrated London News*: 11, 14, 20; The Royal Regiment of Fusiliers Museum (Royal Warwickshire): 12, 35

Acknowledgements

A GREAT MANY people helped me with advice, contacts or information while I was researching and writing this book. My thanks therefore to Dr David Chandler, until recently Head of the Military History Department of the Royal Military Academy, Sandhurst; to Colonel Eric Peters of the Royal Engineers; and to the staff of the National Army Museum, London and the Royal Marines Museum, Southsea.

My thanks also to Geoff Rowcliffe for help in obtaining books I could not readily find in Britain, and to that doyen of Victorian military history, my new best friend, Byron Farwell, whose books on Victorian military life and characters are both highly informative and a pleasure to read. Thanks also to Estelle Huxley for typing and retyping a very complicated manuscript and getting it into shape.

Thanks also to the Royal Engineers Museum at Chatham and the Royal Artillery at Woolwich and a score of Regimental Museums around the country where relics of Omdurman and those other fierce little battles of long ago are kept in surprising quantities. My thanks must also go to John Sim and the staff of Kuoni Travel for their help during my visits to Egypt.

For her enthusiasm for the Sudan and the people who live there, my thanks go to Penny Visman who supplied me with all kinds of books and information from the time that she and her husband Peter lived in Port Sudan and forayed out to Suakin and along the desert road to Berber. I have tried to put together the story of these Dervish Wars and the Mahdiya in a way these friends will enjoy and I hope with their help I have succeeded. If not, the fault is entirely mine.

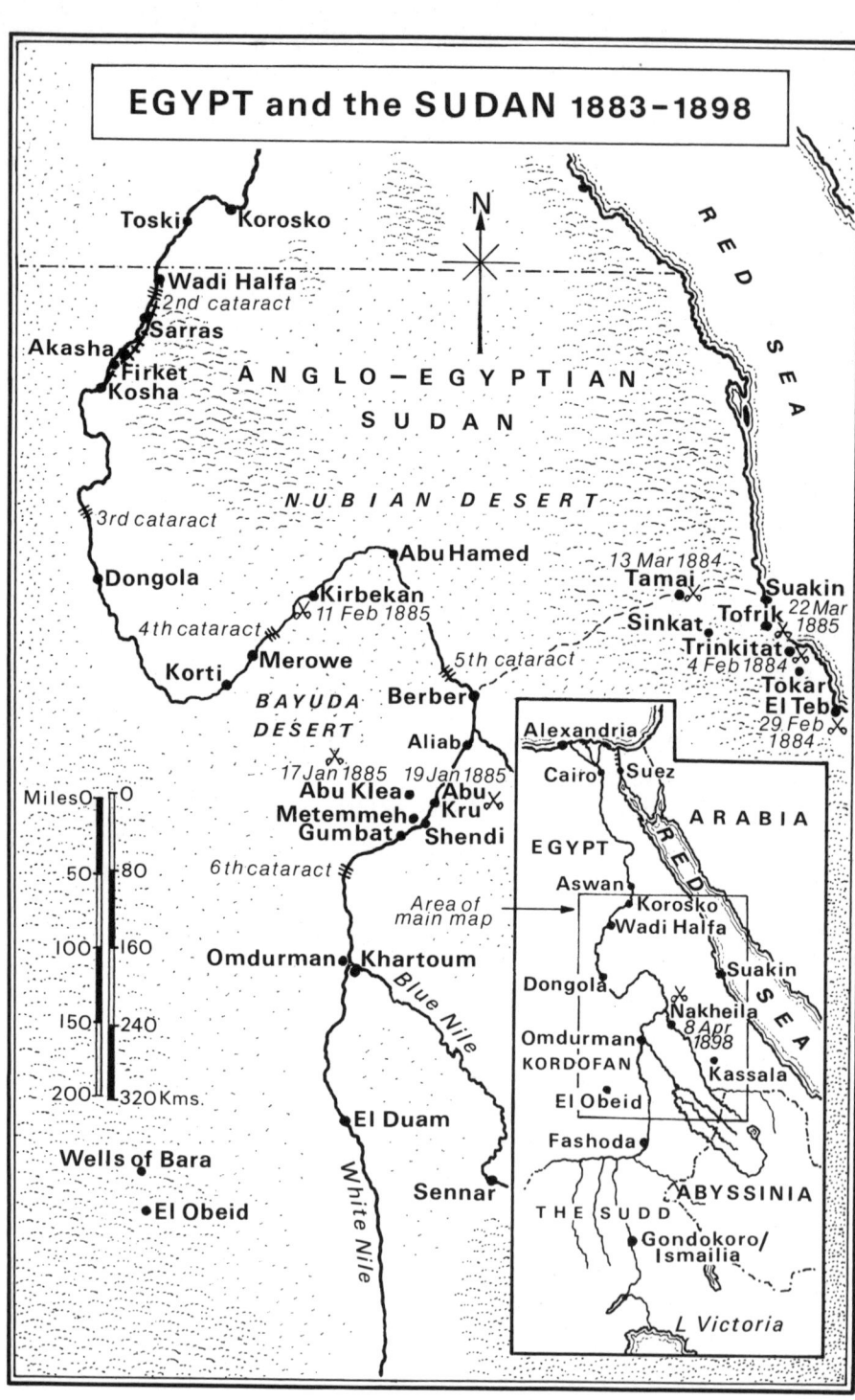

EGYPT and the SUDAN 1883–1898

N

Toski

Korosko

RED SEA

Wadi Halfa
2nd cataract
Sarras
Akasha
Firket
Kosha

A N G L O — E G Y P T I A N

S U D A N

N U B I A N   D E S E R T

3rd cataract

Dongola

4th cataract

Korti

Merowe

Abu Hamed

13 Mar 1884
Tamai
Sinkat

Suakin
Tofrik   22 Mar
           1885
Trinkitat
4 Feb 1884
Tokar
El Teb
29 Feb
1884

Kirbekan
11 Feb 1885

5th cataract

Berber

BAYUDA
DESERT

Aliab

17 Jan 1885   19 Jan 1885
Abu Klea   Abu
Metemmeh   Kru
Gumbat   Shendi

Miles 0   0

50   80

100   160

150   240

200   320 Kms.

6th cataract

Khartoum
Omdurman

Blue Nile

Alexandria
Cairo   Suez

ARABIA

EGYPT

Aswan

Korosko
Wadi Halfa

Dongola

Suakin

Nakheila
8 Apr
1898

Omdurman
KORDOFAN

Kassala

El Obeid

Fashoda

THE SUDD

ABYSSINIA

Gondokoro/
Ismailia

L Victoria

Area of
main map

Wells of Bara

El Obeid

El Duam

Sennar

White Nile

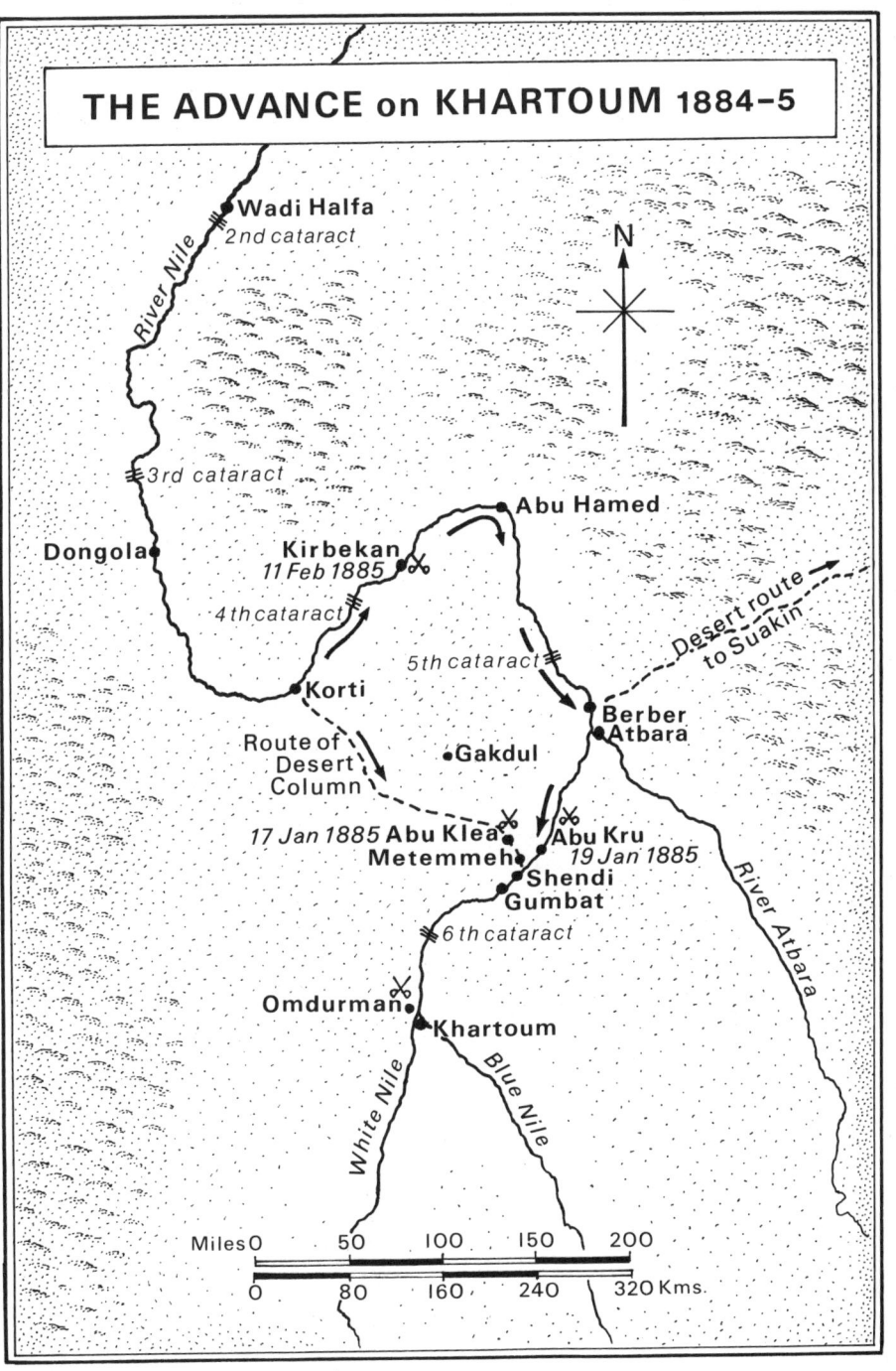

THE ADVANCE on KHARTOUM 1884–5

Wadi Halfa
2nd cataract

N

3rd cataract

Abu Hamed

Dongola

Kirbekan
11 Feb 1885

4th cataract

5th cataract

Desert route
to Suakin

Korti

Route of
Desert
Column

Gakdul

Berber
Atbara

17 Jan 1885 Abu Klea
Metemmeh

Abu Kru
19 Jan 1885

Shendi
Gumbat

6th cataract

River Atbara

Omdurman

Khartoum

White Nile

Blue Nile

River Nile

Miles 0   50   100   150   200
0   80   160   240   320 Kms.

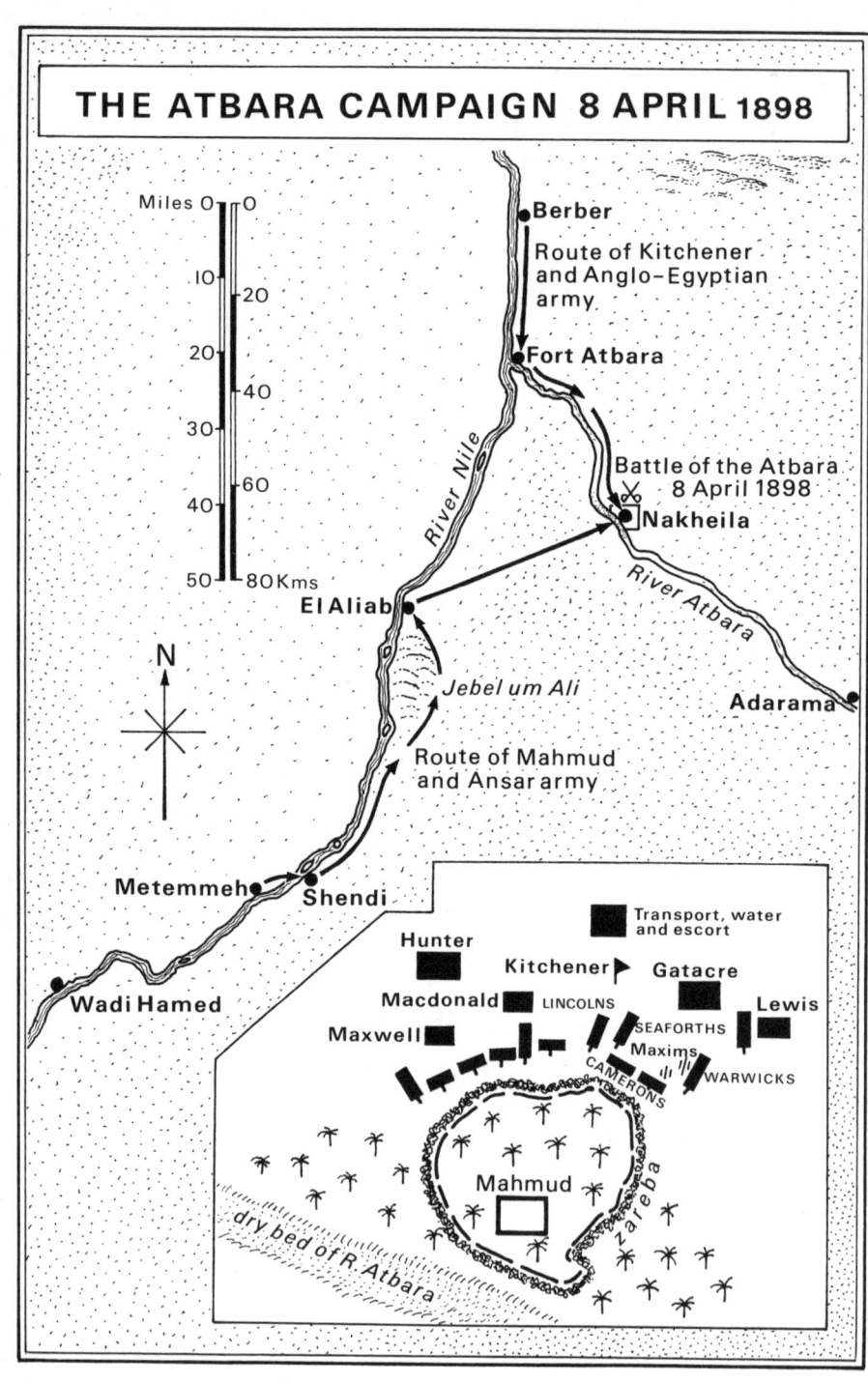

THE ATBARA CAMPAIGN 8 APRIL 1898

Miles 0 ⌐ 0

10 ─ 20

20 ─ 40

30 ─ 60

40

50 ─ 80 Kms

Berber

Route of Kitchener
and Anglo-Egyptian
army

Fort Atbara

Battle of the Atbara
8 April 1898

Nakheila

River Atbara

River Nile

El Aliab

Jebel um Ali

Adarama

N

Route of Mahmud
and Ansar army

Metemmeh

Shendi

Wadi Hamed

Transport, water
and escort

Hunter

Kitchener

Gatacre

Macdonald   LINCOLNS

Lewis

Maxwell

SEAFORTHS

Maxims

CAMERONS

WARWICKS

Mahmud

zareba

dry bed of R Atbara

THE ADVANCE to OMDURMAN,
24 AUGUST to 1 SEPTEMBER 1898

N

Wadi Hamed
23–26 Aug

Wadi Bishara

Shabluka Gorge

Shabluka

Jebel Royan
night of 27 Aug

Wadi el Abid
nights of 28,29 Aug

Sayal
night of 30 Aug

Sururab
night of
31 Aug

Kerreri
Hills

El Egeiga
night of 1 Sept

Jebel
Surgham

OMDURMAN

Blue Nile

White Nile

Khartoum
(ruins)

Miles 0   0
                  5
        5   10
               15
        10   20
               25
        15
        20   30 Kms

THE BATTLE of OMDURMAN, 2 SEPTEMBER 1898

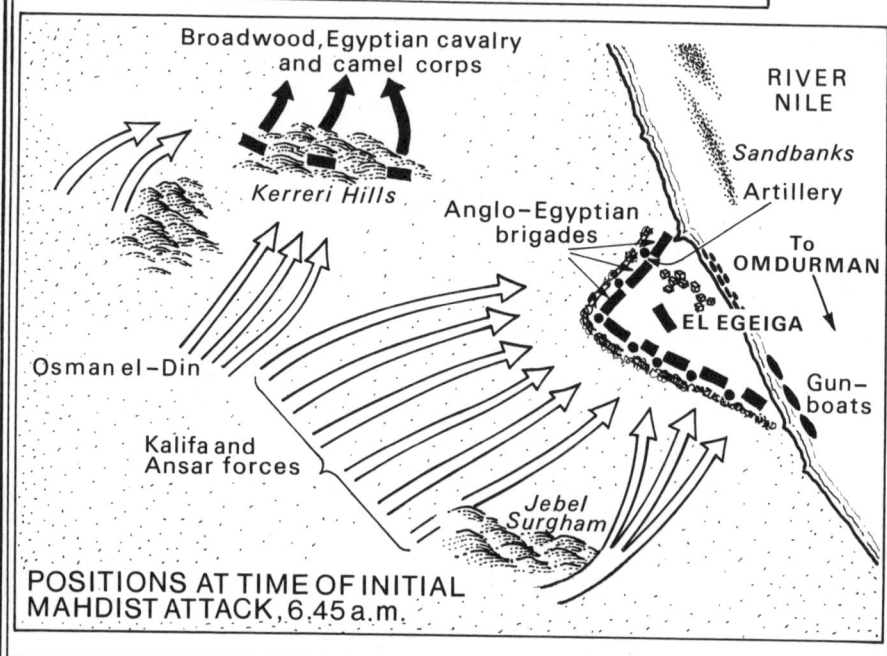

Broadwood, Egyptian cavalry and camel corps

RIVER NILE

Kerreri Hills

Anglo-Egyptian brigades

Sandbanks

Artillery

Osman el-Din

To OMDURMAN

EL EGEIGA

Kalifa and Ansar forces

Gun-boats

Jebel Surgham

POSITIONS AT TIME OF INITIAL MAHDIST ATTACK, 6.45 a.m.

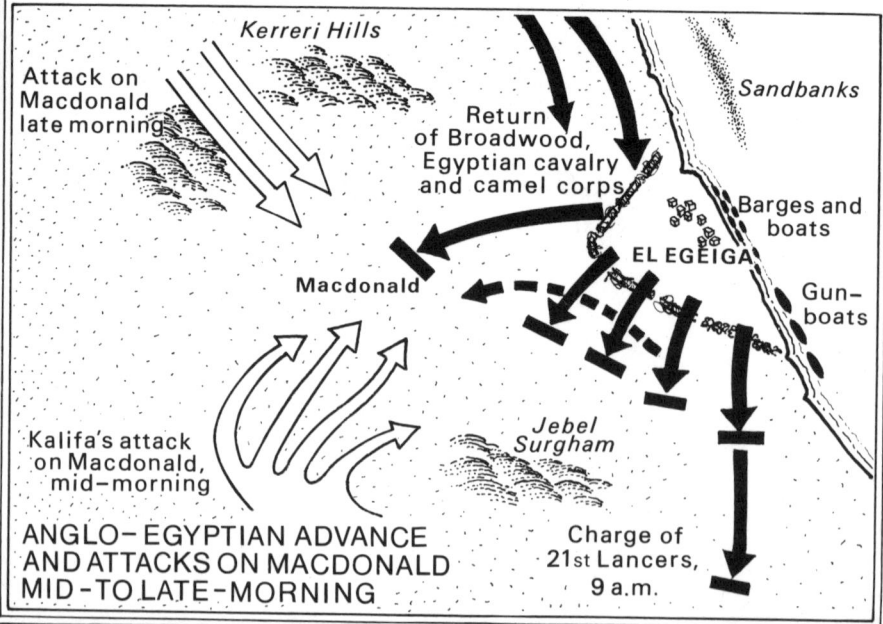

Kerreri Hills

Attack on Macdonald late morning

Return of Broadwood, Egyptian cavalry and camel corps

Sandbanks

Barges and boats

EL EGEIGA

Macdonald

Gun-boats

Kalifa's attack on Macdonald, mid-morning

Jebel Surgham

ANGLO-EGYPTIAN ADVANCE AND ATTACKS ON MACDONALD MID-TO LATE-MORNING

Charge of 21st Lancers, 9 a.m.

Foreword

ABOUT TWO YEARS ago, when I had already started to write
this book, I was visiting Byron Farwell, the distinguished military
historian, at his home at Hillsboro in Virginia. Over drinks before
dinner I asked Byron why, though an American and, as a resident
of Virginia, surrounded on every side by the battlefields and memorials of the American Civil War, he had chosen to devote most
of his time and talent to recording the military history of the British
Empire in the Victorian Age. 'I don't really know,' he said, 'but
maybe because it seems romantic.'

Byron served as a combat soldier in two wars and knows as well
as any, and better than most, that wars are not romantic . . . at
least not at the sharp end. Nevertheless, anyone who studies the
wars of the British Empire will soon come to see what he means,
because the wars of that period, given a little time to heal the
scars, do indeed offer romantic possibilities, not least because of
the officers and men who fought them.

It may seem strange to the modern mentality but in the Victorian age men actually *liked* war. The officers and men in this
book, Gordon, Burnaby, Wolseley, Evelyn Wood, Redvers Buller
and the rest, went out of their way to find action and became
despondent if they were left behind when the regiments sailed off
for another hard campaign.

Terrible odds and terrible wounds did not deter the soldiers of
the Queen doing battle with the Queen's enemies in every corner
of the world, even if some of those enemies had never heard of
Queen Victoria or the British Empire and only wished to be left
alone. The wishes of the enemy rarely bothered the Victorian
soldier; I doubt if the reasons for the fight ever entered his head.

He was a fighting man, and that was enough reason to seek action. Anyway, as soldiers told each other until quite recently, soldiers are not paid to think, they are paid to obey orders.

These Victorian soldiers fought for glory and medals and the honour of their regiments and quite often simply because it was dangerous and exciting and therefore enjoyable . . . and they probably thought it romantic as well. Colonel Fred Burnaby, the fighting Colonel of the Royal Horse Guards – 'The Blues' – who turned up in the Sudan without permission to fight and die among the redcoat infantry, typified the ideal Victorian army officer. Fortunately for people like Colonel Burnaby, there were plenty of wars to enjoy in the British Empire, from the day it was created until the time it finally disappeared in the 1960s.

At a military ceremony some years ago in London, Her Majesty Queen Elizabeth II told the assembled soldiers, 'We are not a warlike nation . . .' All the evidence of history tells us that the British people are, in fact, relentlessly warlike and value military prowess above almost any other quality.

Those words of the present Queen of England would have sounded strange indeed to her predecessor Queen Victoria, who was always interested in the affairs of the army, 'for it is the Queen's army,' as she often reminded Mr Gladstone. Queen Victoria was always demanding news of her army's adventures and devising ways to commemorate its glory. Not for nothing is the most prestigious decoration in the state's gift called the Victoria Cross, a medal given only 'For Valour'.

During the reign of Queen Victoria the British army was almost continually at war somewhere in or around the Empire. One of the last engagements of that gallant red-coated Victorian army was this one, which I have elected to call the Dervish Wars since they were fought in three phases in Egypt and the Sudan between 1880 and 1898.

This book is not just about war. It is also the story of an imperial entanglement, about how, in spite of the wishes and best efforts of Mr Gladstone and his government and that splendid and far-sighted administrator Sir Evelyn Baring, the British became involved in the affairs of Egypt, and through that involvement, with the Sudan. Only then is it the story of a twenty-year campaign, the last war of conquest fought by the Victorian army against a valiant and worthy opponent.

The British Empire has now long gone and most of the British army has gone with it. In the last twenty years the marching regiments that forged the Empire, maintained it and defended it – even as it disappeared – have followed it into oblivion, their memory preserved, if at all, in small regimental museums and in the torn and faded battle flags that hang in country churches. It is curious that just one hundred years ago, in 1898, when the regiments marched out of Cairo on the road to Omdurman, the British Empire seemed as solid as the pyramids they marched by, and likely to last just as long.

It is also curious that the scene of those final triumphs, in the Anglo-Egyptian War of 1882 which led to Britain taking over Egypt and the Suez Canal, also saw the final death throes of Britain's imperial pretensions at the Suez landings of November 1956.

Byron Farwell has written that the British Empire began to decline even as the story told here was starting to unfold, on 'that Sunday afternoon in February 1881 when British soldiers, fleeing from Boer farm boys, ran down the steep slopes of Majuba Hill'. He may well be right, but a significant step in that decline took place on the banks of the Suez Canal where this story opens.

This then, is the story of how it was in one corner of the world, in the last years of the Victorian age, just before the British Empire began its final tilt towards disintegration. Those who seek more enlightenment than these pages can provide are directed to the bibliography.

Robin Neillands
1995

I

Suez

November 1869

The principal obstacles with which M. de Lesseps had to contend were those placed in his way by Her Majesty's Government.

John Marlowe,
The Building of the Suez Canal, 1964

IT WAS A splendid affair, a glorious occasion, by general consent the event of the decade. Africa had become an island, the Mediterranean linked to the Red Sea, the distance between Britain and India halved. The Province of Egypt had been severed from the territorial embrace of the Turkish Empire and a dream of the ancient Pharaohs had become a modern reality. With all that to celebrate the cream of European society assembled at Port Said on 17 November 1869, to undertake the first passage through Monsieur de Lesseps' newly completed Suez Canal.

Since this gigantic undertaking was first and foremost a French enterprise, the Empress Eugenie, wife of Napoleon Bonaparte's nephew, Napoleon III, was guest of honour at all the events. She usually appeared leaning on the arm of the Emperor Franz-Joseph of Austria, though on one occasion she delighted the Egyptian crowds by going for a ride on a dromedary. The reign of her husband would shortly be snuffed out in the Franco-Prussian War but that still lay a year ahead. For the moment the Empress had smiles to spare for the young, awkward Crown Prince of Prussia, who was attending the celebrations accompanied by a train of Junker noblemen.

The Crown Prince and Princess of Holland were there, and to add a little French *gravitas* to the joyful scenes, a group of French *savants*, including Emile Zola and Théophile Gautier. These men were similar to that group of intellectuals who had come to the Delta seventy years before with the army of Napoleon Bonaparte and given Egypt her first intoxicating taste of Western culture.

Ambassadors were there from a score of nations and included Mr Henry Elliot, the British Ambassador to the Sublime Porte, who arrived in the Admiralty yacht *Psyche*, escorted by two steam gunboats of the Royal Navy. Since all the other guests were well aware that for the last decade Great Britain had spared no effort, scientific, technical, financial or diplomatic, to prevent the construction of the Canal, Mr Elliot's demeanour during this time was closely observed by his colleagues.

Other nations sent other talents. From Scandinavia came the playwright Henrik Ibsen, from America a young journalist, Henry Morton Stanley, pausing on his way to Zanzibar from where he would embark on his search for Livingstone in Central Africa, and among a host of Britons the famous explorer Sir Samuel Baker — Baker of the Nile.

All these people were here at the invitation of the Khedive Ismail, Viceroy of Egypt for the Sultan of Turkey, to celebrate this momentous event and pay their respects to the man of the hour, Ferdinand de Lesseps, who had schemed and laboured for twenty years to bring the Canal to completion. De Lesseps himself may have had his mind on other matters. Though already sixty-four years of age on the day the Canal opened, on the following day, in the newly built church by the Canal at Ismailia, he married a young girl from Mauritius.

For the other major celebrant on this occasion, the Khedive Ismail, the opening of the Suez Canal was a major step towards completing the first of his lifelong ambitions: to modernize and Westernize the land of Egypt. His second aim, to expand Egypt's dominion down the River Nile into the Sudan and Central Africa, was proving far harder to achieve. Behind the Khedive's smiles and open-handed generosity to his teeming guests lay a looming problem, for the cost of his ambition was the bankruptcy of Egypt. To pay for his grandiose schemes the Khedive had already mortgaged all the national assets and the bills were about to fall due.

Well, enough of that; those mundane cares could wait for the moment. The bands were playing, the crowds cheering, the champagne flowing. To mark this momentous event, Verdi had been commissioned to write *Aida*, and the younger Strauss had composed his 'Egyptian March' to symbolize the stately progress of royal yachts and iron-clad warships making the first ever voyage through the Sinai Desert from the Mediterranean to the Red Sea.

The world marvelled, and to celebrate such a triumph no expense was spared; there was a banquet for three thousand guests; six thousand people assembled in Cairo for the Celebration Ball. Fireworks and flares illuminated the Pyramids outside Cairo, tens of thousands of Egyptian *fellahin* and Bedouin tribesmen lined the banks of the Canal, dancing, ululating and firing their rifles in the air as the invited dignitaries sailed past; the whole nation was *en fête*. For Ferdinand de Lesseps and his patron, the Khedive Ismail, this was a moment to savour, a last delicious taste of success before reality returned to intrude on this happy and memorable scene.

*

History is not a convenient subject. It does not come in neat packages sealed at both ends, and it is not easy to decide exactly when or for what precise reason Great Britain first became involved in the affairs of Egypt and the Sudan in the closing decades of the nineteenth century. However, it is certain that the British Government of the time, or at least those ministries formed by the Liberal Prime Minister Mr Gladstone, had no desire for such involvement and struggled mightily to prevent it.

Their attempts to avoid any lasting entanglement in Egypt and their total failure to do so provides the central theme of this book. What can also be certain is that from this reluctant beginning, which led to the last major colonial acquisition of the Victorian era – the Anglo-Egyptian Sudan - came that period of colonization and stewardship in Egypt which ended with the Suez débâcle in 1956, an event which fatally exposed the terminal weakness of the British Imperial position. Those proud Imperial generals and red-coated British soldiers who descended on Egypt and the Sudan in the 1880s cannot have imagined how their conquest would end less than seventy years later.

Great Britain went into Egypt for various reasons: to secure the repayment of massive loans granted by British banks to the Khedive Ismail; to suppress the slave trade in the Sudan, a course urged upon government and people by that prototype of pressure groups, the Anti-Slavery Society; to bring order out of chaos; or merely from a desire to meddle. What can be claimed with certainty is that the opening of the Suez Canal in November 1869 played a significant part in the process of entanglement.

Britain – or to be more exact, the British Government – did not want a canal across the isthmus of Suez. British ministers and ambassadors had cast doubt and scorn upon the project for decades, both at the Court of the Sultan of Turkey, the 'Sublime Porte' in Constantinople, and around the governments and financial centres of Europe. No place or opportunity was missed in the attempt to disparage M. de Lesseps' scheme. Diplomats and ministers had raised political objections, scientific experts had cast doubts on the feasibility of the project, rumours had been spread in Europe's financial centres on the commercial viability of the enterprise in order to inhibit the raising of sufficient funds to complete the work. None of these slanders or objections prevented the inexorable progress of M. de Lesseps' dream.

William Gladstone, Britain's Prime Minister for much of this period, had a more personal and far-sighted reason for his objections. He knew that if the Canal was built Britain would inevitably become involved in Egypt. He felt, with certainty, that Britain must take a hand in the shambolic affairs of Egypt, if only to prevent other nations gaining control of such a vital waterway. Gladstone had no wish whatsoever for any expansion of the British Empire. In his view the Empire was already large enough and a growing financial and political liability. Besides, there were problems enough at home. His predecessor, Lord Palmerston, had felt the same way.

Years later, in 1884, a member of the French Senate, Monsieur Lemoinne, agreed with these earlier conclusions: 'The British had always opposed this enterprise and Lord Palmerston had attacked it with every means at his disposal but M. de Lesseps triumphed over all obstacles, until on the day the Canal opened the British said to themselves, "*Il doit être à moi*" – We have got to have it.'

Gladstone was convinced that Britain's far-flung colonies and dominions were of doubtful benefit to the mother country but the British Empire was a maritime one and a link like the Suez Canal must prove either a strategic asset or an enduring problem. Fearing the latter, he spoke out against the Canal and though events were to prove him right, and Britain was inevitably drawn into the problems of Egypt and the Sudan, the spirit of the age was against him.

Exactly *why* successive British Governments were so sceptical of the benefits of the Canal is harder to understand, for the shortening of the route to India, the jewel in the crown of the British Empire, offered Britain many military and political advantages: it halved the time currently needed to send troops to India via the Cape of Good Hope and would bring untold benefits to Britain's large mercantile fleet.

The most obvious reason for the British lack of enthusiasm was simply that the Canal would be French. A Frenchman was constructing it with the active support of the French Emperor and French banks. In the 1860s France was expanding her Empire along the North African shore; she had possessed a cultural and economic foothold in the Levant since the time of the Crusades. The nearest ports to Suez were the French naval bases at Toulon and Marseilles, thus giving France a grip on Britain's lifeline to the East.

There were, besides, some alternative methods of trans-Sinai travel, then securely in British hands, which the Canal would negate. In 1841, a British Naval officer, Thomas Waghorn, had organized an overland route from Alexandria via Cairo to Suez through which passengers and mail now flowed to India with relative ease. In addition, there was the Cape route; any diversion of shipping through Suez must mean a decline in Britain's thriving trade around the Cape of Good Hope and the support that gave to the British settlements in South Africa which were already at odds with the Boers.

All in all, the idea of the Suez Canal was one to be resisted, but now the Canal was completed the British Government was prepared to put a brave face on it. A glowing letter of congratulation arrived for de Lesseps from the British Foreign Secretary, the Earl of Clarendon, and several ships of the Royal Navy joined that first transit through the Suez Canal, dressed overall with flags and bunting.

*

This is the story of an imperial entanglement. It tells how Great Britain, then the most powerful nation on Earth, ruling an Empire containing some 400 million people and reaching into every corner of the globe, became drawn into the affairs of the Sudan, one of the poorest and least desirable territories on the planet, and with that involvement took the first, halting steps towards ruin.

Three factors combined to make such involvement inevitable: the Egyptian foreign debt, and the growing likelihood that it would never be repaid; the urge to suppress the Sudanese slave trade, which was the great cause and the major moral issue of the late-Victorian period; and the need to control the Suez Canal. Whatever the wishes of Mr Gladstone and his government, this combination proved irresistible.

The Suez Canal was the strongest and most enduring of the cables that were to bind Britain to Egypt, which is why the importance of the Canal must be grasped at the start of this story. Although it fades into the background it remains crucial to subsequent events and was to remain important until the British left Egypt and the Sudan for good in 1954–6.

To encompass the events leading to the opening of the Canal and outline the other reasons which pulled the British into Egypt we must go back a little; perhaps not as far as the twelfth-century Crusader Kingdoms of Outremer, when the French – the Franks – first settled in the Levant, but certainly to July 1798, when General Napoleon Bonaparte landed in Egypt and shattered the power of the ruling Mameluke caste at the Battle of the Pyramids. Napoleon's aim was to seize Egypt as his base for an attack on India, but that ambition was thwarted when Admiral Horatio Nelson destroyed the French fleet at the Battle of the Nile in August 1798. This first French sortie finally petered out in 1801 after a short campaign in Syria, but the cultural foothold established by France at that time had a far more lasting effect.

Those *savants* whom Napoleon had brought in his train transformed Egypt. One of these was the scholar Jean François Champollion who, in 1799, interpreted the texts of the Rosetta Stone, unlocked the language of the hieroglyphs and introduced the civilization of Ancient Egypt to a new and fascinated European audience. Champollion's work created a cultural bond between the intellectuals of France and Egypt and as Egypt became more Westernized throughout the middle decades of the nineteenth century, so the influence of France continued to grow.

Egypt's ruling classes sent their children to French schools and the French-run Cairo *lycées*. French became the language of the

Egyptian Government and remained so even after the British took over. The wealthier Egyptians read French books, absorbed French ideas, adopted French ways. Sooner or later, this pervasive French influence astride an important route to India was bound to attract the attention of the British and after that first attack by Horatio Nelson on the French fleet in Aboukir Bay, Britain took steps to advance into Egypt.

The British occupied Egypt after the defeat of the French Army, but withdrew in 1803, only to return in 1807 and be defeated and forced to withdraw by the new ruler of Egypt, Mohammed – or Mehemet – Ali, who had overthrown the surviving Mamelukes.

The Mamelukes, a warrior caste descended from the children of Christian or Circassian slaves, had ruled Egypt much as they pleased until 1798, though they were nominally subjects of the Turkish Sultan. The Mamelukes were unable to regain power after the departure of the French before they were overthrown yet again by Mohammed Ali, an Albanian soldier of fortune in the service of the Sultan. Mohammed Ali conquered Egypt for himself however, not for the Sultan, and proved himself to be both a good soldier and a ruthless ruler. He allied himself with the Mamelukes to expel the British, then massacred the surviving Mamelukes at a celebration banquet in 1811.

Throughout the entire period covered in this book, Egypt was a province of the Turkish Empire. That the Sultan had little influence on events within Egypt was due to the fact that the Turkish Empire was already in terminal decline. Having expelled the Mamelukes, Mohammed Ali expelled the Turkish Viceroy – or Pasha – but was then himself appointed Pasha by the Sultan, who was clearly wary of his warlike, ruthless vassal.

Mohammed Ali was thus able not only to rule Egypt as an independent prince but also to extend his domains by warring in Arabia and in other lands which owed allegiance or paid tribute to the Sublime Porte. In all his actions during the early years of his rule, Mohammed Ali enjoyed the open support of France. He did not however consult the French in 1831 when he embarked on his major imperial adventure and sent his armies south to conquer the deserts and plains of the Sudan, extending his rule to the upper waters of the Nile.

The Sudan was – and is – a bleak, arid and inhospitable country but the Egyptians had long believed that through the Sudan lay the road to riches. Somewhere in Central Africa lay the source of

Egypt's principal asset, the River Nile, and along the headwaters of that river roamed herds of elephant offering a rich bounty in ivory. Somewhere beyond that lay the fabled mines of Solomon and the prospect of unlimited gold. None of this wealth ever materialized and, failing to find riches in gold or ivory, Mohammed Ali and his generals turned to the other asset of the Sudan and the country beyond it: slaves.

Slave trading was not new in Egypt; indeed, Egypt was full of slaves, but this venture into the remote parts of Africa lifted the trade to new and horrific heights. The great days of African exploration, which would reveal the full horror and misery of the slave trade to the civilized world, still lay a decade or two in the future, but by this new and massive involvement in slaving, Mohammed Ali had laid another path down which he led the Europeans into Egypt. Even then the control of Egypt was beginning to interest the active, expansionist British.

Mohammed Ali's Franco-Egyptian alliance did not meet with the wholehearted approval of Great Britain. The British had long suspected the French of intriguing to restore their Empire in the Levant and keeping a wary eye on French ambitions was a long-standing rule for every British government, whatever their political complexion.

With Mohammed Ali's permission, Britain had already established a land route to India across the isthmus of Suez. This enabled her citizens to disembark at Alexandria and hurry south to pick up a ship at Suez on the Red Sea. This route did not at first flourish; the bulk of passengers to India preferred the much slower but far more comfortable voyage via the Cape of Good Hope on transports of the East India Company. This route offered the additional benefit of sustaining British interests in Southern Africa but as the years passed, so the faster, land-linked route to India through the Sinai desert became more important.

It became very important indeed from about 1840, after the development of steamships. The prevailing northerly winds in the Red Sea made it a difficult place for sailing ships but the advent of steamships and then of the propeller rather than the paddle wheel, made the Red Sea ports far more accessible from India and Singapore and cut the travelling time considerably. Moreover, the land route improved: until the middle decades of the century Trans-Suez travellers had to make the transit by mule or camel, but in 1854 the British completed a railway from Cairo to Suez.

They also poured money into developing port and coaling facilities there and at Aden, their new colony at the foot of the Red Sea.

By the 1850s Egypt had become a vital link in the short-sea passage to India. The British believed that the best way to ensure the continuing safety of this vital link – and negating French influence in Egypt – was by maintaining good relations with Egypt's overlord, the Sultan of Turkey. If that meant involving Great Britain in war with Russia, as it did during the Crimean War of 1854–6, that was the necessary price to pay. In fact Russia was always suspected of having designs on British India and no chance to curb such designs could be overlooked. British concerns for the rapid reinforcement of her army in India were increased by the Indian Mutiny of 1857, which the Russians were believed to have supported or even fomented.

For their part, the French believed that the Russians sought the destruction of the Turkish Empire as a way of capturing Constantinople, overrunning the Balkans, and so gaining a clear route to the warm-water ports of the Mediterranean where they would challenge the political and commercial interests of France. This common threat from Russia kept France and Britain from conflict and even made them allies in support of Turkey during the Crimean War.

By the 1850s Britain had secured a vital route to India via Egypt without any great expenditure, but Gladstone's general scepticism about the enlargement of the British Empire was a difficult position to sustain in the 1860s–70s. The nineteenth century was the Age of Imperialism, when all the great nations of Europe sought colonies in the continent of Africa and in the Far East. Britain, however, was in a different position to most of them.

The major powers of Continental Europe, Russia and Austro-Hungary, were land empires. France looked over the narrow Mediterranean towards North Africa, Prussia was currently concerned to unite the German states before tackling French domination of Western Europe. All these nations would snap up territory in Africa or the Far East if they could but while Belgium sought an empire in the swamps of the Congo in Central Africa, and the Dutch were establishing colonies in Java and Indonesia, only the British had already founded a vast colonial maritime empire and needed to protect it and control the trade routes holding it together.

The British Empire was more far-flung than any of her rivals, one linked by her merchant fleet and the Royal Navy. The British might therefore have been expected to welcome the creation of a short sea route to India. If there was a French-controlled canal through Sinai, however, in the event of conflict, the French could cut this route and send troops to the East far faster than Britain could send reinforcements round the Cape. The British therefore much preferred the railway line for mail and passengers while allowing the Royal Navy to control the major sea route round the Cape. Then came Ferdinand de Lesseps with his mad and dangerous ideas.

Political objections aside, the British believed – incorrectly – that constructing a canal across the isthmus would be impossible because of a difference in sea levels. This belief had inhibited the construction of a canal since the time of the Pharaohs, though in fact there is no significant difference between the levels of the Mediterranean and the Red Sea. The minimal difference in sea level was crucial to the plans of Ferdinand de Lesseps, a French diplomat and visionary, who retired from the French Diplomatic Corps in 1854 at the early age of forty-nine and returned to Egypt as a guest of his childhood friend, the Viceroy Mohammed Said.

The conqueror of the Sudan, Mohammed Ali, had died in 1849. He was briefly succeeded by his son Ibrahim, and then by Ibrahim's eldest son, Abbas. These family successions served notice on the Great Powers that the influence of the Porte was waning in Cairo, for in former times the post of Viceroy had been in the gift of the Sultan. Now, although Mohammed Ali's successors sought and obtained the blessing of the Sultan, the succession had become hereditary, and there was no attempt to replace Mohammed Ali's heirs with a Viceroy appointed from Constantinople. Abbas died, or was murdered, in 1854 and was succeeded by his brother, Mohammed Said, who had been befriended in his childhood by the young Frenchman, Ferdinand de Lesseps, son of the French Consul in Cairo. This friendship had endured.

When Mohammed Said succeeded to the Viceroyalty in 1854 he was a portly young man of thirty-two and Egypt had changed from the feudal, semi-savage country of the Mamelukes which Napoleon Bonaparte had conquered sixty years before. Under the rule of Mohammed Ali and his successors, the pace of change began to increase. Egypt began to modernize, to enter the Western world, to entertain dreams of Empire . . . but at a cost.

By 1854 Egypt had already acquired many of the visible trappings of a modern state. There were railways in the Delta, paved streets in central Cairo, a large number of schools, an army equipped with modern weapons and artillery but indifferently led and poorly paid. There was a growing export trade in grain and gum arabic and manufactured goods but especially in a newly introduced crop, cotton.

This brought wealth to the ruling classes, and, under Mohammed Said's successor, the Khedive Ismail, this expansion continued. There was a postal service and a telegraph, more railways were built and tourism began, bringing in curious visitors and useful foreign exchange. Thomas Cook sent steamers down the Nile filled with Western visitors eager to view the wonders of the Pharaohs. Few of these commercial enterprises or the wealth they created extended to the native Egyptians. Commerce was in the hands of European traders and the upper echelons of Egyptian society, occupied by Turks, Syrians, Caucasians, Armenians or Greeks. The native Egyptians, especially the peasant fellahin, worked in the fields or served in the army and had no say in running the country. Their portion was to labour, to fight and to pay taxes. Their rulers, the Viceroys, had wider ambitions.

Mohammed Said needed very little encouragement to fall in with de Lesseps' plans for a Suez Canal. His contribution would be the desert through which the Canal would run and a considerable amount of land on either side for the building of warehouses and ports. The fellahin would be turned off the land and the Viceroy would lease the territory to de Lesseps and his Canal Company for ninety-nine years. Mohammed Said would also provide the labour, tens of thousands of those hapless, now landless, fellahin, though de Lesseps must feed and pay them. In return Mohammed Said would receive forty per cent of the Canal Company shares and fifteen per cent of the profits. It seemed a bargain.

Mohammed Said thought it advisable to obtain the support of his nominal overlord, the Sultan of Turkey, and here de Lesseps' plan received its first check. The British advised the Sultan to reject this scheme for – they claimed – the cost of the Canal's construction would further deplete Egypt's overstretched revenues and lead to a suspension or reduction in the annual tribute paid by the Viceroy of Egypt to the Sublime Porte. They also argued that the Canal would provide a defence line for the Egyptians should the Sultan ever feel inclined to re-occupy the country. Warming to their task, the British then threw in all the other objections they could think of regarding the viability of the project.

Thanks to the entrenched opposition of the British Government, it took de Lesseps four years to raise the money for his Canal, but the initial finance – some £16,000,000, a colossal sum for the time – was finally collected. The work began in 1859, and after ten years of toil the Canal was finally completed in 1869, though Mohammed Said died in 1863 to be succeeded by his eldest son, Ismail Pasha.

Just before his death, Mohammed Said had been told by Sir Henry Buller, the British Ambassador to Constantinople, that 'while Britain has no wish to govern Egypt or exert any prepondering interest over it . . . we can never permit any other foreign power to possess itself of Egypt or gain a preponsdering interest there.' With the death of Said the British may have hoped that the Canal project would be dropped but the new Viceroy Ismail was as interested as his predecessor in the Canal. Ismail also intended to make something of Egypt's disastrous and costly venture in the Sudan.

The problem now was how to do this, for while de Lesseps advanced towards the completion of his dream, Egypt had marched steadily towards financial ruin. By 1860 the Egyptian economy had became fatally overstretched. Ruin was averted in the short term by the outbreak of the American Civil War of 1861–5. This led to a great increase in demand for Egyptian cotton by the European mills and a useful increase in the price. Egypt's revenues soared and Ismail Pasha revelled in the sudden flood of money and the resulting decrease in his problems. Now he could proceed to modernize his country at an even faster pace.

Progress costs money. In Egypt in the 1860s it cost a great deal of money, far more than the national tax revenue could provide, however hard the tax gatherers pressed the hapless fellahin. Failing to make enough from her internal resources and export sales, Egypt therefore began to borrow large amounts from European banks and businessmen, who loaned their money in return for significant trading concessions and at a high rate of interest.

Ismail Pasha, later the Khedive, is usually blamed for Egypt's woes and her subsequent domination by Great Britain, yet all the causes of European intervention – Sudanese slavery, the Suez Canal and foreign debt – began long before Ismail ascended the Viceregal throne. That said, his father, Mohammed Said, was one of Egypt's better rulers. Said attempted to stamp out corruption, ordered the slave trade to cease in the Sudan – though these orders were ignored – and was not personally avaricious. While corruption and the slave trade did not cease, when he died in 1863 his country was still solvent. The dive into ruin really began with his successor, Ismail, whose rule was far less considerate and benign.

During the 1860s London and Paris were the world's great financial and trading centres and before many years of Ismail's rule had passed, the London and Parisian bankers were wondering just how long the Egyptian economy could continue to meet the payments on a spiralling series of loans. These loans could perhaps be justified while the money was being invested in the modernization of the state. An industrialized, efficient Egypt should eventually be able to repay these loans, but Egypt was also pouring money into the bottomless pit of the Sudan.

Mohammed Ali had annexed the Sudan in 1831. It offered no commercial advantages, but with the Nile being so vital to Egypt, to control the river valley from delta to source was an understandable ambition for any Egyptian ruler. Besides, down the Nile came that indispensable aid to the good life: slaves. By the 1860s the full extent of Egypt's involvement in the slave trade was well known to her European creditors.

Slavery had finally been abolished in the British Empire in 1833, after decades of campaigning by William Wilberforce, but slavery had been endemic throughout the Middle East and in the Arab lands around the Mediterranean since the dawn of time. Slavery was still flourishing in Arabia and Africa throughout the nineteenth century, and existed in some Arab countries until well into the twentieth, even though the tide of Western opinion was flowing strongly against it. The French were very active in suppressing the slave trade throughout the nineteenth century but nowhere was anti-slavery opinion stronger than in Great Britain, where the Anti-Slavery Society was a major political force, with representatives throughout the country, in the press and in Parliament.

From 1833, wherever the British could abolish slavery, the trading in slaves stopped. The Royal Navy added slave-ship interdiction to their other duties and harried slavers around the coasts of West Africa and along what was known as the Middle Passage to the Southern United States and the Caribbean. Where slavery could not be stopped, in the United States, the Turkish Empire and among the Arab sheiks of the Gulf, the British expressed their disapproval but put up with it, in the interests of trade and good diplomatic relations. In the case of Egypt and the Sudan, however, the British and French Governments had leverage against the slave trade and they intended to use it.

This leverage was Egypt's growing debt. By 1869 Ismail, the new Viceroy – or Khedive – had been made aware that his continued access to European funds was contingent on his doing something significant about the slave trade, especially in the Southern Sudan. The Sudan was little more than a vast hunting ground for Arab slavers and the terror was spreading. Having ravaged the Sudanese people, the depredations of the slave traders now looked likely to decimate or even wipe out entirely the black tribes of Central Africa.

The Anglo-French demand for the suppression of the slave trade put the Khedive Ismail in a quandary. His vast estates in the Nile Delta were tilled by the fellahin, who were either slaves or little better than slaves, and slaves were the buttress of the Egyptian and Arab way of life, essential for work in the fields or pleasure in the harem. As far as the Sudan itself was concerned, the Viceroy's efforts to extend his dominion there had been largely ineffective and extremely costly, and the economy of the Sudan, such as it was, depended in no small part on the slave trade, which represented about ninety per cent of the Sudanese economy.

From the capital city of Khartoum the Arab slave traders scoured the Southern Sudan and the wild country of Central Africa to Buganda and beyond, gathering in slaves by the thousand. After the British succeeded in closing the slave market at Zanzibar in 1873, the main artery for the disposal of African slaves was down the Nile to Khartoum. From there slaves were sent east to Red Sea ports like Suakin, where those who had survived the journey – more than a third of those taken captive died on the way – were shipped to the fields and harems of Arabia. Before shipment, many of the male slaves were castrated, an operation which led to the deaths of thousands more.

Britain became increasingly involved with the suppression of the slave trade throughout the Victorian era. That Britain – and Britons – should be so concerned about the condition of blacks in Central Africa and largely indifferent to the conditions of the men, women and children labouring in the coal mines and factories at home, is often cited as an example of Victorian hypocrisy, but the African slave had the inestimable advantage of publicity.

During a major part of the Victorian era, from 1856 to the 1880s, the exploration of Central Africa and the search for the source of the Nile supplied the British public with a constant stream of excitement. British expeditions, led by army officers and gallant gentlemen like Burton, Speke, Grant, Sir Samuel Baker, Livingstone and the rest, roved across the Dark Continent and returned to London with tales of hardship and adventure and the abominable practices of the Arab slavers. Public indignation was aroused and the Anti-Slavery Society flourished.

The suppression of slavery was a far more palatable excuse for such roving expeditions than a simple lust for adventure and many explorers added it to their list of objectives. Nor was this excuse entirely false. The travels of at least one man, the Scots missionary David Livingstone, were totally inspired by a love of the Christian Gospel and a detestation of slavery.

The suppression of slavery falls somewhat outside the parameters of this book, but it has a part to play in this story. The suppression of the slave trade, the growing Egyptian debt and the need to secure and control the Suez Canal brought the British into Egypt and at some point in the story, for a longer or shorter space of time, these three causes interlock. Whenever the pressure from one cause abated, the pressure from the others increased.

Left to themselves, causes can achieve very little. It is the people who take them up or are influenced by them that provide the catalyst which sets a train of events in motion. In this story two men predominate, Major-General Charles Gordon of the British army and Mohammed Ahmed, a Sudanese mystic, later called the Mahdi. In November 1869, at the opening of the Suez Canal, they were not yet on stage but between them, without any thought of doing so, these two men conspired to drag Britain into a commitment that was to endure until the middle decades of the twentieth century.

Britain's involvement in Egypt and the Sudan was her last true colonial venture, the last occasion in which her armies and her politicians took over another nation – in this case two nations – and ruled it for purely British purposes, though to the eventual benefit of the subject people. Other colonial territories were acquired later, most notably in East Africa after the Great War, but the great imperial adventure was almost over when that glorious celebratory convoy of ships cruised through the Suez Canal in November 1869.

2

Egypt and the Sudan

1869–1878

'Egypt suffers from the dishonesty, ignorance, waste
and extravagance of the East, such as have brought her
suzerain to the brink of ruin, and at the same time from
the vast expense caused by hasty and inconsiderate
endeavours to adopt the civilization of the West.'

Mr Stephen Cave, MP, 1876

AFTER HUBRIS, NEMESIS. Even as the flags and pavilions were
struck and cleared away along the Canal, the Khedive Ismail
awoke from his euphoria and began to confront the two great
problems of his reign: the colossal extent of the national debt and
his so far futile attempts to control events in the Sudan.

The first problem grew by the hour and the bills for his latest
extravaganza had yet to arrive. On the second count, the Khedive
knew that the best answer to his problems in the Sudan was a
dedicated, incorruptible man, honest enough to resist the profitable
temptations that would be put in his way, strong enough to eliminate the slave trade and remove a great weight from the Khedive's
shoulders.

He had failed to find such a paragon in Egypt. Now he thought
he had met just such a man, a guest at one of the recent receptions,
who had travelled through the Sudan and explored the wilder
parts of Central Africa, Sir Samuel Baker – Baker of the Nile. By
appointing him to suppress the slave trade, Ismail hoped to placate
his critics and creditors in Europe, for Samuel Baker was a hero,
a man famous throughout Britain and the Continent for his courage and resourcefulness.

Sir Samuel Baker was an explorer. Like many Victorian explorers, his travels had made him a great public figure in the middle decades of the nineteenth century, but even among that dauntless band Baker was exceptional. He came from a long line of naval captains and military men and had made his name in a series of long and difficult journeys into Central Africa, following Burton, Speke and Grant in the search for the source of the Nile.

In 1863 he had forced his way along the river past Khartoum, out of the Sudan into the terrible swamp of the Sudd and so to Gondokoro, that dreary outpost on the Upper Nile. He had even gone beyond Gondokoro, as far as the wild tribal country of Buganda, accompanied by his beautiful young wife and a small force of one hundred men. This was the exploit which had made him famous and his account of this harrowing two-year expedition, *The Albert N'Yanza: Great Basin of the Nile*, became a best-selling book.

Baker was awarded the Gold Medal of the Royal Geographical Society, was knighted by Queen Victoria and became a welcome guest at all the great houses in the land. This led to an invitation from the Khedive to attend the Suez Canal celebrations in 1869. It occurred to the Khedive that since Baker knew the Nile valley and its people well he would be just the man for the Sudan. Apart from his experience of the region such an appointment would – must – placate Ismail's more insistent creditors for if Baker could not do something about the Sudan and the slave trade, no one could.

The Khedive was never mean with money and he offered Baker the most generous terms. He would become a pasha, a major-general in the Egyptian army, and receive a salary of £10,000 a year. He would command a force of seventeen hundred men and have a free hand in the matter of weapons and equipment. His task was to annex the Upper Nile Valley to some point well south of Khartoum and suppress the slave trade. This task may not have sounded insurmountable after a few years absence from Central Africa – or a few glasses of champagne – and Baker accepted the position without undue hesitation.

With that problem set aside, at least for the moment, Ismail could turn his attention to the state of Egypt's finances. These, to put it mildly, were disastrous. Ismail had been spending money with great enjoyment for many years, using up all the revenue raised by taxation, using new loans to pay off previous ones, gradually sinking into an unending spiral of debt. He had increased the national debt by about £1 million for every year of his reign and the celebrations for the opening of the Suez Canal alone were estimated to cost £6 million, even today a tidy sum.

Ismail's predecessor, Mohammed Said, had begun the headlong dive into debt in 1858 by issuing bills on the Egyptian Treasury offering interest at up to eighteen per cent. Within a year bills worth 40 million French francs had been snapped up by foreign banks which thereby had obtained a lien on half of Egypt's annual revenue. In 1860 the French government took a direct hand, loaning Said 18 million francs charged against Egypt's customs receipts. Foreign powers now had a grip on Egypt's internal and external finances and by 1880 there were over sixty thousand Europeans living in Cairo or Alexandria, most of them engaged in ventures of very little value to Egypt and great profit to themselves; all were protected by their resident Consuls.

Financial collapse might have come during Said's reign but for the outbreak of the American Civil War in 1861 when Union warships blockaded the coast of the Confederacy and stopped the export of cotton. This led to a worldwide rise in demand for Egyptian cotton, offering a breathing space for the embattled Said and his successor the Khedive Ismail. Nevertheless, the debt continued to mount. When Said died in 1863, Egypt was in debt to the tune of nearly 400 million francs. Most of this was owed to French banks, partly in bonds attached to various parts of the Egyptian national revenue, some of it entirely unsecured.

This pattern of borrow and spend continued under the Khedive Ismail, who also began to borrow from the British; his first British loan, in 1864, was for £5 million at seven per cent interest. By 1865, when the American Civil War ended and the cotton boom collapsed, Egypt's total debt amounted to over £100 million. These sums represented massive amounts at the end of the nineteenth century – the interest payments alone exceeded the annual revenue of the country – and these loans were doing Egypt no good. Most of the new loans went to service the debts on previous loans, and the burden of the overworked, overtaxed fellahin increased continually. It could not last.

Ismail used every device his Levantine advisers could think of to stave off bankruptcy. Taxes were collected in advance, anticipated payments compounded for a smaller sum paid at once, the lash applied to recalcitrant fellahin who might have money to spare.

By 1869 the one national asset that could still be sold off was forty per cent of the shares in the almost completed Suez Canal. However, Canal shares were of little value until the Canal was operating and seen to be returning a profit. When the Canal opened in 1869 Ismail's prospects improved a little.

Britain's unstated fear, that the Suez Canal was a stepping stone for France towards India, was eased in 1870 when France and Germany went to war. The defeat of France in 1871 and the subsequent reparations demanded by Germany effectively removed French influence from the scene, at least for a while. Britain's interest in the Canal continued to grow, not least because most of the ships using the waterway came from Britain's mercantile fleet. In 1870, the first full year of operation, 489 ships went through the Canal, 324 of which were British. Clearly, Britain had a great and growing interest in the security of the Canal and were nervous that the country it ran through was on the brink of collapse. The continuance of Egypt's affairs now depended on the patience of the European banks, but who could tell where the control of Egypt – and the Canal – might eventually reside?

The Canal Company then caused concern in shipping circles by raising the transit tolls, moving from a calculation on net tonnage to one based on gross tonnage, increasing the cost of Canal transit by some thirty per cent. In 1872 de Lesseps so far forgot where the real power lay as to inform the British government that those ship owners who refused to pay could '. . . either avail themselves of the Egyptian Railway or go round the Cape of Good Hope . . . those who do not pay the dues will not be permitted to pass ships through the Canal.' The matter was fully thrashed out at a conference in Constantinople in 1873 when the Sublime Porte, suddenly remembering that Egypt was Turkish territory, agreed fresh but more reasonable charges with the international maritime community and ordered de Lesseps to introduce them.

De Lesseps refused. He went on refusing until Turkey, urged on by Britain, ordered Ismail to send troops to occupy the Canal zone unless de Lesseps complied with the new tariff. This threat proved sufficient but the British had become alarmed, for if a mere former diplomat and amateur engineer could have a veto on the free passage of British shipping, what might some well-armed power do? Even though de Lesseps eventually gave in, Britain had moved another step closer to involvement in Egypt's affairs and the British government, now headed by Benjamin Disraeli, decided to add weight to their concern by acquiring some Canal Company shares.

This was not a new idea. At the end of 1870, a year after the Canal opened, the British Consul-General in Cairo reported a meeting with the Khedive in which Ismail had suggested that the British might care to gain possession of the Canal. This met with a non-committal reply from Lord Granville, the Foreign Secretary, but by 1873, after de Lesseps' intransigence and when the Company was seen to be trading profitably, there was renewed interest. Matters came to a head in 1875, by which time Egypt was teetering on the brink of bankruptcy.

The financial juggling that took place to placate Egypt's creditors during 1875 are too complex for inclusion here. In brief, it became common knowledge that the Khedive wanted – needed – to sell his forty per cent shareholding in the Canal and there were plenty of his creditors eager to urge him on. The problem was to find a buyer acceptable to all parties. This was not easy but one of the first in line was the French bank, Societé Générale. If Societé Générale obtained the balance of the shares the Suez Canal would be a totally French entity and the French Government would be both obliged – and delighted – to protect it.

The British made it very clear that they would oppose any French company acquiring control of the Canal and by now the British government or at least Mr Disraeli, was actively interested in acquiring the Khedive's shares. On 17 November 1875, the Cabinet Secretary sent a message to Major-General Stanton, the British Consul-General in Cairo, stating, 'It is vital that the interests of the Viceroy of Egypt [Ismail] in the Suez Canal should not fall into the hands of a foreign company . . . intimate that H.M. Government are disposed to purchase if satisfactory terms can be arranged.'

Disraeli was well aware that the Khedive needed around £5 million by the end of December 1875 if he was to meet the interest payments on the foreign debt due at that time, but Parliament was not in session and Disraeli needed Parliamentary approval to lay out the necessary funds. Lacking that approval, Disraeli sent his Private Secretary, Mr Corry, to the banker Baron Rothschild and asked for a loan of £4 million.

'What is your security?' asked Rothschild.

'The British government,' replied Corry.

'Very well,' said the Baron. 'You shall have it.'

Britain thus acquired Ismail's shares in the Suez Canal for a small percentage of what the shares were probably worth and remained a major partner in that enterprise for another seventy years, until the Egyptian Government nationalized the Canal and precipitated the Suez invasion of 1956. Two major considerations had now been added to Britain's reasons for involvement in Egypt: the need to secure the repayment of Egypt's debt and the need to secure and protect a vital strategic waterway. There remained the matter of the Sudan.

The Canal and foreign debt were not the Khedive Ismail's only preoccupations during 1875. The problems of the Sudan were again on the agenda. Sir Samuel Baker had returned from the Equatorial Sudan in 1873, given up his position, and returned to London. As soon as he left Khartoum the bad old slaving ways returned.

Baker had spared neither effort nor money to get his 1870 expedition fully mustered and lavishly equipped. He took ten Europeans, including his wife. He had two regiments of soldiers – one Egyptian, one Sudanese, the former useless, the latter excellent – and a personal bodyguard of two score well-armed men who became known, inevitably, as the Forty Thieves. He had boats and paddle-steamers, Sneider rifles, drums, uniforms from the mills of Manchester and a great quantity of stores. By February 1870 Baker's expedition had assembled in Khartoum and was ready for the first stage of their task, the ascent of the Nile to Gondokoro. From that moment on the expedition began to go awry.

It was already apparent to Baker that the Sudan slave trade was thriving and that all the Egyptian garrisons and administrators in the Sudan were actively engaged in it, for they swiftly conspired with the Arab traders to thwart all Baker's attempts at suppression. That apart, he could not get to his post at Gondokoro. The great reed swamp of the Sudd barred his path up the river, and in 1870 all the channels through the Sudd were jammed with vegetation and the river was low. After two months of effort, tormented by swarms of flies and mosquitoes, he decided to abandon any attempt to advance upriver until it was in flood.

The expedition duly set sail again in December 1870. By March 1871 they were still caught in the Sudd, plagued by mosquitoes, felled by malaria, tormented by flies. It was not until May 1871, six months after leaving Khartoum, that Baker ran up the Turkish flag at Gondokoro and announced the annexation of the Upper Nile Valley. He also declared that the province south of the Sudd would henceforth be called Equatoria and that Gondokoro would be renamed Ismailia, in honour of the Khedive.

To achieve the hoisting of a flag and the renaming of a wilderness had taken Baker the best part of two years. His next task was to extinguish the slave trade. Before he could even begin that Augean task, Baker had trouble with the local tribes, for the blacks of 'Equatoria', roused to fury by the Arab slavers, harassed his patrols relentlessly. Most of his Egyptian soldiers deserted, and having stolen a quantity of his shipping, fled back downriver to Khartoum.

When Baker finally marched south into Buganda he discovered that the tribes of Central Africa had no wish to be annexed by Egypt. The main tribal leader in what is now Uganda, the Kabarenga of Bunyaro, put up strong resistance, leading to an all-out battle in June 1872 between Baker's Sudanese riflemen and the Bunyaro tribesmen. Baker won that battle but the tribespeople continued to harass his lines of communication until he was forced to retreat.

The Kabarenga was finally defeated in March 1873 but by December of that year Baker had resigned his post and taken his wife back to Britain. Whatever he had managed to achieve in Equatoria soon crumbled away and the slave trade he had been sent to destroy continued to flourish – to the anguish and fury of Western politicians and the vocal British Anti-Slavery Society. Fortunately, in February 1874, the Khedive found another British champion to tackle the problems of the Sudan, Colonel Charles George Gordon of the Royal Engineers.

3

Enter General Gordon

1874–1880

'Gordon is one of our National Treasures.'
Lord Cairns in a speech in the House of Lords,
August 1884

CHARLES GEORGE GORDON is the pivotal figure in the story
of Britain's involvement with Egypt and the Sudan. It is highly
probable that but for Gordon, Britain might not have become
involved there at all. Gordon was born in 1833, the son of a British
general. He seems to have been a normal, lively child, much
given to practical jokes and in 1848, when he was fifteen, he
passed without remark into the Military Academy at Woolwich.
Four years later he emerged as a second-lieutenant in the
Royal Engineers, that ingenious corps which was to produce a
surprising number of remarkable officers during the Victorian
era.

The Victorian army was in the habit of producing, and tolerat-
ing, strong, forceful, independently minded officers. Few officers
in any army at any time were as forceful, as independent, or as in
need of tolerant superiors as Charles George Gordon of the Royal
Engineers, and he began to make his mark soon after receiving his
commission.

Gordon served in the Crimean War where he was wounded,
displayed great gallantry under fire and made many friends,
including Garnet Wolseley. He then took various routine assign-
ments until 1860, when he volunteered for service in China. China
made Gordon famous; after China he was regarded in Britain as

the epitome of the muscular Christian, the Victorian warrior, the gallant English gentleman.

He was a slight, wiry man, five feet five inches tall, with startling blue eyes, at twenty-six years old already noted for his charm, his deep interest in religion and a certain reluctance to obey orders. Had he stayed with his corps he might have spent his life in honourable but unremarked service, but in China he was offered a singular opportunity and he seized it with both hands.

In 1860 China was another country under commercial siege by the Western imperial powers, but one also riven by internal conflicts. One of the most severe had arisen in 1850 when a Chinese Christian convert, Hung-Sen-Tsan, proclaimed himself to be a brother of Jesus Christ. Taking the title of 'Heavenly King' he decided to convert the Chinese to Christianity and when they proved unwilling to accept his word, resorted to force. Ten years later the Heavenly King's 'Great Peace' – or Taiping – had brought bloody war to large parts of China.

The Taipings enjoyed considerable military success. They defeated various government armies and massacred the entire population of Nanking. Massacres and the torture and execution of those who refused to be converted to Christianity became a feature of the Taiping Wars but the Heavenly King enjoyed a decade of success before he aroused any significant opposition. At first the powerful European community in China had even supported this evangelical Christian, but when the Taiping Wars began to interfere with trade, they decided he had to be stopped. The merchants therefore raised an army by subscription and to command it hired an American mercenary, Frederick Ward.

By 1862 Ward's 3,000-strong force, known for no good reason as the 'Ever-Victorious Army', had achieved some successes but now they needed a new commander. The British commander in Shanghai, Colonel Stavely, was approached by the business community and he allowed his young subordinate, Major Charles Gordon RE, to accept the post.

Even by the standards of the time, when a certain eccentricity in a public figure was almost expected, Major Gordon was a strange man. He was an efficient officer of the Royal Engineers and considered brave in an army where bravery was taken for granted. What set him apart were his personal qualities. Celibate, frugal, deeply religious, he prayed for hours each day and when in need of guidance, even in military affairs, tended to consult the Prophet Isaiah rather than his superior officers.

Yet Gordon's character was full of contradictions. He drank heavily, though without apparent effect; a bottle of brandy often stood next to the Bible on his table. He was also inordinately interested in young boys. Throughout his life Gordon kept himself surrounded by small boys, usually waifs or orphans. He would pick them up on the streets or in hovels, take them to his quarters, wash, feed and dress them, provide them with pocket money and send them to school; he delighted in their company. There is no hint or suggestion from his contemporaries that his interest in these boys was motivated by anything other than kindness and Christian charity. As far as is known his interest in them was both benign and total. He supported them as long as he lived, followed their careers with interest and kept a map dotted with small flags, each marking the place where every one of his boys – his 'Kings' as he called them – was living or working.

Everyone who knew Gordon found him impressive. Some thought him slightly mad, others thought him a saint. Even blunt soldiers like Sir Garnet Wolseley, Sir Evelyn Wood and Herbert Kitchener regarded Gordon as remarkable. His latent genius, or whatever quality fired this curious, unpredictable man, came into full flower in the wars against the Taipings.

Gordon led the Ever-Victorious Army like a medieval hero, heading every charge against the Taiping lines, armed only with his officer's cane – his 'wand of victory'. He drove the Taiping army away from Shanghai, defeating their field armies, capturing city after city. After fifteen months of fighting the Taiping rebellion was broken and the Heavenly King was dead. When the Chinese army entered his palace in Nanking in 1864 they found the 'King' and his numerous wives swinging gently from silken ropes.

The campaign against the Taipings was not won without some typically Gordon incidents. On appointment he had amazed the merchants and the mandarins by refusing to accept a salary, though he eventually took a small sum in order to keep up payments to his 'Kings'. He quarrelled with all his superiors and when a Chinese commander shot some Taiping chiefs who had been offered quarter by Gordon, Gordon went after this officer, revolver in hand, and threatened to kill him. Gifts of money, women, and profitable appointments were all rejected. When the body of the Heavenly King was discovered in Nanking, Gordon wept. He then swiftly disbanded the Ever-Victorious Army and sailed for home where, to his considerable surprise, he discovered that his adventures and activities in China had made him famous.

The generals at the Horse Guards – later the War Office – and the Queen were impressed. Gordon was promoted to Lieutenant-Colonel and made a Companion of the Bath, while to the press and public he was a hero – for the rest of his life the British knew him as 'Chinese' Gordon. However, as they got to know him, the generals and the government became wary of this strange, charismatic officer with his cavalier attitude to orders; it was more than twenty years before they gave him a field command and his appointment to the Sudan arose by accident.

In 1872, Nuba Pasha, the Khedive's Chief Minister, met Gordon in Constantinople where he was part of a British mission to the Porte. Knowing that Baker Pasha was unlikely to renew his contract in the Sudan, Nubar asked Gordon if he could think of anyone willing and able to take up the task and accept the post of Governor-General of Equatoria. Gordon had spent the last six years building fortifications along the Thames and Medway, compensating for this routine, boring work by giving free rein to the great passions of his life, the promotion of the Christian Gospel and the welfare of boys. He therefore replied that if he could obtain the requisite permission from his government, he would be happy to accept the post himself. This permission obtained, Gordon arrived in Cairo in February 1874 and so began the connection with Egypt and the Sudan that eventually led to his death.

Gordon was a complex, many-sided character, a superb leader of irregular troops but a mystic, hard to understand and harder still to command. He always went his own way, carried forward by faith in God and in his own ability to overcome any difficulty. Whether he was the right man to handle the delicate, complex affairs of the Sudan is quite another matter.

The Khedive Ismail's first intimation that Gordon was not as other men came when Gordon declined Baker's generous salary of £10,000 a year and said £2,500 would be more than sufficient. Gordon's eccentricity also revealed itself in his choice of companions, most of whom he recruited in Cairo in a couple of days. He chose an international assortment, including an American, Charles Chaillé-Long, who turned out to be useless, and John Russell, son of the famous Crimean and American Civil War correspondent for *The Times*, William H. Russell, who turned out to be a drunk.

Only a young Italian, Romolo Gessi, who had learned to soldier with Garibaldi, was to prove a stout ally in the time ahead. The most controversial of Gordon's appointments was an Arab former slaver, Abu Saoud, whom Gordon found languishing in gaol. Gordon claimed that Abu Saoud knew the Sudan and was a reformed character; only half of this turned out to be correct. Saoud was actually an unrepentant slaver and far too wily for Charles Gordon. Saoud's release also infuriated Samuel Baker who had originally put Abu Saoud in prison, regarding that act as one of the few successes of his service in Sudan.

Gordon took up his charge by sailing through the Suez Canal and disembarking at the Red Sea port of Suakin. There he climbed on to a camel for the first time in his life and rode for hundreds of miles across the desert to Khartoum. On the evening of his arrival he received a foretaste of what he would be up against. A welcome banquet arranged by his superior, Ismail Ayat Pasha, Governor-General of the Sudan, concluded with a performance by naked dancing girls and degenerated into an orgy. Gordon left the banquet in disgust.

Gordon remained in the Sudan as Governor of Equatoria from early 1874 until the end of 1876, but it was neither a happy nor a successful time. The climate, the corruption of the Egyptians, the relentless hostility of the slavers and his own restless energy combined to wear Gordon out. Sessions with the Bible soon combined with evenings on the brandy, and this together with the loneliness, tested his temper severely.

When he first arrived at Gondokoro he found that the garrison left by Baker had not been paid for a year and were only kept at their posts by periodic gifts of rum or slave girls sent from Khartoum. Gordon made a series of decisions, the most far-reaching of which was to return to Khartoum and telegraph fresh terms to the Khedive: briefly, that Equatoria should be separated from the rest of the Sudan and that Gordon should report directly to the Khedive, ignoring Ismail Ayat Pasha in Khartoum. The Khedive agreed and Gordon returned to Gondokoro with *carte blanche* to do what he wanted. His first task was to dismiss the slaver Abu Saoud, who had swiftly returned to his former ways.

Then came war with the river tribes. They had been exploited by Baker's Egyptian troops as well as the slavers and they attacked Gordon's patrols and garrisons with all their old ferocity; in one skirmish the élite of Gordon's little army, Baker's old bodyguard, the 'Forty Thieves', was almost annihilated. Only Romolo Gessi seemed up to his duties and together he and Gordon set out to bring some sort of order to the Upper Nile Valley and Equatoria. This was no easy task. Order in Khartoum was maintained by Ismail Ayat Pasha with the gallows, the prison cells and the *courbash* – the fearful hippopotamus-hide whip. Gordon had no taste for such methods and outside Khartoum there was no order of any kind.

The root cause of the trouble was slavery. Profitable and deeply corrupting, it offered the slave-holder not only wealth but also power, labour, and women. It was the mainspring of Sudanese life and until it was rooted out Gordon stood no chance of achieving his ends. He therefore elected to make stern war on the slavers, the chief of whom was Zobeir Pasha, the virtual ruler of Darfur, the Western province of the Sudan.

Zobeir was a prince of slavers. He maintained an army of Arab horsemen who scoured Darfur and the country alongside the Bahr-el-Ghazal, the 'River of Antelopes', one of the great tributaries of the Nile, his raiders roving far into Central Africa to capture slaves by the tens of thousands and bring them north to Khartoum. Zobeir became fabulously wealthy. What he could not obtain by threats or force, he obtained by bribery. Gordon's lack of interest in money meant he could not be bribed but the Khedive's Egyptian administrators in the Sudan were all in Zobeir's pay: without their compliance Gordon's task was hopeless.

Gordon flung himself against the slavers with Christian zeal and ferocious energy but the problem was too great, the country too large, his resources too few; he could not make any real impact on the situation. He explored and mapped the Upper Nile and freed thousands of slaves, but very little was actually achieved. Once freed, these Africans sat around listlessly, not knowing how to find their way home again, and were soon snapped up by other slavers. At the end of 1876, worn out with overwork and malaria, Gordon made his way back to Cairo and resigned his post.

The Khedive was aghast. Gordon was one of the planks under-lying his shaky position, one reason why his creditors stayed their hand, the only evidence that he was serious about ending the slave trade. These two factors were linked and Egypt's debts, secured and unsecured, now amounted to around £94,000,000. He *had* to retain the services of Colonel Gordon, who had now returned to England and in January 1877 he sent Gordon a telegram: 'I refuse to believe that when Gordon has once given his word as a gentle-man, anything would ever induce him to go back on his word.'

That comment was enough. Gordon returned to Cairo in Febru-ary 1877 and stated fresh terms. This time there must be no half measures. The corrupt Ismail Ayat Pasha must leave Khartoum and Gordon must be made Governor-General of the entire Sudan. The Khedive agreed.

Then there was the matter of Zobeir. The slaver had recently arrived in Cairo with a great quantity of money, seeking the Khedive's blessing on his rulership of Darfur and confirmation of his *de facto* rule of that much-ravaged province. Gordon wanted Zobeir hanged or imprisoned, but the Khedive, having taken Zob-eir's money, proposed a compromise. Zobeir was placed under house arrest in Cairo; Gordon departed again for Khartoum.

During this brief stay in Cairo, Gordon met a man who was to play a leading part in Egyptian and Sudanese affairs in the coming decades, Sir Evelyn Baring, later Lord Cromer, who had just taken up the post of British Representative in Cairo. Baring was a strong-willed man with powerful political connections. Rather more to the point, given the state of Egypt's finances, he was one of the banking Barings.

Baring's Bank had been created by Sir Francis Baring at the end of the eighteenth century, while Sir Francis was Chairman of the East India Company. The bank rose in fortune as British trade expanded and became a linchpin of British influence abroad, rivalling the Rothschilds in power and wealth. The Duc de Riche-lieu said in 1812 that 'there are six great powers in Europe, England, France, Austria, Prussia . . . and the Baring brothers', and the Duke was probably right. Baring money funded British armies in the Napoleonic Wars and financed the American 'Louisi-ana Purchase' from France in 1803, a deal that doubled the size of the United States.

In the 1870s the Baring Bank was at the height of its powers and Sir Evelyn Baring was a scion of that powerful and astute family. One of his brothers was the Ambassador to Washington; his cousin, Lord Northbrook, was currently Viceroy of India but even without his family connections Sir Evelyn Baring was a most remarkable man. His book, *Modern Egypt*, which details his time in Egypt from 1876 to 1907, is a model of autobiography and extremely readable. In that work Baring reveals himself as a tolerant, far-sighted but grimly purposeful man, who did not suffer fools at all, let alone gladly, and his time in Egypt was driven by a commitment to efficiency and economy.

Baring occupied a pivotal position in Anglo-Egyptian affairs for more than a quarter of a century, enduring some trying times and dealing with some remarkably difficult people, but he never lost his sense of proportion or his ability to reason. With all that, he was a man with a steel core; wise men did not fall out with Sir Evelyn Baring. By his sound common sense and fair dealing Baring earned and enjoyed the trust and respect of everyone, both British and Egyptian, who came in contact with him. While Gordon may have gained the historic headlines, it is Baring who must be credited with the organization, indeed with the creation, of modern Egypt and the Anglo-Egyptian Sudan.

Baring had just been appointed British Representative in Cairo – the country, nominally a province of Turkey, did not warrant an Ambassador – and he was deeply sceptical about Gordon's latest commission. 'Even assuming that the Khedive is sincere in his desire to suppress slavery and bring order to the Sudan, nothing is more certain than that he is powerless to do so,' he noted drily in his diary.

Gordon thought otherwise. Equipped with the Khedive's fresh commission, he descended on the Sudan like a whirlwind. Unlike his Egyptian predecessors who wallowed in what small luxury Khartoum could afford Gordon was rarely in his capital. Riding a swift camel he ranged far across the Sudan, arresting slavers, freeing slaves, dispensing justice. Romolo Gessi returned to his service in 1878 and was despatched to bring order to Darfur, where Zobeir's son, Suleiman, was in the field against the new Governor-General.

Gessi fought Suleiman in the Bahr-el-Ghazal and, having dispersed the slavers' army, had the young Suleiman and eleven of his followers shot. This was the sort of language the Sudanese slavers understood and the slave trade faltered. In a further strike against the endemic corruption Gordon appointed his own officers to fill the provincial posts: Gessi became Governor of the Bahr-el-Ghazal, while an Austrian soldier, Rudolf Slatin, was sent to rule Darfur. Equatoria went to a German doctor, Edouard Schnitzer, who became known as Emin Pasha, and an English seaman, Frank Lupton, was being groomed for a senior administrative post by Gordon in Khartoum. All was going well and all might even have been well, but for the fact that the Khedive Ismail's chaotic rule was coming to an end in Cairo.

The parlous state of the Egyptian economy had been analysed in the Cave Report of 1876, a document commissioned by the Khedive Ismail. Mr Stephen Cave was a British Member of Parliament sent to examine and report on Egypt's finances and his report was published in May 1876. It made gloomy reading but it did not, as confidently expected, lay all the blame for Egypt's financial misfortune at Ismail's door.

According to Cave, while the Khedive Ismail had been both extravagant and foolish, the rates of interest demanded by his European creditors were little short of usury. He therefore proposed that the Egyptian debts should be rescheduled and paid back over a much longer period, at greatly reduced rates of interest. Unfortunately this report gave great encouragement to the Khedive Ismail. Three days after the Cave Report was published Ismail announced a suspension of all foreign debt repayments pending the new deal.

This action proved unwise. The Khedive's French and British creditors at once appealed to their governments to put pressure on Ismail and get the payments restarted, on pain of sanctions or military intervention. As France and Britain were to find, again, in 1956, economic sanctions could not be effective without the threat or use of force. The first steps towards an armed confrontation between Egypt and the West had been taken.

The Khedive and his advisers attempted to divert this impending action by creating a new body, the Caisse de la Dette, a Commission which would contain delegates from all the creditor nations, France, Britain, Italy, Germany and Austria, as well as Egypt, and be charged with managing and reducing the national debt. This was a formidable task, for the total debt stood at some £91 million. Paying the annual minimum seven per cent interest alone would eat up about two-thirds of Egypt's revenue, without touching the capital debt at all.

The British Government at first refused to play any part in the Caisse de la Dette and this attempt by Ismail to keep some control over his national affairs finally foundered, to be replaced with a system called 'Dual Control', in which two commissioners, one British in the person of Sir Evelyn Baring, one French, a Monsieur de Blignières, took control of Egypt's Ministry of Finance and Ministry of Public Works, thus controlling both the country's income and public expenditure. Another Englishman, Sir Edward Malet, became Consul General. Ismail may have been forced to accept Dual Control but he did not have to like it. He liked it still less when the Dual Control commissioners began to disentangle the national finances and separate the country's money from his personal Treasury.

In an attempt to delay or divert this action, in March 1878 Ismail invited Gordon up from Khartoum to chair a fresh committee looking into the causes of the national debt. Given Gordon's contempt for money it is hard to think of a more bizarre appointment but his proposals were quite sensible. Gordon suggested that representatives of the creditors, as interested parties, should be excluded from the committee. He also proposed a moratorium on the debt repayments, a move already proposed by Mr Cave and rejected by everyone else.

Gordon also fell out with Sir Evelyn Baring, whom he found pretentious and patronising. 'When oil and water mix, we will mix together', he declared. Baring's thoughts on their exchanges are not on record, but he put his finger on one of Gordon's fixations when he noted in his diary that 'It is not easy to deal with a man who, in moments of difficulty, takes his instructions from Isaiah.' Gordon returned to Khartoum, and the debt commissioners continued to wrestle with the Khedive.

Without Ismail's co-operation, Dual Control could not be fully effective, and in 1879 Ismail's continued resistance to the commissioners' enquiries led to his downfall. The French and British governments put pressure on the Sultan to depose Ismail and replace him with his more complaisant son, Tewfik. Their aim was to secure total co-operation in the running of the country; they forgot that Egypt was not their country.

The Khedive Ismail was finally driven out of office in June 1879. He left in style in his private yacht after removing £3 million from the Egyptian Treasury to bolster his retirement in Constantinople. With his departure and Tewfik's accession the troubles of Egypt began to multiply. One of the first to follow Ismail out of Egypt was Colonel Charles Gordon.

The overthrow of Ismail was the last straw, but Gordon was already heartily sick of his work in the Sudan. Worn out with years of overwork in a terrible climate he was clearly in the grip of a chronic, even suicidal, depression. 'I have lost every desire for the things of this life and have no wish for eating, drinking or comforts.

If I have a wish for anything it is for a dreamless sleep,' he wrote in his diary. In July 1879 he sent in his resignation and by January 1880 he was back in Britain. The Khedive Tewfik promptly appointed Raouf Pasha, a man known to be both corrupt and incompetent, as the new Governor-General of the Sudan, and slave trading and public corruption rapidly returned.

Henry Morton Stanley has described the Khedive Tewfik as 'most amiable'. In fact, Tewfik was a weak, vacillating person, the kind of man who agrees with whomever he has spoken to last, and he proved quite unable to control the events which now engulfed him. In practice, Tewfik had little to do, since the government of Egypt was effectively in the hands of Baring and de Blignières. The two commissioners could dominate Tewfik far more easily than they had the Khedive Ismail but the Egyptian people soon became unhappy with the Dual Control system.

The Khedive Ismail had been profligate, incompetent and a harsh ruler but he had what we now call charisma and the Egyptians were used to him. Besides, he was Egyptian and a Muslim. It would be another century before it dawned on the colonial powers that their subject peoples might prefer to be ruled incompetently by one of their own than ruled efficiently by strangers. Once Ismail had gone, the fact that their country was being run by foreigners, and Christians to boot, could no longer be concealed from the Egyptian people.

The common people of Egypt and, more importantly, the officers and soldiers of the Egyptian army, had certainly become tired of the avarice and inefficiency of the ruling, French-educated, Turkish-Armenian-Circassian aristocracy, but the activities of the British and French administrators, probing into every corner of the country, attempting to change every aspect of their lives, were to prove highly unpopular. Egypt might be deeply in debt but it was *their* country and the Dual Control commissioners were not over tactful in carrying out the much-needed fiscal and political reforms.

It seems strange today that any nation should allow another nation to move in on part of its territory and take control of its affairs but Egypt was not then a sovereign nation. It was a province of the Turkish Empire and a ruined one; if the Turks had no wish to rule there and the British were eager to take charge, there was no power available to the people of Egypt, legal or military, to prevent them.

This insensitive attitude towards the Egyptians was typical of the view taken by colonial administrators towards their subject peoples in the heydey of the Victorian Empire: that they were usually corrupt and generally incompetent and needed strong Western guidance. This belief may have been based on reason, and held in the name of justice and efficiency, but in this case at least it ignored the fact that the ways of Egypt suited the Egyptians perfectly well.

Before long, loud murmurs of discontent were heard, most often and most loudly from the officer corps of the Egyptian army. More complaints came from the Chamber of Notables, a body of leading Egyptians set up by Ismail after some urging from the Dual Control commissioners, in an attempt to introduce Egypt to the beginnings of Parliamentary Government. This attempt at democracy provided the spark that ignited a military revolt and led to the Anglo-Egyptian War of 1882.

4

Arabi's War

1881–1882

'The sole aim of this Government is the prosperity of
Egypt and its full enjoyment of the liberty which it has
obtained from the Sultan.'

Lord Granville, British Foreign Secretary, 1880

ALTHOUGH THE EGYPTIAN population had been simmering
with resentment against the intrusive foreigners for many years,
the first sign of revolt appeared on 1 February 1881, and over an
internal matter. Two infantry colonels, Colonel Arabi of the 4th
Infantry Regiment and Colonel Fehmi of the 1st Infantry Regiment, were summoned to the Ministry of War in Cairo to explain
why they had organized a petition attacking Osman Pasha, the
Minister of War, as incompetent – which he certainly was – and
demanding that the qualifications of all those officers recently selec-
ted for promotion should be carefully re-examined.

Apart from disparaging the performance of the Minister of War,
the petition alleged that Colonel Fehmi and Colonel Arabi, though
clearly far more qualified than the majority of those favoured, had
been left off the promotion roster, mainly because they were not
members of the ruling Turkish-Circassian élite. Both accusations
were quite true; the petition had been strongly backed by most of
the army; and the Minister of War would not tolerate it.

The Minister intended to arrest the two colonels as soon as they
arrived at his office and put them before a court martial, but this
was Cairo and his intention had swiftly leaked out. The colonels
had therefore instructed their regiments that if they had not

returned from the Ministry within two hours their soldiers were to march into Cairo and obtain their release. The army rank and file, underpaid, poorly disciplined and disregarded, was ripe for mutiny and the two colonels were popular. Following the colonels' arrest, their regiments duly arrived in the city, there was a most unseemly riot and the Khedive Tewfik duly capitulated, dismissed Osman Pasha as Minister of War and appointed Baroudi Pasha in his place. This may have been a sensible decision for Baroudi Pasha was well-liked, but the officers had tasted power and were soon back with further demands.

Their next move came on 9 September 1881 when a group of Egyptian officers, again led by Colonel Ahmed Arabi, marched their regiments to the residence of the Khedive Tewfik at the Abdin Palace in Cairo. Their demand now was for the dismissal of the government, an increase in the size of the army and the setting up of a new national government with Colonel Arabi as Secretary-of-State for War. The ever-compliant Khedive Tewfik promptly agreed to these demands.

Having done so he sent for Sir Auckland Colvin, the British Commissioner of the Debt. Colvin had recently replaced Evelyn Baring, who had gone to India to join the Council of the Governor-General, Lord Northbrook. Colvin and the British Consul-General in Cairo, Sir Charles Cookson, currently deputizing for Sir Edward Malet, began to negotiate directly with Arabi. No one paid much attention to the words or wishes of the Khedive Tewfik and by taking this action the British confirmed Arabi's worst suspicions, that they were the *de facto* rulers of his country.

In 1881 Colonel Ahmed Arabi, the hero of the army, was forty-two years of age and a most unlikely revolutionary. The son of a sheik, he was a slow-speaking, cautious man, unimpressive in appearance but a good soldier, a committed nationalist and, a rare thing for an officer in the Khedival army, a native-born Egyptian: a later generation has compared Arabi to the 1950's Egyptian leader, Colonel Nasser.

Arabi had completed his education at the Azhar University in Cairo, where he remained a hero to the native Egyptian students. Mohammed Said had noticed this fellah officer and appointed him as one of his Viceregal ADCs, promoting him to the rank of Lieutenant-Colonel. Said's successor, the Khedive Ismail, had little time for fellah officers. Arabi remained a colonel for the next sixteen years, took part in Egypt's disastrous war with Abyssinia and grew steadily discontented with the Khedival government and the interference of the European powers.

The commissioners protested to the Khedive Tewfik about Arabi's appointment to the government but their objections only served to make Arabi even more popular with the general population and the army rank and file. Before long, Colonel Arabi was generally regarded as the hope of the nation, and from the time he appeared on the scene, local resistance to the Khedive Tewfik, to Dual Control, to foreign interference and expatriates in general, began to harden.

Under the guidance of the Dual Control commissioners it should have been possible to restore the country to some kind of financial stability, reduce the foreign debt and ease the burdens of taxation on the fellahin. To their credit, the commissioners were partially successful in these ends. By 1881 they had reduced the size of the foreign debt, eliminated some of the worst exactions of the Egyptian tax gatherers and tidied up the shambles that passed for a civil service. This should have gained them a measure of popularity but none of this earned the commissioners much in the way of gratitude; they were foreigners and Christians and their actions were inevitably seen as interference, which indeed it was. Their collusion with the Sultan of Turkey to expel the Khedive Ismail had aroused the enmity of the population and violence began to brew in the hot, dusty streets of the capital and the Delta towns.

The British Consul-General in Cairo, Sir Edward Malet, had some sympathy with Colonel Arabi but was worried about where this growing discontent would lead. Nor was Arabi without support in Britain. The writer and traveller Wilfred Blunt was one Englishman who openly supported Egyptian independence, deplored the actions of the speculators, regarded the commissioners' actions as unwarranted interference in Egyptian affairs and thought the British should leave Egypt entirely alone. Blunt was a passionate Arabist and a strong opponent of Mr Gladstone, currently the Prime Minister of Britain, a man who, said Blunt, 'was capable of any treachery or any crime . . .'

Gladstone was as anxious as anyone to avoid any overt interference in Egypt's affairs but matters were now rapidly getting out of hand. It was becoming ever more clear that if Arabi was to be stopped, the expatriates protected, the Canal secured, and the debt repaid, then force must eventually be applied. As Sir Edward Malet feared, the actions of Colonel Arabi and his supporters led to a series of capitulations by Khedive Tewfik and a steady slide into anarchy, which in turn brought the prospect of foreign military intervention more likely.

In January 1882, the French and British governments issued a Joint Note which they hoped would indicate their strong support for the Khedive Tewfik and so quell the growing discontent. This confirmed that the two Governments would '. . . oppose all internal and external threats to the Khedive and the current order of things in Egypt.'

However well meant, the Joint Note had a disastrous effect. The Khedive Tewfik thought it patronizing. Arabi and the army saw it as a threat to their position, and the ruling Turkish-Circassian élite in Egypt regarded it as a declaration of intervention. The timing alone was insensitive, for the Muslim world, including the normally complaisant Turkish Sultan, had recently been outraged by the French seizure of Tunisia. Now – or so it appeared – the British and French proposed occupying Egypt and imposing their will by force. The position of the Khedive and the Chamber of Notables was at once thoroughly undermined while the influence of the army, and especially of Colonel Arabi, grew in proportion.

Civil disorder then broke out in towns across the Nile Delta. The Egyptian press was quick to fan the flames of smouldering resentment. 'We are the prey of two lions, France and England,' wrote one newspaper 'who are waiting for the favourable moment to realize their designs, hidden under a deceptive policy. One day we hope to see our administration cleared of all Europeans and on that day we can say that England and France have done us great service'. To bring that day closer Europeans were soon being reviled, spat at, insulted, even attacked, in the streets of Cairo and Alexandria.

Such incidents provided the British and French governments with all the reason they needed to intervene. They called a meeting of Egypt's creditor nations – a 'Conference of the Powers' – in Constantinople and sent the Khedive a note demanding the dissolution of the national government. To give weight to these demands an Anglo-French squadron of warships sailed for Alexandria and anchored in Aboukir Bay. Tewfik complied with these demands and his government resigned. Then the Egyptians demanded a new national government and this was established amid great acclaim with Colonel Arabi as Prime Minister. Colonel Arabi, with the backing of the army and the bulk of the population, had no

difficulty overawing the Khedive and the Chamber of Notables.
Arabi was now, in effect, the dictator of Egypt.

The Conference of the Powers assembled in Constantinople on
23 June 1882, but soon ran into trouble. The Sublime Porte had
already protested against the Joint Note and became further
alarmed at the prospects of direct intervention into what was, after
all, a Turkish possession. The Sultan became even more annoyed
when Russia, Austria, Germany and Italy declared that the maintenance of the (Anglo-French) *status quo* in Egypt was in the
interests of the creditor nations and the European powers in general, a broad hint that if either nation decided to launch a military
intervention in Egypt, the rest of the European nations would not
protest.

The Sultan of Turkey declared that he would not attend this
Conference since the affairs of Egypt were an internal matter and
the concern of the Turkish Empire alone. The Conference delegates
hurriedly declared that none of the nations represented had any
territorial interest in Egypt and, having stated that, the Conference
adjourned.

In Egypt matters were now deteriorating fast. On 11 June 1882,
even before the Conference went into session in Constantinople,
an anti-foreigner riot broke out in Alexandria. This resulted in the
death of some fifty expatriates. Rioting soon broke out in other
Egyptian cities. Most foreign residents had the sense to flee and
some found shelter in the ships of the Anglo-French naval squadron
now anchored off Alexandria from which news of their plight was
telegraphed to Paris and London.

With rioting in the streets and their warships on hand, the
British and French Consul-Generals and the Dual Control commissioners demanded that the Khedive dismiss Colonel Arabi. The
Khedive duly complied only to have his entire government tender
their resignations. The Khedive was totally out of his depth in
these turbulent waters and when Arabi demanded reinstatement,
Tewfik again complied. These constant shifts lost Tewfik all authority over his government, army and people.

The rapid deterioration of public order in Egypt was fast pushing
the British and French governments towards direct intervention,
a course of action both were most anxious to avoid. Intervention
was nevertheless becoming inevitable. Egypt contained a large
mercantile community containing many French and British citizens. Although the actions and demands of this community had

played a large part in reducing Egypt to penury, both the French and the British governments, and especially their Consuls on the spot, had become accustomed to protecting their citizens and elevating them above Egyptian law. This was in the High Victorian days of 'gunboat diplomacy' when any foreigner or foreign government daring to raise his hand against a French or British citizen could expect to find warships offshore or redcoats in the streets. The Anglo-French community in Egypt were now demanding similar protection.

Colonel Arabi clearly intended to expel the most exploitative expatriates and cancel the foreign debt, and the Egyptian mobs were giving practical effect to this policy by attacking foreigners in the streets and burning their houses and warehouses. Neither the Dual Control commissioners, the Khedive, or Colonel Arabi now seemed able to impose order on the mobs or control escalating violence in Egypt.

Those Anglo-French expatriates who could leave were already fleeing the country – more than fourteen thousand had left by mid-June 1882 – but there remained the matter of Egyptian foreign debt and the country's internal financial affairs – which the commissioners still controlled – as well as the protection of the Suez Canal. If the men on the spot or in Constantinople were unable to restore order and return Egypt to tranquillity, sterner methods might have to be employed.

At this point the interests of the French and British governments began to diverge. Both were interested in seeing their banks and businessmen recover their money but the French had enough on their hands conquering and occupying Algeria and Tunisia and wanted no further commitment in North Africa – at least for the moment. Even on the matter of the Canal, the two nations failed to agree. The British were quite prepared to fight for the now-vital maritime link; the French were not.

On 24 June, Arabi announced that any military intervention at Alexandria would be met with force and the two Dual Control commissioners were excluded by soldiers from attending a meeting of the national government. The growing tumult in Cairo was a most unwelcome distraction for the Gladstone government in London, for the Prime Minister was not interested either in expanding the Empire or in the problems of Egypt. He had problems enough at home, most particularly the question of Home Rule for Ireland – 'One prayer absorbs all others: Ireland, Ireland,

Ireland,' he said later, but the state of affairs in Egypt could not be ignored.

There was the Suez Canal to protect, British lives to defend, and rather closer to hand, Queen Victoria to placate. Mr Gladstone was not the Queen's favourite Prime Minister. He was a Liberal, a retiring, stubborn radical, totally uninterested in imperial adventures or national glory. He was, in addition, quite capable of standing up to the Queen's demands. Her Majesty's most famous complaint was that 'Mr Gladstone addresses me as if I were a public meeting,' but a study of their correspondence reveals that Gladstone was almost saintly in his patience with the Queen and her continual demands for British action, especially over any problems affecting the Empire.

The Queen saw fit to send the Prime Minister several warnings over the progress of events in Egypt, and she was not the only one. Opposition MPs arose from the Tory benches in the House of Commons and the Lords to attack the spineless conduct of Her Majesty's Liberal Ministers. Businessmen lobbied their MPs for action to protect their interests, the press became excited and the War Office began to rumble with anticipation. On 3 July 1881 the Adjutant-General of the British Army, Sir Garnet Wolseley, sent Gladstone a draft plan for the invasion of Egypt and the seizure of the Suez Canal. Gladstone deplored the necessity for such a move and remained very reluctant to commit troops to Egypt but he permitted Wolseley to make some cautious preliminary moves.

A force of two infantry divisions and a cavalry brigade were put under embarkation notice and shipping was assembled on the Clyde and the Thames. In the Mediterranean the garrison of Cyprus was reinforced by a company of Royal Engineers and two battalions of infantry. These troops arrived in Cyprus on 10 July 1882, by which time events in Egypt had developed into open war.

Step by step, whether Gladstone wanted it or not, the British were being drawn into Egypt, though even outside Parliament, British opinions on intervention were sharply divided. The British public were well aware that Egypt had been looted and misgoverned for decades; there was little sympathy for the expatriate business community in Cairo and a certain understanding of the Egyptian desire for independence. Arabi even had his supporters in London where his resentment of the Turkish-Circassian élite and the foreign speculators was well understood. Many British people were willing to assist him in his struggle, and spoke out in

the streets and in Parliament against those urging military intervention in Egypt. These voices were soon drowned in the rising
clamour for decisive action to protect British property and lives.

On 10 July 1882 the British Admiral commanding the squadron
off Alexandria, Sir Beauchamp Seymour, noted that the Egyptian
army was moving coastal artillery batteries into position along the
shoreline at Alexandria and digging entrenchments. Considering
this a potentially hostile act, Seymour sent an officer ashore to
demand that the artillery be removed and the trenches filled in.
These demands were promptly rejected. After a brief consultation
with London, Admiral Seymour informed the garrison commander
at Alexandria that unless the Egyptians complied with his demands
he would open fire on their works.

This sudden British bellicosity alarmed the French Admiral
Conrad. After consulting his superiors, who ordered him to withdraw, the French portion of the allied squadron upped anchor and
sailed away towards Port Said and the northern entrance of the
Suez Canal. If the British intended to make war on the Egyptian
people, they must do it on their own. The British Admiral's warning also alarmed the Khedive Tewfik, but he made no attempt to
intervene or prevent what was clearly about to happen. He withdrew to a palace outside Alexandria and remained there, silent,
while war descended on his country.

On 10 July Admiral Seymour sent ashore a final ultimatum
demanding the dismantling of the shore batteries at Alexandria.
When this was rejected, the British warships duly opened fire on
the defences of Alexandria, at 7 a.m. on 11 July 1882.

The Egyptians had mounted nearly two hundred guns along the
shoreline but they could not match the weight of shot available to
Admiral Seymour. Seymour had nineteen ships of the Mediterranean fleet anchored off Alexandria. These included his flagship
HMS *Invincible*, and her sister ship HMS *Inflexible*, both mounting
11-inch guns. The other battleships – all of them the newly
designed ironclads – were equally well-armed. In the course of the
day their fire systematically destroyed all the Egyptian batteries
around the shore.

The bombardment of Alexandria went on for a full ten hours.
By the evening of 11 July all the shore batteries had been silenced
but they had nonetheless been well handled, scoring seventy-five
hits on British ships. The bulk of Alexandria's citizens had meanwhile fled south into the desert or down the road to Cairo,

abandoning the city to the mob. Over the next couple of days large areas of Alexandria were looted and much of the city was burned by the time Royal Marines and naval bluejackets were landed from the fleet on the evening of 13 July. These forces, accompanied by fire control parties, soon had the city under martial law.

Seymour's precipitate action met with strong disapproval from the French but the British were unrepentant. Even Sir Evelyn Baring, the most reasonable of men, later declared, 'There can be no doubt that the bombardment was justifiable . . . not merely on the narrow ground of self-defence but because it was clear that in the absence of effective Turkish or international action, the duty of crushing Arabi depended on Britain alone.'

Certainly no other nation was anxious to intervene. Most of them hastened to distance themselves from the British action and whatever consequences might follow. The French naval squadron hurriedly left Port Said and withdrew to their bases at Marseilles and Toulon. Apart from voicing their disapproval, the French took no further part in Egypt's affairs. Britain and Egypt, or to be more exact the Egyptian army, now moved swiftly towards war, while the bulk of Egyptian citizens and the Khedive Tewfik attempted to stay out of the way.

Following the bombardment and landings at Alexandria, Arabi mustered his army around Cairo, where he proposed to make a stand against any invasion force. Now head of the Egyptian government, he declared a cancellation of all overseas debts and a determination to block or destroy the Suez Canal. He made no move to carry out this latter threat but even before it was made, a British army was at sea and bearing down fast on Egypt's shores, a strong force of horse, foot and guns, an army of disciplined, professional, fighting men under the command of a stout-hearted soldier, Lieutenant-General Sir Garnet Wolseley.

5

Wolseley's War

1882

Ensign Garnet Wolseley believed that the best possible way to get ahead in the Army was to try to get killed every time he had the chance.

Joseph H. Lehman, *All Sir Garnet*, 1964

IN JULY 1882, General Sir Garnet Wolseley, Adjutant-General and second-in-command of the British Army, was just forty-nine, Britain's best-known general, and a soldier at the height of his powers. He was also extremely glad to get out of London for a while and return to the job he loved best, commanding troops in the field. Wolseley was the product of an army that was just emerging from the most traumatic decade in its history; for the last ten years he had been at the centre of military controversy over army reform and the arguments were far from over. However those disagreements could wait; for the moment there was an enemy to fight and a war to be won.

Garnet Wolseley was born in Ireland in 1833, the eldest of seven children, the son and grandson of army officers. At the age of seventeen, after several direct appeals from his mother, Wolseley was commissioned in the 12th Foot – later the Suffolk Regiment – through the direct intervention of the Duke of Wellington, for the Wolseley family had no money to buy him a commission. Displaying conspicuous courage was the way poor men got on in the Victorian army and since joining up Wolseley had pursued action and adventure with particular assiduity.

He fought in Burma, where he was wounded, and in the Crimea, where he was severely wounded and Mentioned-in-Despatches. In the Crimea, while attached to the Royal Engineers, he met and became friends with Charles Gordon and for the rest of his life regarded Gordon as one of the two most remarkable men he had ever met; the other was the American Confederate General, Robert E. Lee. Wolseley served in the Indian Mutiny in 1857, where he took part in the relief of Lucknow and rose to the rank of Lieutenant-Colonel by the age of twenty-two, a remarkable achievement at any time. He served in China in the 1860s, where he was considered for command of the mercenary Ever-Victorious Army, that post eventually going to his friend Charles Gordon.

Wolseley also took every opportunity to learn more about his profession, a rare attribute for an officer in the Victorian army. Posted to Canada in 1862, during the American Civil War, he found time to visit Robert E. Lee's splendid army of Northern Virginia, which was then engaged in the Antietam campaign. The sight of those large volunteer armies, Union and Confederate, so unlike Britain's small army of long-service, professional soldiers, made a considerable impression on him.

In 1867 he married Miss Louisa Erskine and in 1879 he published a book, the *Soldier's Pocket Book*, full of information and diagrams on military life and military skills. The book was not uncritical of current army practices but it remained in print for many years, bringing Wolseley to the attention of those interested in army reform and also those who were totally opposed to it. Meanwhile, Wolseley was rising fast in his chosen profession. In 1869 he returned to Canada to command the Red River Expedition, a force sent against a 'Meti' half-caste, Louis Riel, who had raised a rebellion in the West. Wolseley's force made their way across the wilderness to Manitoba in canoes paddled by French-Canadian *voyageurs*. The rebellion had collapsed before they reached Fort Garry but the *voyageurs* were to enter Wolseley's mind again in the Sudan a few years later. During this expedition he began to gather around his headquarters a group of efficient and forward-looking officers.

In 1870–3 he commanded the British Expeditionary Force during the Ashanti campaign in West Africa. By then he was a local Major-General and, at forty years old, the youngest General in the British army. The Ashanti campaign was hard but successful and Wolseley returned from West Africa to the plaudits of his countrymen. He was confirmed as Major-General, appointed

GCMG and KCB, awarded the thanks of both Houses of Parliament and granted the useful sum of £25,000 to support his rank and position. He had also, perhaps more usefully, put together a group of like-minded compatriots, including some of those clever young officers he had met on the Red River Expedition. These officers, all of them Wolseley's personal friends, later became known as 'The Wolseley Gang', or the 'Ashanti Ring'.

Among these were a number of men who will appear later in this tale, fighting in Egypt or the Sudan. They include John McNeill VC, Sir Evelyn Wood VC, Redvers Buller VC, Herbert Stewart, William Butler, Hugh McCalmont and many more, men chosen, said Wolseley, for their competence and reliability. Other men, less favoured or less generous, said they were chosen for appointment or advancement because they were Wolseley's cronies and supported his views on reform. Wolseley freely admitted that he kept a list of officers he intended to take on his campaigns. Since Britain was then without a General Staff, commanders were permitted to recruit their own staff for any particular campaign, but Wolseley stressed that he was always on the lookout for talent and any soldier worth his salt might earn a place on his list.

Wolseley had need of friends. A small, upright man with bright blue eyes and a pleasing manner, everyone admitted he had a first-class brain. However, he was not an easy man to like, being both arrogant, ambitious, and a thorough-going snob. He was also a clear-thinking, fighting soldier who had spent the greater part of his career railing at the outmoded anachronisms which dogged the British army. Although he was undoubtedly right in these observations, his comments found no favour with his ultimate superior, the Duke of Cambridge, Commander-in-Chief of the British Army, or indeed with Cambridge's dear friend and cousin, Her Majesty Queen Victoria.

Since the end of the Napoleonic Wars in 1815, the British army had been trapped in a time-warp created by the Duke of Wellington, Field Marshal, Commander-in-Chief, conqueror of Napoleon, victor of Waterloo. After Waterloo, Wellington's influence hung heavily over the British army and while he lived this was perhaps no bad thing, for the Duke was a military genius.

Those who followed in his path were rather less gifted and the growing inadequacies of the British army, in equipment, training, leadership, manpower, logistics – indeed in every facet but courage and fighting ability – were painfully revealed during the Crimean War. During that war the incompetence of the general officers and the terrible sufferings of the men outraged the British public but army reform, however necessary, still took time. Few organizations in the world were, or are, as conservative as the British army.

The world was changing fast as the nineteenth century advanced, and the scale of everything, including military endeavours, was steadily growing. In the American Civil War of 1861–5, more than three million men took to the field in huge volunteer or conscript armies; more than six hundred thousand were killed. In the Franco-Prussian War of 1870–1 the short-service army of Prussia rapidly doubled, trebled, quadrupled in size, growing to a total strength of some nine hundred thousand men as reservists flocked back to the colours. In 1870 the British army, with a vast Empire to police, contained around one hundred and seventy thousand men and had no reserves at all.

Ten years later, when Wolseley sailed for Egypt, the British army was still tiny and entirely volunteer in composition, but a great deal had changed for the better in the previous decade. Wolseley and his supporters in the campaign for reform gained a useful ally in 1868 when Sir Edward Cardwell became Secretary of State for War in the first Gladstone government. Cardwell, a pacifist, was an unlikely choice but though he detested war, he knew that Britain must have an army and he determined to make it a good one, a task that would have daunted a lesser man.

The first snag with the British army of the 1860s was that no one was actually in charge of it. The Commander-in-Chief, the Duke of Cambridge, was uncertain to whom he was responsible, the Queen or the government. As a member of the royal family he tended to prefer the Queen and paid very little heed to his political superior, the Secretary of State for War. This might have made Cambridge a very powerful figure indeed, but for the fact that he controlled only a small part of the army. The army overseas was responsible to the Foreign Office or the Colonial Office. The British army in India, as well as the Indian army, were both accountable to the Governor-General, the Viceroy of India.

Neither was the Commander-in-Chief responsible for the logistical elements of the army, supply, pay, transport; such things cost money and were therefore the responsibility of the Chancellor of the Exchequer. The militia was responsible to the Home Office and the artillery and engineers reported to the Master-General of the Ordnance, who was apparently responsible to no one. The army could not stir out of Britain without the support of the Royal Navy but the two services were barely on speaking terms.

A better recipe for chaos could hardly have been devised and yet the British army clung to the system with all the power at their command, and since army officers were gentlemen or aristocrats, often connected with those in high office, their power to delay or resist reform was considerable.

Cardwell had to drag the British army into the latter half of the nineteenth century with the diehards fighting him every inch of the way. The fight became especially bitter over Cardwell's three main reforms: the abolition of purchase for commissions or promotion; the introduction of short-service enlistment to create a trained reserve; and the abolition of numbered regiments to introduce the 'linked or county battalion' system. Each reform provoked uproar.

To abolish purchase, Cardwell had to repay the sums the officers had laid out for their rank, or in the words of the historian Byron Farwell, 'Buy the British Army back from its officers.' This cost the country around £6 million and caused a great deal of resentment. The Iron Duke himself had always sworn by purchase, declaring that purchase provided the army with aristocratic officers, gentlemen accustomed to command by right of birth. It was also economical as rich men did not require much pay. This of course overlooked the fact that purchase either kept out or kept back men of ability who could not afford to pay for a commission or advancement. While this weakness was openly admitted, the British army fought for the retention of purchase, mainly because they were used to it.

For over two hundred years commissions in the British army for all formations other than the artillery and engineers had been obtained by purchase. This may account for the fact that a surprising number of successful generals came from the Corps of Engineers, where ability was the main criteria for promotion.

In the cavalry and infantry, promotion could only be purchased up to the rank of Lieutenant-Colonel. After that it depended on seniority but that was no guarantee of ability either. Many officers stayed in the army until they died and had no thought of another career. Even in the 1860s there were a number of senior serving officers who had fought at Waterloo fifty years before, and Cardwell's insistence that all officers must either 'get on or get out', achieve promotion or retire after a certain number of years in one rank, caused yet another outcry.

All purchase depended on the necessary vacancy, but the overall result was that money rather than ability governed the selection and advancement of officers in the Victorian army. There was a price scale and the prices rose according to rank and the prestige of the regiment, so that poorer men in good marching regiments, unable to obtain promotion, were often obliged to sell out and start again in some other regiment or enter the Indian army where the cost of living in the Mess was much cheaper. The British army was not a career open to talents.

The Bill abolishing purchase had a particularly difficult passage through Parliament for the House of Lords, which could then veto Bills, let it be known that they would never pass it. Gladstone then discovered that the Act establishing purchase had been passed by Royal Warrant rather than by Statute and to prevent a consti-tutional crisis – for Gladstone was quite determined that purchase should be eliminated – Gladstone prevailed on the Queen to repeal the Warrant.

Cardwell diffused much of the opposition to the abolition of purchase by paying the market rate for the commissions rather than the much lower prices suggested by the official list, but a worse row was to follow over short service. The British army was made up of regular soldiers who, in theory, entered for life and in practice served for about thirty years. Promotion was slow and recruitment difficult since not everyone wanted to enlist for life. The main problem was that thanks to long-service enlistment there was no reserve of trained soldiers to recall to the Colours in time of trouble; by the time a soldier retired or was discharged he was too old for further service. Cardwell's Army Enlistment Act of 1870 aimed to change all that but produced another storm of opposition, both in the army and in Parliament.

Cardwell introduced short-service enlistment, where men signed on for twelve years but could be released after seven years and placed on the Reserve List, from which they could be recalled in time of need. An infantry battalion then consisted of between eight hundred and a thousand men mustered in eight or ten rifle companies, a cavalry regiment of around four hundred men in five or six troops; it was never easy to attract sufficient recruits to keep the battalion or regiment up to strength. Short service allevi-ated this considerably and also attracted a better class of recruit.

Short service was also planned to create a trained reserve, but again there was solid opposition from the Commander-in-Chief, the Queen, Rudyard Kipling, and most of the rank and file. They felt that only long-service soldiers could do the job that British soldiers had to do, fighting hard for very little pay in the remoter parts of the Empire. Gladstone and Cardwell had their eye on a closer problem, the large citizen armies of France, Germany, Austria, even Italy, and were determined that Britain should have adequate military reserves to fight such armies if need be. They saw a large reserve of trained soldiers as essential to Britain's security and were determined to reform the army into a modern fighting machine. Between 1868 and 1874, Cardwell re-shaped the British army into a pattern that largely holds good to this day, at least in the infantry arm.

Cardwell kept the soldiers' pay to one shilling (5p) per day but stopped the deductions of money for food and clothing and introduced special allowances for particular trades and skills. He improved the barracks and took steps to abolish flogging, in spite of objections from the Queen. These reforms were met with general approval, unlike – and this proved perhaps the most difficult task of all – abolishing the old method of numbering regiments – the 3rd Foot, the 79th Highland, the 60th Rifles and so on – and replacing it with the 'linked battalion' system.

The British soldier of Victoria's time was very proud of his regimental number, which indicated his regiment's long history and place among the regiments of the line. Soldiers of the 1st Foot, or Royal Scots, thought themselves and their regiment vastly superior to privates in the 34th Foot – later the Border Regiment – and soldiers of these regiments could both look down and take pity on the Johnny-come-lately men of the 100th Foot, later the Leinster Regiment or Royal Canadians.

To the civilian these numbers might have seemed an anachronism, but the soldiers cherished them and when Cardwell abolished the numbering system there was opposition from every rank and quarter of the army – an opposition that endured in one way or another up to the Second World War, when men of the King's Royal Rifle Corps, to give just one example, would still refer to their gallant and distinguished regiment as 'The 60th'. Cardwell himself was not able to force this system through and it was left to his successor, Hugh Childers, to finish the task, which was finally completed in 1881, just before Arabi's Revolt began.

Cardwell and Childers replaced the numbers with a two-battalion territorial system usually based on counties. Each infantry regiment would now consist of at least two battalions; one would be in the field, probably soldiering in some part of the Empire, while the other, usually the 2nd Battalion, would be at the home depot, recruiting and training; every few years these battalions would change round. All regiments would be linked to a county, city or region, from which they would draw recruits. Cardwell and Childers never managed to force this change on the cavalry, which retained their numbers, until the 1970s, but it was established in the infantry and soon proved a great success. It was also to prove a valuable link between the British public and the army and greatly improve the standing of the private soldier.

Tommy Atkins, that much despised red-coat Kipling wrote about, now became a local hero, someone to be proud of. The exploits of the county regiment was, and still is, followed with close attention by local people because their fathers, husbands, brothers or sons served in it. When the county regiment went to war the public turned out to wave or weep as the columns marched to the railway station, and when they came home again the people were there in the streets, cheering the lads on their way back to barracks.

Cardwell also improved military education, especially for the officers, and improved the curriculum at the Staff College. It was another forty years before the British army took up the idea of a General Staff to run the army and plan campaigns, even though the Prussian army had a staff who proved notably efficient in planning and delivering victory in the Franco-Prussian War of 1870–1. Finally, to decently dispose of old or useless officers, he introduced retirement schemes.

To achieve all this Cardwell fought a deadly battle with the Duke of Cambridge, not least in the far-reaching matter of submitting the army to political control and placing the office of Commander-in-Chief firmly in the gift and under the control of the Secretary of State for War. In all this Cardwell and Childers enjoyed the support of Garnet Wolseley, who in 1882 became Adjutant-General of the Army and the Duke's right hand.

The Duke of Cambridge had served in the army all his adult life and commanded a division during the Crimean War, though with no particular distinction. The horrors and disasters of that squalid campaign seem to have made no impression on him. He abhorred radicals and reformers, declaring that 'Change should only come when it is absolutely necessary and it is only necessary when it can no longer be avoided.' The Duke liked the British army exactly how it was and spent his entire life trying to preserve it in the model bequeathed to him by the Duke of Wellington and his much-admired commander in the Crimea, Lord Raglan.

The Duke of Cambridge adored the British army; that was part of the problem. He liked the bands and the parades and the glorious uniforms and evenings in the Mess over dinner and port, discussing the good old days and deeds of valour with sword and bayonet, times when the men of the British army stood and fought and died as soldiers should, for the honour and glory of Queen and Country. The army was his life, and his life was perfect just the way it was, without any new-fangled tinkering by civilian politicians or young upstarts like Garnet Wolseley and his gang of 'reformers'. Wolseley and his 'Gang' were enthusiastic supporters of the Cardwell-Childers reforms and this alone made them very unpopular with the Duke of Cambridge and consequently with the Queen.

Queen Victoria is an English icon but she must have been a very tiresome woman. While fully aware that Britain was a constitutional monarchy she did not let that fact deter her from challenging the government and insisting on her various prerogatives whenever she thought the former in need of it or the latter threatened. She also enjoyed immense prestige, great public affection and considerable powers of influence; when she took against anyone in public life, his life became difficult and his prospects dim. The Queen took against Major-General Sir Garnet Wolseley quite early in his career, a fact which he knew and resented. He had done the State good service; why then was his Sovereign so reluctant to acknowledge the fact and allow him due praise and promotion?

The Queen considered Wolseley conceited and a braggart. When he was caricatured as 'The Very Model of a Modern Major General' in Gilbert and Sullivan's *Pirates of Penzance* and appeared to enjoy the notoriety, the Queen saw this as evidence of his low popular tastes. When Wolseley was appointed High Commissioner for South East Africa and raised to the rank of full General in 1879, the Queen refused to 'approve' the appointment and said she would only 'sanction' it. The reason for the Queen's attitude probably lay in the fact that she regarded Wolseley as a 'political general', more loyal to the government than to herself, and an enemy of her adored cousin, the Duke of Cambridge.

The Queen's views on Wolseley were not shared by the Commander-in-Chief. With all his faults the Duke of Cambridge was a fair and honest man. He disliked Wolseley's support for reform but liked him personally and acknowledged his ability. When it came to his ears that the government intended to send an Expeditionary Force to Egypt with Wolseley in command, he wrote a letter to the Queen urging her not to oppose this appointment, '. . . for Wolseley is very decidedly as able a man for the field as we have got.' Her Majesty duly approved this appointment and in August 1882 Wolseley set sail for Egypt.

*

The Anglo-Egyptian War of 1882 lasted a little over a month but it had far-reaching consequences and revealed a new British army, one vastly improved from the force that had fought in the Crimea twenty-five years before.

There were, of course, a few residual snags. Wolseley's final muster of 40,000 men was over-endowed with generals, no less than forty of them managing to attend the war in various capacities. Everyone who was anyone wanted to go on the Egyptian Expedition, including Prince Edward the Prince of Wales; the Queen forbade him to go but there was another scion of the House of Saxe-Coburg, the Duke of Connaught, third son of Queen Victoria and the apple of her eye. His desire to fight was harder to resist for Connaught commanded the élite 1st Guards Brigade which Wolseley was very anxious to employ. Well aware of his unpopularity with the Queen, Wolseley was in dread of something happening to the Duke if and when the Guards Brigade was committed to battle.

That problem apart, Wolseley relied on the members of his 'Gang' who were there in force. Redvers Buller was in charge of Intelligence, a not entirely suitable appointment. Buller was not over-endowed with brains, but having recently won the Victoria Cross during the war in Zululand he could have any appointment he wanted. Also on the Staff was Colonel William Butler who was the Quartermaster-General, the officer responsible for supply. Sir Evelyn Wood was there, as was Hugh McCalmont and General Gerald Graham VC, who was commanding an infantry brigade while Colonel Drury-Lowe commanded a brigade in the cavalry division. With these fighting friends at his back, Wolseley was confident of success.

Wolseley knew exactly what he needed to do in Egypt and had no intention of blundering about in the cotton fields and watercourses of the Delta. His priority was first to seize and secure the vital Suez Canal before Arabi could carry out his threat to block or destroy it; only then did he intend to meet and defeat Arabi's army. He therefore began his well-crafted campaign with a little deception.

Wolseley's plan for the invasion of Egypt was to feint at Cairo from Alexandria before putting his army ashore elsewhere. A landing at Alexandria was expected and he used this expectation to deceive the Egyptian forces mustering south of Alexandria. Part of this deception involved one of his senior commanders.

Major-General Sir Edward Hamley, one of Wolseley's Divisional Commanders, was author of the strategic manual, *The Operations of War*. Hamley was Professor of Military History at the Staff College and a very opinionated man who felt that Wolseley might stand in need of his experience and advice. Wolseley appeared to agree with this and on arrival at Alexandria, Hamley and his staff were soon seen everywhere about the town, interrogating prisoners and consulting maps.

Hamley's main proposals, to land the army at Aboukir Bay and advance south on Cairo, were therefore soon well known on both sides of the line. Hamley was nonetheless furious when Wolseley ignored his advice, kept to his original intention and sailed with the main force for Port Said and the Canal, leaving Hamley and his division to cover this diversion and garrison Alexandria. Though Hamley caught up later and took part in the campaign he never forgave Wolseley for using him in what he judged a cavalier fashion.

British warships entered the Canal at Port Said without difficulty. The Canal Company offices there and at Ismailia were captured by a young midshipman and parties of Royal Marines without a shot being fired. De Lesseps appeared from his villa at Ismailia to berate the British for this armed incursion but was soon mollified and invited Wolseley to dine. The British army was fully ashore at Ismailia by 26 August and Wolseley was soon preparing to advance north and west towards Cairo, with a fighting force of seventeen and a half thousand men.

The land phase of the Anglo-Egyptian War began on 28 August 1882, when large Egyptian forces attacked the infantry brigade at Mahsama commanded by General Gerald Graham. Graham was outnumbered five to one, but had no difficulty in beating the Egyptians off. Redvers Buller, Wolseley's Chief of Intelligence, had meanwhile been scouting forward across the desert towards Cairo and reported that Arabi was digging in to defend the city at Tel-el-Kebir. On 10 September 1882, Wolseley and his entire force began marching cautiously north-west across the desert, knowing that Arabi's army lay somewhere to their front, entrenched around the village at Tel-el-Kebir, about half-way between Cairo and the Canal.

Colonel Arabi knew his business. He had chosen a good defensive position, dug-in on it and manned the position with twenty-five thousand men, including a number of the crack Sudanese battalions. He also had some seventy guns of various calibre. His troops had a clear field of fire over a flat, open desert, and if they stood their ground they could hope to beat off any force flung against them. Wolseley and his Staff had been able to study these defences for some days, and although the bellicose Colonel Redvers Buller proved less than satisfactory in the Intelligence role, he had made the interesting discovery that the Egyptians did not man their defences after dark. Wolseley therefore decided on a night attack, a manoeuvre then considered the height of daring, and it was indeed fraught with risk.

Fortunately, officers of the Naval Brigade were on hand with their compasses. Their ability to navigate, coupled with the fact that the desert was flat, made a night attack feasible. Sometime after midnight on the morning of 13 September 1882, the Expeditionary Force – seventeen thousand, five hundred men, with sixty guns – set out across the desert towards the Egyptian lines.

The advance was led by the Highland Brigade – the 1st Battalions of the Camerons, the Gordons and the Black Watch – commanded by General Alison followed by the Duke of Connaught's 1st Guards Brigade. The advance went well and smoothly after a drunken Highlander had been forcibly subdued, and by 0300 hrs the outline of the Egyptian trenches could be seen in the darkness ahead. The attack went in at dawn, the British attacking with the sun on their backs, and although the Sudanese infantry put up a stiff fight, holding off the Gordon and Cameron Highlanders until the Black Watch and the Guards Brigade came up, the defences were soon overwhelmed and the rout began.

Colonel Arabi left the battlefield with the remnants of his army and fled to Cairo with the British cavalry hard on his heels. Arabi reached Cairo on the afternoon of 14 September and was arrested that afternoon. He was tried by court martial and sentenced to hang but eventually sent into exile in Ceylon, where he remained until 1902; when he returned to Egypt he found that he had been totally forgotten. The Khedive Tewfik, who had been lying low in his villa near Alexandria, re-entered his capital ten days after the battle at Tel-el-Kebir, to find the British in effective control of his country, although the bulk of the British army, including General Wolseley, had sailed home immediately after the fall of Cairo. They came home to find themselves heroes.

As far as the British people were concerned, the Arabi War of 1882 was a neat, well-fought little campaign costing very little in blood or treasure; from start to finish the whole affair took less than two months. The army and the government were also pleased with the results, feeling that the torments of reform had clearly been justified. Total casualties were less than four hundred. On his return Wolseley found that even the Queen had thawed a little. The Duke of Connaught had written to his mother praising his commander and she made no difficulties when Wolseley was raised to the rank of baron and given a grant of £30,000 by Parliament.

On the other hand, another step had been taken towards British involvement in Egypt. As Blunt had warned and Gladstone had feared, destroying Arabi had left Britain in charge of Egyptian affairs. The nominal overlord of Egypt, the Sultan of Turkey, had no interest in the country apart from receiving the annual tribute and, on balance, the Egyptian people themselves preferred the rule of any European power to that of the Turks. Arabi had gone, the Khedive was discredited and the British were therefore committed. They had taken over the country, defeated the Egyptian army and imprisoned the chosen man of the people. If the objects for which this war had been fought were to be attained, the British must stay on and restore order. No one suspected just how long that stay would be.

The British were in fact to remain in control of Egypt for the next seventy-two years. Gladstone's worst forebodings had come to pass. The present situation was, in fact, rather worse than he had supposed for the Arabi revolt and the subsequent British campaign in Egypt had distracted general attention from an additional and far greater problem in the Sudan.

Britain was now impaled on the horns of a self-imposed dilemma. She had acquired Egypt and time would reveal the wisdom of that action, but with Egypt Britain had also acquired the Sudan and a host of as yet unappreciated problems. What they needed on the ground was a tactful diplomat and a good man of business, and the man chosen for this task was Sir Evelyn Baring. His appointed task was to rebuild Egypt and create a modern state; the job was immense and the means to complete it limited. However, as Baring himself remarked, 'It was not the first time an endeavour had been made on the banks of the Nile to make bricks without straw.'

Baring had left Egypt in June 1880 to serve on the Staff of his cousin, Lord Northbrook, the Governor-General of India. When it became clear that the situation in Egypt would require a man of quite exceptional resourcefulness and ability, Baring's previous service on the Dual Control Commission led to his being offered the post of Resident. He arrived in Cairo on 11 September 1883, and was to remain there until he returned to England as Lord Cromer in 1907. During that time he transformed the country from a bankrupt province of the Turkish Empire to a stable, viable, modern state.

One of the most important tasks facing the new Resident was the rebuilding and retraining of the Egyptian Army. The committed supporters of Arabi were stripped of their rank and sent to serve a newly appointed British General, Hicks Pasha, in the Sudan. To re-order the remainder, one of the Wolseley 'Ring', Sir Evelyn Wood VC, accepted the post of 'Sirdar' – Commander-in-Chief – of the Egyptian army. To assist him Wood recruited a number of able and experienced officers, including Major Hector Macdonald of the Gordon Highlanders, and the up-and-coming Major Herbert Kitchener of the Royal Engineers, who had taken a small part in the Arabi war, serving as an intelligence officer in Alexandria. Kitchener obtained his release from survey work in Cyprus and he joined the Egyptian army as a cavalry commander.

Evelyn Wood was another of those battered, hard-fighting Victorian Generals. He had begun his military career as a midshipman, serving in the naval brigade in the Crimea, where he was severely wounded and recommended for the Victoria Cross – all before his seventeenth birthday. Finding the military life much to his taste, Wood was allowed to transfer to the army, where he obtained a commission in the 13th Dragoons. He returned to the Crimea, served in the Indian Mutiny where he won the VC in a cavalry action and by 1861 – when just twenty-three – he was already a Captain, having paid £2,500 for the promotion. In 1864 he passed the course at the Staff College and from then on his career accelerated.

Wood was a member of the Wolseley Ring and like the rest of that coterie, relentless in the pursuit of action. After Crimea and the Mutiny he served with Wolseley in the Ashanti campaign, where he was wounded yet again – Wood was always getting wounded – and in the Zulu war of 1879. Then came the Egyptian campaign of 1881–2 and his appointment as Sirdar of the Egyptian army.

Wood was not a lucky man. He was wounded in nearly every campaign and when he was not wounded in action he managed to get hurt on the hunting field or by pure accident. He was hit in the chest by a musket nail in the Ashanti war, had his face mashed while attempting to ride a giraffe in a zoo, and broke a score of bones in one accident or another. He remained a cheerful, feisty officer, and although now forty-four and growing increasingly deaf, he assembled a reliable band of officers and NCOs and took up his new command with enthusiasm. Provided he kept a tight hold on the purse strings he knew he could rely on the full backing of Sir Evelyn Baring, though the Sirdar was, at least in theory, responsible only to the Khedive. This new army might soon be needed, for trouble was brewing in the south.

Evelyn Baring lost no time in taking up his responsibilities and found them immense. All the financial problems once tackled by the Dual Control fell on his shoulders as well as all the rest of the nation's woes for he was, to all intents, the dictator of Egypt. Added to that, since he had been in India a new problem had arisen in the Sudan, Egypt's great colonial possession, where a serious revolt now appeared to be in progress.

As yet, precise details were scanty, but it appeared that this sudden eruption – a jihad or Holy War – was led by a shadowy figure, a poor man, a scholar and a mystic from the province of Dongola in the Northern Sudan. Called by some the Messiah, or 'Expected One', Mohammed Ahmed-Ibn-el-Sayed-Abdullah would become best known to history as the Mahdi.

6

Enter the Mahdi

1881–1882

When Allah made the Sudan, Allah laughed.

Sudanese saying

THE SUDAN IS a vast, harsh, empty land, the largest country in Africa, covering an area of about a million square miles, almost the size of Western Europe. A stony, arid desert occupies the country in the north and a great expanse of swamp, waterless scrub and mimosa thorn blankets the country to the south. The principal physical feature of the Sudan is the river Nile, which bisects the country, running from the southern border with Uganda to the Egyptian frontier at Wadi Halfa. However, unlike Egypt the river Nile is of no comparable importance to the people of the Sudan.

To the Sudanese the Nile is an artery, a river road leading from south to north. It has sometimes been seen as a strategic liability, for the river is the way by which invaders or slave traders have always entered the Sudan. The riverine tribes trade along the Nile and are great boatmen but many Sudanese have no connection whatsoever with the river. More than half the population live on the dry, rolling plains of Kordofan and Darfur, the provinces south and west of the river, or in the province of Kassala away to the east, where they earn a thin living as nomadic herdsmen, driving flocks of sheep or herds of goats about the plains, rearing camels, trading with the Arabs or the Egyptians for those necessities they cannot make or grow for themselves. For the Sudanese people, life was, and is, harsh and simple. Having little, they need little and ask only to be left alone.

The principal towns lie on or close to the Nile and the entire country is plagued with a quantity of flies and mosquitoes and the ailments and diseases such insects bring with them: malaria, bilharzia, trachoma. It is, by any standards, a most inhospitable country but the people themselves are just the opposite. Such natural attractions as there are in the Sudan lie in the space and silence of the desert but those Europeans who have ever worked or travelled there are loud in their praise of the kindness and hospitality of the Sudanese people. The Sudanese have two other qualities: they are, in the main, devout, even fervent Muslims and the people of the Sudan are warriors.

At the end of the last century, such external trade as the Sudan possessed depended on the export of ivory, principally for the manufacture of billiard balls, and on sales of gum arabic, a substance extracted from the acacia tree which provided the thickening agent in ink. The chief source of revenue, however, came from the slave trade.

In the closing decades of the nineteenth century the Sudan was still virtually a medieval country, totally undeveloped. There were no roads or railway lines. There was only one telegraph line, running from Khartoum up the Nile to Berber and Cairo. The country had neither been mapped nor fully explored nor even legally defined. The name itself lacks definition for 'Sudan' means simply 'land of the blacks'; Balad-el-Sudan in Arabic. To the east lay the Red Sea and the Abyssinian province of Eritrea. To the west, far across the desert, lay the territory of French Equatorial Africa. The southern boundary lay beyond the great reed-clogged barrier of the Sudd, that great, insect-humming swamp astride the Nile and along the frontier of what is now Uganda and was then simply part of Central Africa, valuable only as a source of ivory – and slaves.

The northern boundary lay along the Tropic of Cancer, with the Libyan or Western Desert running off to the north-west. Beyond that northern border, past the river town to Wadi Halfa, lay Egypt, the source of all the Sudan's problems. Egyptian rulers had always sought to dominate the Sudan, to exploit the country and its people for the greater good of Egypt.

In the 1880s this sprawling, hostile land was home to a population roughly estimated at around nine million people. The bulk of these were nomads but there was a smattering of wealthy, urbanized Sudanese and rather more Egyptian and Circassian expatriates who clustered in the few small, mud-walled towns like

Khartoum or El Obeid, the capital of the province of Kordofan, in river ports like Wadi Halfa or Berber, or in Red Sea towns like Suakin. These people were generally referred to by the Sudanese as 'Turks', and this period in their history is therefore known by the Sudanese as the 'Turkiya', the time of the Turks. The Sudanese population is racially mixed, a composition of Arabs and blacks, with the Muslim Arabs dominating in the north and the pagan blacks being predominant in the south. Whatever their racial origins, all the Sudanese resented their Turko-Circassian rulers from the north.

Mohammed Ali had sent his Egyptian armies to occupy and annex the Sudan in 1821 and the Egyptians had been ruling – or rather misruling – there ever since. By the 1870s Egypt had about forty thousand poorly paid, ill-trained and undisciplined troops dotted about the Sudan in scattered garrisons, where they passed their time terrorizing the local people and trading in slaves. 'The entire country,' wrote Sir Samuel Baker in 1870, 'was leased out to slave-hunters by the Khartoum Government.' The Sudan was run as a tyranny, and ripe for revolt.

In 1880 the Egyptian garrisons in the Sudan included a garrison of some ten thousand men at Khartoum and a further six thousand men in El Obeid, away to the west. None of these garrisons was of much military value added to which Egypt's ability to resist or prevent any trouble in the Sudan was more than usually impeded at this time, as the attention of Egypt's rulers was focused on events in Cairo where Colonel Arabi was at odds with the Khedive Tewfik and the British army.

When this story opens, the Sudan was a political, administrative and economic shambles. The population was either prey to Arab slavers or actively engaged in making slave raids down the Nile, ravaging the black tribes of Central Africa, sending men and women by the tens of thousands to labour in the cotton fields of Egypt or serve in the harems of Arabia. The Egyptian administrators, from the Governor-General in Khartoum down to the most minor official in the remoter parts of Darfur or Kordofan, neglected their duties and devoted their time entirely to the support and practice of slavery.

While the people of the Sudan can be broadly divided into the Hamitic Arabs and blacks there were many tribal groupings. Some estimates endow the Sudan with more than three hundred tribes; others say the Sudan contained more than twice that many, and all the tribes contained sub-groups. The most significant of the larger tribes were the Beja people who lived on the Red Sea coast around the port of Suakin and the Baggara nomads of Kordofan, who were to provide most of the Mahdi's cavalry and camel troops. One of the sub-groups of the Beja were the Hadendowa people, the famous 'Fuzzy-Wuzzies', who provided the best soldiers in the Egyptian Army. These tousled-headed warriors became the most redoubtable opponents of the invading British, able to 'break the British square', a feat that had eluded the veteran soldiers of Napoleon Bonaparte.

Even if anyone in authority had time to notice the critical state of affairs in the Sudan, it is not likely that anyone would have cared. To the Egyptian administrators the Sudan was a dreadful place, a country to be exploited, nothing more. Those Sudanese who complained about their treatment at the hands of their rulers were either flogged with the courbash, jailed and tortured, hunted down and sold into slavery, or killed. This had gone on for decades but it could not last if the Sudanese found a leader who could ignite their warlike spirit and channel their resentment at alien rule on a path to liberation.

By 1880 the Sudan was ready for revolt and when the Egyptians returned their attention to the Sudan in the autumn of 1882, the country was already in the grip of a religious rising led by Mohammed Ahmed, calling himself the Mahdi, the Expected One. To the people of the Sudan the Mahdi offered a glimpse of freedom and his call for a jihad against the Turks, the people from the north, met with an immediate, growing and nationwide response.

Mohammed Ahmed-Ibn-el-Sayed-Abdullah, who came to fame as the Mahdi, was born in 1844 on an island in the Nile near Dongola, where his father was a carpenter and boat builder. Mohammed Ahmed's father also claimed to be a direct descendant of the Prophet but when he died, three of his sons dropped this claim and were content to carry on the family business. Not so Mohammed Ahmed, who had been interested in religion from his childhood days and had been allowed, and even encouraged, to follow this calling by attending Muslim religious schools or 'khalwas' in Khartoum.

Education in a khalwa had existed throughout the Sudan for centuries and still exists to this day. In a khalwa the entire day is devoted to the study of the Koran under the guidance of a 'fakir' or holy teacher. The fakir insists that his pupils learn the Koran by heart and the endless hours of study necessary to achieve this induces a degree of fanaticism. The young Mohammed Ahmed spent years at the khalwa in Khartoum before moving north to the famous khalwa of Sheik Mohammed-El-Khair at Berber. There his labours increased, devotional exercises, fasting and meditation being added to long hours of study. Gradually, by his dedication and asceticism, this young man came to be noticed by his teachers and the local people. His reputation spread and he acquired disciples.

There are no dates available charting the progress of Mohammed Ahmed towards the status of Mahdi but the process clearly took years. In his twenties he moved south of Khartoum to the island of Abba on the White Nile. There his asceticism increased. He fasted, fell into trances and dreamed strange dreams. These activities attracted many visitors, who poured off the Nile ferries to see this strange young man and hear his preaching.

The broad thrust of Mohammed Ahmed's teaching followed that of other reformers in other religions. His Islam was one devoted to the words of the Prophet and based on a return to the original virtues of prayer and simplicity as laid down in the Koran. Any deviation from the Koran was therefore heresy. There was also a political edge to this doctrine. Mohammed Ahmed's contempt for the Egyptians and Turko-Circassian people, who oppressed the Sudanese, co-operated with the slavers and led a life of indolence and luxury, was all too plain but he offered hope as well. The way to paradise lay through humility and a strict observance of the tenets of Islam.

There was nothing particularly new in Mohammed Ahmed's doctrines but he was an inspiring teacher. His message – that this world was but a testing ground and paradise awaited those who followed the Muslim faith – had a strong appeal to a people who found their daily lives hard in the extreme and welcomed the promise or prospect of a better life if not in this world then in the one to come. As far as this life was concerned, a better life depended on getting free of the 'Turks'.

As Mohammed Ahmed's fame spread, questions arose. Who was this young man? On what grounds did he presume to interpret the Word of Allah and the teachings of the Prophet? Mohammed Ahmed's answer, first given to a small group of disciples, was that he was the Missing One, the 'Expected Guide', the 'One who is Conducted on the True Path', the Mahdi.

Muslims believe that the leader of Islam must be a direct descendant of the Prophet through his daughter Fatima. Fatima and her husband Ali had twelve children but the twelfth died without issue, or so it is believed by the Sunnis, one of the two main sects of the Muslim religion. This belief is contested by the other main sect, the Shi'a, who hold that he did have issue, a man who vanished without trace but will some day reappear. This man is Al-Mahdi-al-Muntazir, the Expected One. The Shi'a believe that the Mahdi will be recognized by certain physical signs, among them a gap in his front teeth, a black mark on one cheek and long, thin hands. The Mahdi must accept his role with reluctance, be of the line of Fatima, be proclaimed in the Great Mosque in Mecca and, most important of all, his arrival will signal the start of the time when all people will be converted to the Muslim religion. Mohammed Ahmed filled all these criteria. His disciples became convinced that he was indeed the Mahdi.

The Mahdi and his disciples began to spread the word of his coming, along the river Nile, on the plains of Kordofan and in the mountains of Nubia. From there the news spread to Khartoum and soon reached the ears of the Egyptian Governor-General, Rais Pasha. Rais Pasha had followed Gordon as Governor-General of the Sudan and under his rule slaving had returned, and other ills besides. Bribery, corruption, the courbash, prison and torture were all reapplied to the long-suffering population; if any man can be said to have primed the Sudanese explosion, that man is Rais Pasha. On hearing of the new prophet the Governor-General consulted the learned men of the city and they offered the opinion that this was a 'false Mahdi', but still a danger to the true religion and the established authority. Pontius Pilate did much the same thing when he consulted the Pharisees; like Pilate, Rais Pasha decided to have Mohammed Ahmed arrested.

Rais Pasha was not a religious man but nor was he a fool. He felt that this new 'prophet' required investigation and he elected to move slowly. He first sent a delegation to interview the Mahdi on Abba Island, a small party of soldiers and mullahs under the guidance of Abu Saoud, the former slaver dismissed for corruption by Gordon but now restored to office.

Abu Saoud duly met with the Mahdi but matters did not go well. The Mahdi refused to explain his beliefs to the religious leaders from Khartoum, declined to come to the capital for further investigation by the Governor-General and threatened Abu Saoud with a *jihad* unless the rulers in Khartoum accepted his teachings and changed their ways at once.

This was a clear call to revolt and Rais Pasha saw it as such. His response was to send Abu Saoud back to Abba Island, this time accompanied by two steamers crammed with soldiers, and charge him with the task of arresting the Mahdi and bringing him back to Khartoum in chains. This action proved most unwise.

The Mahdi's first military success came on the night of 12/13 August 1881, when his small force of three hundred ill-armed men, equipped with swords and spears, wiped out Abu Saoud's much larger body of Egyptian soldiers armed with Remington rifles. Most of the Egyptian soldiers were clubbed to death or cut down on the river bank; only a few survivors succeeded in swimming back to the steamer, where Abu Saoud had wisely decided to stay on board. He returned to Khartoum with the news of this disaster and Rais Pasha then called for a larger expedition. However, Arabi's revolt was now engaging all attention in Cairo. By the time the Egyptians and their British masters turned their thoughts back to the Sudan at the end of 1882, the Mahdi's revolt was in full swing.

Following the destruction of Abu Saoud's force, the Egyptian Commander at Fashoda had sent twelve hundred well-armed men downriver to retake Abba Island. In October 1881 this force was cut to pieces by the Mahdi's army which had risen to eight thousand men since their initial victory two months before. Six months later, in June 1882, another Egyptian force of six thousand men was overwhelmed in a night attack by a Mahdist force now estimated at fifteen thousand men. On this occasion it was the Mahdi's men who attacked and overran the Egyptian camp, slaughtering all the soldiers and making off with a large quantity of arms and ammunition, including several cannon. This was no longer a tribal rising but a full-scale national revolt.

The people of the Sudan did not all support the Mahdi or adhere to Mahdist doctrines. From the many who did, the Mahdi swiftly built up his forces, and equipped and organized them into armies. At first the Mahdi ordered his men to have no truck with Western weapons and rely solely on the sword and spear but he was soon equipping his men with breech-loading rifles and captured field artillery.

The Mahdi referred to his followers as 'Ansar' or 'helpers', the term used in the Koran to describe the disciples of the Prophet.

This term was also used, as it is used in this book, to describe the sword- and spear-armed infantry of the Mahdi's armies, the element which made up the bulk of his force. The British usually referred to all the Mahdi's followers as 'Dervishes', a term picked up from the Levant where it was often used to describe groups of religious mystics – hence the famous 'Whirling Dervishes' of Konya in Anatolia, just one of many Dervish groups.

Before long the Mahdi had acquired sufficient men to form several armies. He began to divide his forces into separate divisions and smaller fighting units, despatching them under the command of his emirs to attack Egyptian garrisons and overrun the smaller provincial towns.

The principal generals of the Mahdi, the men commanding large forces, were called the 'Kalifas' or 'followers'. One of these was the Kalifa Abdulla, a devout Muslim and a good soldier who was one of the Mahdi's first followers and his eventual successor. Under these men were many battalion-sized units called 'rubs', each commanded by sheiks or emirs, and these in turn were divided into smaller companies of around one hundred men commanded by ra's mia – the equivalent of a centurion. About ten per cent of the Ansar were armed with rifles; the rest carried the traditional weapons of dagger, sword and spear. Many of these sub-units had their own battle flags in various colours, green and white and red, covered with sayings from the Koran, with the black standard of the Mahdi – and later of the Kalifa Abdulla – always being the largest in the field.

The Dervish cavalry usually came from the nomadic Baggara people who were fine horsemen or camel riders while the Ansar riflemen – or jihadiya – were usually non-Arab Sudanese from the south, the west or the Nuba Mountains. These were armed with single-shot, .45 calibre Remington breechloaders taken from their fallen opponents or from captured Egyptian arsenals. The artillery pieces came from the same source and were usually manned by captive Egyptian soldiers converted to Mahdist doctrines. Rifles and artillery fire actually played a small part in the battlefield tactics of the Dervish armies though they used artillery in sieges and against steamers sailing along the Nile.

The principal Dervish tactic was to skirmish forward under cover until they could launch a massed charge to close-quarters, where they would lay about their opponents with razor-sharp swords and spears. The Ansar were formidable at such close-quarter fighting. The secret of the early Mahdist successes lay in the valour of the Sudanese Ansar warriors and the lack of discipline in their Egyptian opponents, who in spite of their superiority in weaponry fell apart and fled before the Ansar onslaught.

By 1883, after three crushing defeats in six months – though details were scanty since there were very few survivors – the Egyptian Government was thoroughly alarmed. Their new British overlords, Baring and Sir Evelyn Wood, the Sirdar of the Egyptian army, were ambivalent about the Sudan, not knowing a great deal about what was involved there and anxious to avoid further stresses on the fragile Egyptian economy. In this they were following the cautious doctrines laid down by Gladstone and the British Government. The British may have acquired Egypt – and Egypt possessed the Sudan – but Britain had no intention whatsoever of being sucked into any Sudanese quagmire.

Gladstone insisted, and Baring concurred, that the Sudan was a purely Egyptian problem, and it would be wiser for Britain to remain uninvolved. A sensible wish, certainly, but clearly something had to be done about the Mahdist rising and the Egyptians alone could not do it. The Egyptian Government was therefore allowed to look around for a British officer, some competent soldier who could take charge of their forces in the Sudan and stamp out the Mahdist revolt. The man they chose was Colonel William Hicks, a soldier of the Indian army.

William Hicks had joined the Indian army in the Bombay Presidency in 1849. He had served through the Indian Mutiny of 1857–8 and on Napier's Abyssinian Expedition of 1868. Now aged fifty-two, he was a respected if undistinguished officer. Having decided that his prospects of promotion were limited in the British army, which had taken over the army of the East India Company after the Mutiny, he was now looking for profitable employment elsewhere and jumped at the opportunity of becoming Chief-of-Staff of the Egyptian army in the Sudan.

Hicks received his commission from a stout-hearted Egyptian soldier, Abd el-Kadar, once the Commander of Samuel Baker's 'Forty Thieves' and the man who had replaced Rais Pasha as Governor-General of the Sudan in January 1883. Hicks' first task was to re-train and re-enthuse his existing troops and muster more men before trying conclusions with the Mahdi.

Hicks' heart must have sunk when he first encountered the men of his new command, so different from the keen, disciplined sepoys of the Indian army. According to Colonel Herbert Stewart, one of the Wolseley Ring who was then examining the situation in the Sudan, 'The Egyptian officers are ignorant and incapable of grasping the meaning of the slightest movement. A third of the troops cannot use their rifles and would be more formidable if armed with sticks . . . they also entertain superstitious ideas about the Mahdi . . . and it is impossible to criticise too severely the conduct of the Egyptian troops – both officers and men – towards the natives.'

Before Hicks could take up his appointment in Khartoum, the Mahdi had struck again. His objective this time was El Obeid, the capital of Kordofan province and the second city of the Sudan. El Obeid had a garrison of six thousand men and a resolute commander, Colonel Mohammed Sayed. In October 1882, when the Mahdi sent in a delegation ordering the garrison to surrender, Colonel Sayed responded by tearing up the Mahdi's summons and hanging the Mahdist envoys from the walls. The Mahdi's army promptly assaulted the town but were driven off with great loss by Sayed's artillery and rifle fire. The Mahdists then settled down to a siege which became a small-scale version of the later siege of Khartoum.

Within weeks, hunger and disease began to stalk the town but El Obeid held out for four months before it fell to assault on the night of 17 January 1883. The fall of El Obeid was followed by a massacre of the population and the execution by torture of Colonel Sayed and those of his soldiers who declined to join the Mahdi's army. Nor was this the only disaster. A relief force of three thousand men sent to El Obeid from Khartoum was massacred by the wells of Bara, some miles from their destination. With the capture of El Obeid and the following massacres, the Mahdi acquired both national recognition and a great quantity of arms and ammunition, including more artillery and a great number of modern rifles. The Mahdi also acquired some European prisoners, including a German missionary, Father Ohrwalder, and a number of Greek nuns. The Mahdist revolt had also spread to other parts of the Sudan.

Along the Red Sea coast the Hadendowa tribe were up in arms under a redoubtable Beja chieftain, Osman Digna. Osman Digna was to become one of the heroes of the Mahdist wars, respected, even admired by his enemies. Osman Digna had been a slaver, until the arrival of British gunboats in the Red Sea had severely curtailed the trade and the profits. Osman Digna took to Mahdist doctrines with enthusiasm and by the end of 1882 had already begun to eliminate the Egyptian garrisons along the coast and astride the vital camel route from Suakin to the town of Berber on the Nile. Clearly the Mahdi's revolt was spreading and had to be stopped before it spread into Egypt. All eyes now turned impatiently to Hicks Pasha and the Egyptian army in Khartoum.

7

Gordon for Khartoum

1883–1884

'An Army has not vanished in such a fashion since
Pharaoh's host perished in the Red Sea.'

Lord Fitzmaurice, in a speech in the House of Lords,
November 1883

COLONEL HICKS HAD not been idle since taking up his appointment in Khartoum. He had found a few good European officers and they had set about trying to improve his army. This was not a task that could be easily accomplished and very little had in fact been achieved. The reinforcements he had requested from Cairo proved disappointing, being either the sweepings of military gaols or sullen prisoners-of-war from Colonel Arabi's defeated army. These men arrived at Khartoum half-starved and in chains. Hicks would have preferred to spend more time training and inspiring his army, but with the Mahdists sweeping forward on every front, time was not on his side.

On 29 April 1883, Hicks Pasha marched out of Khartoum with a field force consisting of four battalions of Egyptian infantry, some Sudanese cavalry and four Gatling machine-gun detachments, a total of ten thousand men. A few days later he defeated a large Mahdist force at the Jebel Ard, south of Khartoum, killing at least five hundred Ansar and driving the rest off, all for the loss of just seven men. It was a triumph, the first sign that the Mahdi could be defeated. Elated with this success Hicks' army returned to Khartoum and prepared for a further advance on the Mahdi's headquarters at El Obeid.

Hicks waited nearly four months before he advanced again. He remained in Khartoum, telegraphing Cairo all the time for more men, weapons and camels, his patrols plagued by Mahdist scouts, his numbers steadily depleted by malaria and desertion. Discipline and morale did not improve. The Mahdi was clearly biding his time, lying low in El Obeid while these elements worked on Hicks' army, but Hicks was finally obliged to take the field. He marched out from Khartoum on 9 September 1883, leading an army of ten thousand soldiers into the full heat of the Sudanese summer. Very few of these soldiers were ever seen again.

Hicks' army was simply not a fighting force. Frank Powers, the British Consul in Khartoum, who was also the local correspondent for *The Times*, saw it march out and wrote: 'Here we have nine thousand infantry that fifty good men could rout in ten minutes, one thousand cavalry and bashi-bazooks [irregulars] that have never learned to ride, and a few Nordenfeld guns – and this to beat the sixty-nine thousand men the Mahdi had got together.'

Powers' estimate of the Mahdist armies was a little on the high side. By the summer of 1883 the Mahdi had an army of forty to fifty thousand men. The bulk of these were the Ansar, wild tribesmen armed only with sword and spear. Many carried shields and some wore medieval chainmail but the bulk of them dressed only in the patched jibbah they were ordered to wear by the Mahdi as a mark of humility, that was eventually to become the uniform of the Mahdist armies.

The Mahdi could now also call on at least five thousand riflemen, many of them former soldiers in the Egyptian army, armed with Remington rifles, plus five thousand Baggara cavalry, drawn from the nomadic tribes south of Khartoum. He also had a great many warriors mounted on camels and a growing quantity of field artillery also manned by prisoners from the Egyptian army. Somewhere in the scrub-covered desert south of El Obeid, this force fell on Hicks' army and slaughtered it to the last man.

Hicks' army had left his forward base at El Duam on the Nile, south of Khartoum, on 27 September 1883. From there they marched south-west across the desert and through dense thickets of thorn and acacia scrub towards the village of Sherkirla. His last despatch came from the village of Zureiga, fifty miles from El Duam. This reported a great shortage of water and constant harassment from Ansar and Baggara patrols.

Hicks' army continued to advance through the scrub and mimosa trees, in an unwieldy 'hollow-square' formation, gradually losing all cohesion and discipline. They found water at Ageila and there was plenty of scrub with which to construct zarebas, thick thorn-bush hedges, around their camp each night, but morale continued to fall, not least after hearing of proclamations from the Mahdi, warning the Egyptian soldiers that those who opposed him were sure to die.

The end came on 5 November. Having harassed Hicks' army closely for the last three days, the Ansar now put in an all-out attack. After heavy sniping the Ansar came sweeping from the cover of the scrub with sword and spear. Hicks' thirsty and dispirited troops were marching slowly in three irregular squares and within minutes all three had collapsed. The Egyptian soldiers and bashi-bazooks made little effort to retaliate and there was yet another fearful massacre. Of the ten thousand soldiers in Hicks' army a handful of camel riders got away and only a few hundred prisoners were taken by the Mahdi. Hicks and all his officers died sword in hand, and their men were butchered all around them.

This latest disaster horrified Egypt and caused great dismay in London. It also had an immediate effect in the Sudan. With Kordofan gone, Slatin Pasha, the Gordon-appointed Governor of Darfur Province further to the west, now totally cut off from Khartoum, could not hope to hold out. On 23 December 1884, he surrendered to the Mahdi and to save his life became a Muslim. He was to remain a prisoner of the Mahdists for the next twelve years. Meanwhile, the Mahdi's lieutenant in the Eastern Sudan, Osman Digna, had cut the caravan route from Suakin to the town of Berber on the Nile, laid siege to the towns of Tokar and Sinkat and destroyed an Egyptian column sent to their relief. The country was being overwhelmed by the Mahdist tide, and with the death of Hicks Pasha the British sank deeper into the quagmire of the Sudan.

*

The Egyptian government simply had no idea now how to cope with the Mahdist insurrection. The army in Egypt was as yet little better than the one slaughtered in the Sudan, and to send it against the Mahdi without a great deal of further training was unthinkable. Besides, it was led by British officers and after Hicks' death no one in Cairo or London was keen to send them to a similar fate. The 'advice' offered to the Egyptian government by Sir Evelyn

Baring was nevertheless unpalatable to the Khedive Tewfik. Baring needed no urging from Gladstone to advise the Khedive that Egypt should simply abandon the Sudan and give up all attempts at controlling the Nile valley south of Wadi Halfa.

Egypt had spent a great deal of blood and treasure in the Sudan over the previous fifty years in an attempt to build an empire along the Nile and the Khedive Tewfik was reluctant to lose this investment. Furthermore, the first breath of the British proposal in Cairo led to the immediate resignation of the entire Egyptian government. There was also a well justified protest from Abd-el-Kadar, the Governor-General in Khartoum. He pointed out that if the Khedive and the British announced their intention of abandoning the Sudan, the population would be left with no choice but to defect at once to the Mahdi and the Egyptian troops and the expatriates in Sudan would be left entirely at the mercy of the Dervishes.

The truth of this statement did not concern Sir Evelyn Baring. He had to answer to his political masters in London and Gladstone's instructions were unequivocal: there was to be no British involvement in the Sudan. A new Egyptian government was soon in place, one which took a much more pragmatic look at the problems of the Sudan and their first suggestion was a compromise: to extract the Egyptian garrisons but maintain a claim on the country which could be enforced again at some future date, when the Mahdist storm had passed.

This apparently sensible proposal left the problem of extracting the Egyptian garrisons and much of the expatriate population of Khartoum across a thousand miles of country swarming with Mahdist supporters. Moreover, following the slaughter of Hicks Pasha and his army, the British press and public – and Her Majesty Queen Victoria – had become interested in the Sudan. On 1 January 1884 *The Times* published a letter from Sir Samuel Baker urging military intervention in the Sudan.

The British were not accustomed to having their generals slaughtered and certain sections of the press were soon putting forward the view that the man for the job in Khartoum was Major-General Charles Gordon – Chinese Gordon – an upright Christian gentleman, dauntless and heroic, who had served with distinction in various theatres of war, knew the Sudan well and could handle this tricky task with comparative ease.

This suggestion had first been mooted by William Thomas

Stead, editor of the *Pall Mall Gazette*, a political journalist who saw a great deal of hard-selling copy in a Parliamentary row. Stead was the leading journalist of the day and is credited with inventing the 'interview'. Before Stead, journalists gathered the material for their articles from sitting in on debates or collecting gossip in the clubs of St James's. Stead believed in going to the source for his information and opinions – a revolutionary idea at the time – and, on hearing that Gordon was staying with his sister Augusta, he took the train to Southampton and sought out the famous general's views on the current problems of the Sudan and the prospects of the Mahdi.

Gordon did not regard the Mahdist revolt as serious, at least at the moment. He felt that if a resolute commander was sent to hold Khartoum, the Mahdist revolt would soon peter out; in any event, the idea of withdrawal was unthinkable, damaging to British prestige, risky to those attempting to flee. These opinions, as reported and published by Stead, are interesting, partly because they are contradicted by future events, partly because they inspired the government to offer Gordon a role in the Sudan.

Gordon had not spent a happy or productive time since his return from the Sudan in 1879. He had wandered the world from India to China and South Africa and spent some months in the Seychelles, where, gripped by religious mania, he had declared the island of Praslin to be the original site of the Garden of Eden. Back in Britain, he had briefly fallen out with his beloved sister Augusta and annoyed his chiefs at the War Office. Gordon was not an easy man or a reliable subordinate and even his friend and admirer, Sir Garnet Wolseley, was too canny to employ him. When the Sudan proposal arose Gordon was on the point of resigning his commission and accepting a post with the King of the Belgians, assisting Henry Stanley to develop a Belgian Empire along the Congo river.

Gordon had even sent in his resignation to Wolseley, who flatly refused to accept it. 'I hate the idea of your going to the Congo. If I ever have the power, the first man I shall employ will be yourself.' This was neither kind nor truthful; as Adjutant-General of the army, Wolseley had ample opportunity to employ Gordon anywhere at any time, but he chose not to do so. He admired Gordon greatly as a man but declined to accept him as a subordinate, well aware that Gordon usually took a very flexible view of orders.

This new idea of 'Gordon for the Sudan' met with considerable support in Britain, especially amongst the press and public. It was greeted with rather less enthusiasm by Sir Evelyn Baring in Cairo. Baring had met Gordon and found him far from easy to understand. He also felt that Gordon's strong Christian beliefs alone should bar him from intervention in a Muslim quarrel. The subsequent negotiations between London and Cairo over Gordon's appointment were complex. Indeed they were to prove so fatal that they need to be spelled out in some detail.

The weight of responsibility for the Sudan rested, in the end, on Sir Evelyn Baring. This being so, the decision to accept Gordon for the Sudan depended on his agreement. Baring was most reluctant to allow it. The pressure on Baring over this issue was immense, as he himself records: 'During the course of an official career which extended over a period of nearly fifty years I, at times, had some hard work. But I never had such hard work, neither was I even in a position of such difficulty nor in one involving such a continuous strain on the mind, the nerves or – I may add – the temper, as during the first three months of 1884.'

The difficulties arose on 1 December 1883 when Baring received a telegram from the Foreign Secretary Lord Granville: 'If General Gordon were willing to go to Egypt, could he be of use to you or the Egyptian Government, and in what capacity?'

Baring consulted the Egyptian Prime Minister, Sherif Pasha, and they had little difficulty in rejecting this proposal, giving as their grounds that since the root of the Sudan problem was a Muslim revolt, the appointment of such a devout Christian would be less than helpful. This exchange occurred *before* William Stead published his article in the *Pall Mall Gazette*.

Then on 22 December, Baring sent a telegram to Lord Granville, advising him that the British government should insist on Egypt withdrawing from the Sudan, adding, 'It will be necessary to send an officer of high authority to Khartoum with full powers to withdraw the garrisons and make the best arrangements he can for the future of that country.'

The Egyptian government still had no intention of withdrawing from the Sudan and rather than comply with Baring's dictat, Sherif Pasha resigned. On 7 January 1884, Granville sent another telegram to Baring: 'Could General Gordon or Sir Charles Wilson be of assistance under altered circumstances in Egypt?'

Baring could still think of no good reason to send Gordon or

Wilson, another experienced officer, to Khartoum, and had meanwhile discussed the entire matter again with the new Egyptian Prime Minister, Nuba Pasha. They had decided that the former Governor in Khartoum, Abd-el-Kadar, would be the right man for the job. Unfortunately he failed to press this point with Lord Granville, and on 14 January Granville sent yet another telegram: 'I hear that Gordon is ready to go to Suakin to report to H.M. Government on the military situation in the Sudan and to return without any further engagement ... He might be of use in informing you and us of the situation. It would be popular at home, but there may be countermanding objections. Tell me your real opinion, with or without Nuba Pasha.'

It is more than likely that the prospect of public popularity at home weighed more heavily with Lord Granville than Gordon's suitability for the Sudan. Granville had now offered Gordon to Baring three times and Baring's resistance began to crumble. Baring capitulated because, 'With this array of opinion against me, I mistrusted my own judgement. I did not yield because I hesitated to stand up against the storm of pubic opinion. I gave a reluctant assent because I thought that as everyone differed from me, I must be wrong.' British press and public opinion had prevailed and Gordon would go to Khartoum.

Gordon accepted the post on 18 January 1884. His acceptance was met with cheers in the House of Lords and headlines in the newspapers. He was briefed for the task, first by Lord Granville in London and then by Baring in Cairo. Therein lay the roots of the approaching problem, for Gordon's instructions varied. The British government in London ordered Gordon to go to Khartoum to 'advise and report' on the problems of the evacuation. Sir Evelyn had, however, requested that a British officer should '. . . go to Khartoum and conduct the retreat.'

Baring and the Egyptian government assumed that Gordon would again become Governor-General of the Sudan and make himself responsible for any course of action within that tortured country. There remained of course General Gordon's own views, which he had not yet made apparent. With this fatal mixture of conflicting expectations already brewing, Gordon left London on the evening of 18 January 1884.

There is something wonderfully tragic and typically Victorian about Gordon's departure from London. He spent the last few hours dining with friends and playing with their children. He then went alone in a hansom cab to catch the boat train at Victoria Station. There he was met by his aide, Colonel J. H. D. Stewart of the 11th Hussars, who was to accompany him to Khartoum, and a small knot of frock-coated dignitaries.

At the station it was discovered that Gordon had no money. Lord Granville therefore went to buy his ticket while Lord Wolseley, after giving Gordon his watch and all the cash he had with him, took a cab and scoured the gentlemen's clubs of St James's, raising about £200 from the members who were then at dinner or playing cards. Many of the members accompanied Wolseley back to Victoria. There on the platform to say goodbye was the Commander-in-Chief of the army, the Duke of Cambridge, who held open the door of Gordon's compartment while the rest passed in his luggage.

The whistle blew, the guard waved his flag, and the train taking Gordon to his destiny chugged slowly away. A few hours later, taking a brandy at his club, Lord Granville posed the question to his colleagues: 'Are you sure we have not committed a gigantic folly?'

8

Graham's War

1884

'It has yet again been shown that a small body of British troops can defeat a horde of courageous savages. But no other important object has been obtained.'

Sir Evelyn Baring, Cairo, 1884

WHILE BARING AND the British government debated the wisdom of sending Gordon to Khartoum, matters had moved on in the Sudan. The destruction of Hicks Pasha's army was not the only defeat suffered by the Egyptians in 1883, nor was it the only one involving a British officer. On the Red Sea coast the Mahdi's local lieutenant, Osman Digna, was in arms, raiding the Suakin-to-Berber caravan route and besieging the garrisons of the coastal ports. This eastern rising was no light matter: if the Sudan garrisons were to be evacuated, the Red Sea ports were vital. From Berber to Suakin was only around two hundred miles and from Khartoum to Berber by the Nile route was about the same distance. River steamers could ship the refugees from Khartoum up to Berber in comparative safety and if the camel route from there to Suakin could be kept open, a satisfactory withdrawal with minimum losses was at least possible.

In their path was Osman Digna. Like Zobeir in Darfur, Osman Digna had made a thriving living as a wholesaler for the slave trade, collecting slaves from Berber and marching them east to small ports along the Red Sea coast. There those men and boys destined for service in the harems were routinely castrated – an operation from which many did not recover – before they were shipped in dhows to the sheiks of Arabia. Osman Digna grew wealthy from the slave trade and surrounded himself with a large armed following which enabled him to dominate the desert around Suakin when the Mahdist revolt broke out in 1881. By 1884 his army numbered around eighteen thousand men, including a thousand riflemen and perhaps five thousand Hadendowa swordsmen – the formidable Fuzzy-Wuzzies.

Kipling was to immortalize these dauntless Hadendowa warriors in a poem which expressed a view widely held by the British troops who encountered them in battle:

> So 'ere's to you Fuzzy-Wuzzy, at
>   your 'ome in the Sudan.
> You're a poor benighted 'eathen but
>   a first-rate fighting man;
> And 'ere's to you, Fuzzy Wuzzy, with
>   your 'ayrick 'ead of 'air –
> You big, black, bounding beggar – for
>   you broke a British square.

Osman Digna's strength and audacity was mounting by the day so, following the destruction of the Egyptian columns sent to the relief of Sinkat, the Egyptians mustered another force to put him down. This one was composed of Sudanese volunteers and Egyptian gendarmes, commanded by a former officer in the British army, Major-General Valentine Baker.

Valentine Baker is one of those colourful figures who haunt the pages of military accounts in the latter days of the Victorian Empire, a hard-riding, hard-drinking cavalry officer who sought out wars all over the Empire in search of adventure, medals and military glory. In Baker's case the reason for his appearance in Egypt, commanding a scratch force of gendarmes and bashibazooks, was an attempt to regain his once-thriving professional and personal reputation at home.

Valentine Baker was the younger brother of the famous explorer Sir Samuel Baker and started public life with a considerable flourish. Joining the 13th Lancers, he served with distinction in South Africa and the Crimea. He explored the remoter parts of the Empire and observed the Franco-Prussian War of 1870–1. By the early 1870s his career was going well: he had risen to the command of the élite 10th Hussars at Aldershot, leading his splendid regiment in reviews before the Queen and the Prince of Wales.

Then disaster struck: in 1875 Baker was accused of indecent assault on a young lady in a railway carriage. Subsequently tried and found guilty, he was cashiered from the army, fined £500 and sent to prison for a year.

On his release, Valentine Baker found there was no place in British society for an officer and gentleman who assaulted young ladies in railway carriages. Fortunately, such actions were no bar to appointment or promotion in the armies of the Turkish Empire and Baker therefore became an officer in the armies of the Sultan. He did well in Turkey's war with Russia, reaching the rank of Major-General before coming to Egypt in 1882 as Commandant of the newly-formed Egyptian gendarmerie, a semi-military force charged with enforcing law and order in the countryside and on the frontiers.

Baker's ambition was to regain his rank and position in the British army, and as a step to that end he had hoped to obtain command of the Egyptian army. That appointment went to Sir Evelyn Wood, for Sir Evelyn Baring – and Queen Victoria – felt that the British officers seconded to revitalize this force after the fall of Arabi would not agree to serve under Baker. He thus made what shift he could with the gendarmerie and in December 1883 this force was training in Suakin when news arrived of the Egyptian defeat outside Sinkat and the investment of Tokar by Osman Digna's warriors.

Baker hurriedly embarked his force in transports and sailed for Trinkitat, a small port some distance to the south of Suakin; from here they would advance to lift the siege of Tokar, twenty miles to the south-west. Baker's force resembled that of Hicks Pasha, a mixed bag of Sudanese soldiers, bashi-bazooks and Egyptian gendarmes, commanded by British officers, none of them particularly eager to try conclusions with the formidable Osman Digna and his fanatical Hadendowa swordsmen.

Baker advanced from Trinkitat with around three thousand men, a third of them his reluctant Egyptian policemen, who had joined the gendarmerie mainly to escape this sort of campaigning. There were three hundred Turkish bashi-bazooks armed with muskets, and a thousand Sudanese blacks, rightly regarded by Baker as the best troops in his force. For support he had four hundred Egyptian cavalry, four pieces of field artillery and two Gatling guns. Placing this force 'in-square' Baker advanced towards Tokar.

The square, the tactical formation most frequently adopted by all the forces campaigning against the Mahdi in the years to come, was a hollow, four-sided formation with infantry and guns composing the sides and all the animals and stores gathered in the centre. This formation had been employed by armies for centuries and offered at least a sense of security when advancing over open ground in the face of cavalry or assaulting infantry armed with edged weapons.

The square was ideal for all-round static defence on the open desert, but was difficult to maintain on the move. It should be pointed out that only the front and rear faces were in line. The sides marched in column but had only to turn right or left when attacked in order to fall into line, while the rear rank merely turned about. The formation was always unwieldy and offered a large target to enemy forces armed with rifles.

Victorian generals were familiar with fighting irregular or tribal forces and did not adopt the square formation lightly. Baker was well aware of the tactical limitations of the square during an advance and knew that to hold a square firm under attack required steadiness, training and discipline. These qualities, alas, were not currently available in Baker's little army. Nevertheless, it was in this formation that Baker's force advanced out across the desert from the port of Trinkitat.

They had only gone a few miles, meeting sniping and light opposition from Dervishes concealed in the scrub, and were close to the small village of El Teb, when Baker, who was riding some distance before the front face of the square with his Staff, became aware that Dervishes on camels and horseback were threatening the flanks of the square somewhere to his rear. Before Baker could ride back and take charge, the square was already starting to buckle. Within a few minutes it had become a confused mass of men, camels and supply carts, the soldiers starting to run about in panic, the whole formation collapsing into a mob of men shouting for help.

Before this mess could be sorted out and the Egyptian riflemen pushed back into formation, Dervish cavalry came sweeping down on every side of the square. They were supported by thousands of screaming Hadendowa Ansar armed with sword and spear, who came storming up out of wadis and from the scrub, falling on the square from every quarter . . . and the square collapsed. Within seconds the Hadendowa warriors were chopping their way into the mass of frightened soldiers, killing Egyptians with every stroke of their terrible swords.

The brief fight at El Teb was another frightful massacre, for most of the Egyptians made no attempt to defend themselves. They either threw away their arms and lay down to be slaughtered, the Dervishes hauling up their heads the easier to cut their throats, or they fell under the whirlwind of sword and spear thrusts. Those who held out fired until their ammunition pouches were empty and then fled across the desert only to receive a spear between the shoulder-blades or be cut down by a Hadendowa sword. Baker recorded some details of the fight a week later in a telegram to Baring: 'The Egyptians made no attempt to fight but threw down their arms and ran, carrying the Black troops with them and allowing themselves to be killed without resistance. More than 2,000 were killed and the Europeans also suffered terribly.'

Baker and some of the Egyptian cavalry managed to stay clear of this shambles and cut their way back to the coast five miles away, where the pursuing Dervishes were finally deterred by the guns of British warships anchored offshore. The Ansar then returned to scour the battlefield, searching for slaves among the survivors, killing and mutilating the wounded and gathering up a useful quantity of rifles and ammunition. Of the three thousand men who marched out of Trinkitat that morning, only five hundred were alive and free by the end of the afternoon.

Nor was this the end of the tragedy. After Valentine Baker Pasha and his few surviving soldiers re-embarked and returned to Suakin, the garrisons of Sinkat and Tokar were left with the option of surrender or retreat. The garrison commander at Sinkat, Mohammed Tewfik, elected to march for the coast. Drawing up the soldiers in a hollow square, placing civilians, women and children in the middle, the garrison left the town on 8 February 1884. They did not get a mile before Osman Digna's Hadendowa warriors swept down on them and once again the Egyptian square collapsed.

There was another fearful slaughter of the soldiers and the civilian men, while the captured women and children either vanished into the slave markets and harems in the Mahdist camps or were sold to the sheiks of Arabia. Two weeks later, to avoid a further massacre, the garrison of Tokar surrendered. Of all the Egyptian settlements along the Red Sea coast, only Suakin remained secure, protected by a small British-officered garrison and the guns of some Royal Navy warships.

These repeated defeats and massacres put Sir Evelyn Baring and his masters in the British government in a difficult position. They had taken over Egypt, destroyed the Egyptian army, and made a puppet of the Khedive Tewfik. The British were now running Egyptian affairs and the whole world knew it. Like it or not they had to accept responsibility for Egypt's problems, the most pressing of which was undoubtedly the Mahdist rising in the Sudan.

The British government, and especially Prime Minister Gladstone, were still attempting to stay out of further involvement in the Sudan but the Queen now became involved and her attitude was decisive. It is difficult to underestimate the influence exerted on military affairs by Queen Victoria but it was immense, persuasive . . . and highly effective.

In Her Majesty's opinion, and in the opinion of most of her soldiers, the British army was really the Queen's army. The soldiers' Oath of Allegiance was to the Queen and through her to the country, not to any government or politician currently in power. Although the generals were appointed by and responsible to the politicians and Parliament, the views of the Queen carried considerable weight at the Horse Guards and the Ministry of War.

Her Majesty took a very poor view of armies led by British officers being cut to pieces by sword-armed savages. This opinion even stretched to armies led by former officers like Valentine Baker. Baker was clearly not a gentleman; he may even have been a bounder and was currently serving in the forces of another power, but he was British and relentlessly brave. In Her Majesty's opinion repeated massacres of forces led by British officers in the Sudan were deleterious to British prestige. If they continued it might set a bad example to discontented folk in other parts of the Empire. Something had to be done to restore British military standing and Her Majesty expected someone – possibly the Prime Minister – to do it. The Queen's view was widely shared by the British public and the British press and they were not to be denied.

The Queen, the press and the public put increasing pressure on Gladstone and his ministers and eventually the Prime Minister began to cave in. Sending the famous fighting general, Charles Gordon, to the Sudan had been one attempt to satisfy public demands for action and Gordon was already on his way to

Khartoum. Evidently something more dramatic was called for on the east coast of the Sudan, and in late January 1884 Gladstone decided to send a small fighting force to the Red Sea coast. This decision was greeted with joy by the Queen: 'We are delighted that my Government has finally decided to act,' she wrote. 'May it not be too late to save other lives, for the fall of Sinkat was terrible.'

Mr Gladstone was rather more ambivalent about the fate of the Egyptian garrison of Sinkat and not at all sure that a further commitment of British troops was entirely wise. It could be said, and Mr Gladstone was not the only one in Britain to say it, that the Egyptians had no business in the Sudan and were clearly not welcome there. The rising of the country under the Mahdi was simply the inevitable outcome of decades of Egyptian exploitation and Mr Gladstone's oft-expressed opinion was that Britain should stay out of it and restrict her involvement to Egyptian territory. This, however, was easier said than done.

It was therefore with some reluctance that he sent instructions to the senior officer at Suakin, Admiral Sir William Hewitt, then commanding the Red Sea squadron of the Mediterranean Fleet. Hewitt, who had already seen what happened to the Mahdi's enemies and knew the situation in the Eastern Sudan in some detail, was ordered to muster his forces, send troops ashore, and see off Osman Digna's warriors with as much speed as possible.

Hewitt cannot have welcomed this instruction; his 'forces' consisted of three small warships and their crews. By stripping the crews to the bone he was able to muster about one hundred and fifty men, either bluejackets or gunners of the Royal Marine Artillery, the latter equipped with two Gatling guns. Even had the remnants of Valentine Baker's force, now licking their wounds within the walls of Suakin, been ready and willing to fight, this force was clearly not adequate for the task of thrashing Osman Digna. Hewitt did have one advantage: as Commander of this force he had a remarkable officer, Captain Lord Charles Beresford of the Royal Navy.

Beresford was currently Commander of the steam gunboat HMS *Condor*, a ship he had captained at the bombardment of Alexandria during Arabi's revolt. Beresford was also a warrior, a man as happy to fight ashore with rifle and bayonet as afloat with heavy guns. Hewitt gave him command of the bluejackets and Royal Marines and Beresford soon had his small command at the peak of efficiency and spoiling for a fight. Hewitt sent this force ashore on 10 February 1884 and they joined the garrison of Suakin to await further orders.

In an attempt to augment Beresford's brigade, a further one hundred and twenty Royal Marines, homeward bound from India, were snatched from a passing troopship and two hundred and eighty Royal Marines and volunteer bluejackets were recruited from British warships in Port Said and sent through the Suez Canal to Suakin. This was a comfort to the garrison but the Suakin force still hardly mustered a sufficient number to venture far beyond the walls. Fortunately, more men were on the way, for in spite of Gladstone's thinly veiled opposition to involvement the British Lion was starting to stir.

Troopships were on the sea, bringing fighting men from India, Aden and the British army in Egypt, to form a force in Suakin that finally totalled three thousand men. Eventually five first-class battalions came ashore: the Black Watch, the Gordon Highlanders, the Royal Marine Light Infantry, the King's Royal Rifle Corps, the Yorkshire and Lancashire Regiment and the Royal Irish Fusiliers, plus a small cavalry force provided by the 19th Hussars and Valentine Baker's old command, the 10th Hussars. The force also had Gatling and Gardner guns and some field artillery.

There were also a number of supernumerary officers, including Lieutenant-Colonel Frederick Burnaby, the tall, languid, elegant commanding officer of the Royal Horse Guards, 'The Blues'. Burnaby had no business being in the Sudan at all but was unable to resist the prospect of action. His Commander-in-Chief, the Duke of Cambridge, had in fact specifically forbidden him to go but Burnaby simply took leave from his regiment and went anyway. Such conduct was not unprecedented from a Victorian officer and Colonel Burnaby was a noted adventurer. A famous romantic, he had already explored Central Asia and written a best-selling book, *A Ride to Khiva*, which is still in print today. He was also a noted swordsman, though his chosen weapon was a double-barrelled Purdey shotgun loaded with buckshot. A fighting man to match the Hadendowa, Burnaby was to do good service in the hand-to-hand battles of the Sudan.

The confidence shown by the British in committing this small force of men to battle is remarkable. The Suakin force, little more than a small brigade, was expected to fight a large Dervish army which had outfought and massacred large numbers of Egyptian troops in recent months. No one thought the task too great at the time, for British soldiers were expected to fight and win, whatever the odds against them.

Once assembled, these men were mustered in three 'brigades' two infantry and one cavalry, the whole commanded by a very experienced officer, Lieutenant-General Sir Gerald Graham VC, KCB. Graham was one of the Wolseley 'Ring' and a personal friend of Gordon, a friendship dating back to Crimea days. Graham had seen Gordon off to Khartoum before coming down from Egypt to take up his command at Suakin. Graham was accompanied by two senior officers, Colonel Herbert Stewart who had distinguished himself at Tel-el-Kebir in 1882 and was to command Graham's cavalry, and Colonel Sir Redvers Buller VC, who had also distinguished himself in the Arabi campaign. Like Graham, they too were members of the Wolseley 'Ring' and highly regarded by the Adjutant-General. Buller was to be Second-in-Command of the force and command one infantry brigade while a Colonel Davis commanded the other.

Graham was a giant of a man, over six feet tall, a tough old soldier and one of Wolseley's confidants. Like Gordon and Kitchener, who was now serving as a 'bimbashi' or major in the Egyptian army, Graham had been commissioned in the Royal Engineers, a corps that provided many fighting generals in Victoria's army. He had served in the Crimean War where he had been wounded twice and won his VC leading an assault on the Redan at Sebastopol. He had been with Wolseley at the taking of the Taku Forts in China and commanded a brigade in Wolseley's army during the Anglo-Egyptian War of 1882.

Graham had been a fighting soldier and he remained a fighting general: 'Six foot four inches tall and brave as a lion,' according to Wolseley. Like Colonel Burnaby, General Graham was an officer who preferred to be in the thick of the fighting, sword and pistol in hand, rather than in the rear with his Staff, commanding the battle. Such gallant conduct might be considered meritorious in a subaltern but is rather less desirable in a commanding general who is expected to keep clear of the ruck in order to get an overview of what is going on and issue the necessary orders. Like his second-in-command, Redvers Buller, Graham was not the most intelligent of generals and his eagerness for personal combat was to prove a liability in the weeks ahead.

The original intention was that Graham should use this force to relieve Tokar. Before he could do so, Tokar surrendered and his new orders simply required him to advance into the desert, give Osman Digna a good dusting and so restore the prestige of British arms. There was no strategic objective, no thought of aiding Gordon or advancing to Berber. Graham's war would be a punitive raid, no more. With that intention in mind, Graham disembarked his men at Trinkitat on 28 February 1884 and prepared to advance into the desert.

General Graham led his army out of Trinkitat on 29 February and formed it up outside the walls in the same square formation used a month before by Valentine Baker. The front face of the advancing square was composed of the Gordon Highlanders, the rear face by the Black Watch. The Royal Marines and the Yorks and Lancs provided the left face and the Royal Irish Fusiliers and the riflemen of the King's Royal Rifle Corps were on the right. These side-face battalions were all marching in column-of-fours, ready to turn or wheel into line if the square was attacked, while the service elements, the ordnance, food, medical and transport camels, together with the rest of the force, marched in the centre.

Graham knew his business and took sensible precautions against a surprise attack. A squadron from the 10th Hussars skirmished ahead, quartering the scrub-covered desert, while the rest of Colonel Stewart's cavalry brigade, some five hundred men of the 10th and 19th Hussars plus some mounted infantry, were kept intact in the rear. The corners of the square were occupied either by 7-pounder field pieces or by Gatling or Gardner machine-guns. These hopper-fed and crank-fired machine guns could enfilade the faces of the square and cut down any Ansar warriors charging in to the attack. Graham knew that only a good weight of fire could halt a Dervish charge if it was mounted from close range and in sufficient numbers.

This British square formation sounds very unwieldy, as indeed it was. It is best imagined as a fort on the move, with the walls made up of fighting men, but it was a sensible enough formation when the main danger was from infantry charging home with edged weapons from some as yet unknown quarter. The force amounted to about three thousand infantry and artillerymen and nine hundred cavalry and mounted infantry. With this force went Valentine Baker — one wonders how his old regiment, the 10th Hussars, welcomed their former commanding officer — and a number of his gendarmerie. These last elected to stay inside the square.

Osman Digna had been investing Trinkitat at a distance and was well aware that Graham had come ashore with a small army. He had therefore sent his nephew Madani and the emir of the coast, Abdullah-ibn-Hassan, to occupy the ruins of an old sugar mill by the village of El Teb, some miles south of the port. There they took up positions in rifle pits overlooking the vulture-covered corpses of Baker's army, which were still lying out in the desert.

Osman had a Gatling gun, some Krupp field pieces captured from Baker's army and about ten thousand men, including his own Hadendowa tribesmen. Many of these were now armed with .45-calibre single-shot Remington rifles. These Dervishes were in position around the sugar mill, occupying trenches or hidden in wadis, when Graham's ponderous expedition came rolling across the open desert towards El Teb, bagpipes wailing from the ranks of the Scottish battalions. The action began about noon, with a blast of cannon and machine-gun fire from the Dervish position.

Osman's artillery, served by the Egyptian gunners captured at Tokar, opened fire at a thousand yards on the advancing British square and began to score hits. Artillery fire was not the sort of thing Graham had expected from sword-armed savages and there was a pause while the British artillery deployed, found the range and returned the fire. During this pause the British infantry lay down in square, but when the Ansar artillery had been silenced they rose and moved forward, advancing in enfilade to the left, intending to outflank the Dervish position.

This made the Royal Marines and the Yorks and Lancaster battalions the advancing face of the square, with the Black Watch on one flank, the Gordon Highlanders on the other and the King's Royal Rifle Corps and Royal Irish Fusiliers in the rear. While the British infantry were getting up and starting forward again, some two thousand Ansar sword and spearmen rose from cover in the scrub and charged in against the British square.

Given a sufficient field of fire and well-handled weapons, a British square should have proved a more than adequate bulwark against charging swordsmen but the British infantry carried single-shot Martini-Henry rifles and the Ansar had less than two hundred yards to run. They also had covering fire from their own riflemen until they were close in and their charge struck home hard. Stabbing with their leaf-bladed spears, swinging heavy, razor-sharp swords, the Ansar smashed into the Yorks and Lancs battalion and drove them back thirty yards or more.

The Ansar broke in the left front face of the British square, turning it from four firm ranks into a mass of men fighting off the Hadendowa with sword and revolver, rifle and bayonet. Thanks to their stout resistance the square did not collapse. The Ansar engaged with the Yorks and Lancashire battalion were promptly raked with fire from the Royal Marine Light Infantry on their flank and from the troops on the other sides of the square.

While the Yorks and Lancs and the Royal Marines were thus closely engaged, more Ansar warriors came thudding in against the other faces of the square. Here, too, in spite of the Martini-Henrys the Ansar charged home, rolling under the bayonets to rise at the feet of the British infantry and lash out with sword and spear. Colonel Burnaby of the Blues was fighting on his own outside the square, armed with a 12-bore shotgun, firing blasts of buckshot into the charging mass of shrieking Hadendowa. There was a brief swirl of hand-to-hand fighting, a roar of rifle, pistol and Gatling fire; then the Ansar broke off, the Yorks and Lancs and the Marines charging after them across the desert to overrun Osman Digna's artillery position and shoot down the gunners.

The Ansar were now falling back towards the mud houses of El Teb but though in retreat they were not routed. They withdrew in good order, those with rifles turning to fire at the reforming British square. Stewart's cavalry were now coming up from the rear at a fast trot and, mistaking this Ansar withdrawal for a rout, Stewart ordered his troopers to charge.

This charge went in over broken, scrub-covered ground, where the cavalry could not be kept in line. The scattered troopers soon found themselves under individual attack from groups of Ansar infantry, who hurled spears or ran in with swords. Some lay down to hamstring the horses, slashing at their hocks, or tried to fetch the chargers down by throwing sticks of mimosa wood against the horses' legs. Stewart's sword-armed troopers could not reach the Ansar spearmen on the ground and were charged in turn by a squadron of Sudanese horse, well-mounted Baggara tribesmen, many clad in chainmail, wielding sword and spear.

This sudden apparition must have seemed like a relic of the crusades but was a most effective one. These armoured warriors speared or cut down a number of British troopers before the cavalry remembered they had carbines, dismounted and shot the Baggara off their horses.

The British square had by now reformed and, rolling forward yet again, soon overran the Ansar position around the sugar refinery. In the village, the ever-adaptable gunners of the Royal Marines Artillery turned captured Ansar cannon round to blast the more tenacious warriors out of their trenches. Then the Gordon Highlanders and the Royal Navy bluejackets came sweeping through the scrub, flushing out lone swordsmen from hiding, dauntless warriors who fought and stabbed and slashed, even when wounded, fighting until they were shot down and killed. Graham's men had the El Teb position now and had only to mop up. Very few prisoners were taken.

By early afternoon the battle of El Teb was over: British losses were surprisingly light – five officers and thirty-four men killed, sixteen officers and thirty-six men wounded. The latter included the unfortunate Valentine Baker who had been severely wounded in the face. The Ansar had lost fifteen hundred killed and as many more wounded, but these figures give little indication of the fierceness of the Dervish resistance. Every man in Graham's army had acquired a great respect for these valiant Sudanese warriors, who came on in spite of cannon, machine-gun and rifle fire, fought hand-to-hand and did not know when they were beaten. It was a thoughtful little army that left some of the Black Watch to garrison the village of El Teb and moved on cautiously towards the town of Tokar.

The Ansar did not attempt to hold Tokar which Graham's men reached on 3 March. Graham found a few Egyptian survivors from Baker's gendarmerie and gathered them up before marching back to the coast, picking up the Black Watch at El Teb, arriving back at Suakin on 5 March. Here there was news of a fresh Ansar force mustering to the south, astride the road to the other main town nearby, Sinkat. Graham had no orders to cease campaigning and therefore prepared to attack the Dervishes again.

Five days later, on 10 March 1884, Graham sent the Black Watch battalion out of Suakin, ordering them to advance about ten miles and then construct a large zareba on the Sinkat road. These compounds made up of thorny mimosa branches were a method of creating a defensive position in country where stones for building walls, known as sangars, were in short supply. The rest of Graham's force came up to occupy the zareba on the following day. Graham's force moved out on 12 March and engaged the Ansar again on the following morning at the village of Tamai.

The composition and arrangement of Graham's army was much the same as at El Teb, but this time the British advanced in two infantry brigade squares commanded by Redvers Buller and Colonel Davis. Graham had around three thousand five hundred officers and men while the Ansar forces at Tamai were commanded by Osman Digna's cousin, Mahsud Musa. Mahsud commanded around ten thousand men, most of them armed only with sword or spear, but some with rifles. The advancing British were soon met by Ansar snipers concealed in wadis, hidden in the scrub, or dug-in in rifle pits, with a large number of Hadendowa, perhaps two thousand, hidden in a ravine which lay directly across their line of advance. These Hadendowa waited in cover until Graham's force was only two hundred yards away; then they burst from the ravine and opened the battle with a ferocious close-quarter charge against Davis's brigade.

The British infantry had met such a charge at El Teb and were not over-eager to meet one again. They greeted the Ansar onslaught with a blast of musketry and machine-gun fire from the Gatlings, but their firing was wild and high and many of the Hadendowa were able to run in under it. Thick clumps of scrub provided further cover for the Dervish attack and suddenly there was a gap in the British square.

Just before the Hadendowa appeared, the 1st Battalion the Black Watch, leading the advance, had been ordered forward to clear the ravine. This created a gap between the Black Watch and the Yorks and Lancs and put the Gatling and Gardner guns and gunners at the front of the flanking columns out in the open. As the Black Watch advanced, the Ansar rose from cover and charged home against the British square. According to General Graham: 'A large body of natives, coming in one continuous stream, charged with reckless determination on the 1st Yorks and Lancasters, – the contingent making up the other half of the front face of the square – The brigade fell into total disorder and the enemy captured the guns of the Naval Brigade which were locked by the men, who stood by them to the end.' This was the scene depicted by Rudyard Kipling in which the 'Fuzzy-Wuzzies' did the impossible and 'broke the British square.'

For a few minutes all was chaos. The Black Watch were hit in the flank by this sudden Dervish charge, and driven back into the square, the men fighting singly or in small groups. There was no time for volley firing or sophisticated tactics. This was hand-to-hand fighting at its most brutal, the British infantry firing into the shrieking faces of the Ansar warriors, parrying sword cuts with rifle butts, trading bayonet thrusts with their stabbing and slashing opponents. Whoever ran died, so there was nothing left to do but stand and fight it out.

The Gatling and Gardner gunners of the naval brigade blazed off their ammunition, chained the weapons and fled back to the deceptive safety of the square, with yelling Ansar warriors bounding at their heels. The Ansar then struck hard at the Royal Marine Light Infantry and the British square again gave ground, falling into a vast mêlée of British infantry and Sudanese warriors, a mass of fighting men reeling back for about half a mile, cutting, shooting, clubbing and stabbing at each other. The British commander, General Graham, had been well forward when the Dervish charge came in. Within minutes his horse had been shot down, his escort dispersed, and he was now on foot in the scrub, fighting with sword and revolver among his soldiers, surrounded by the enemy and in no position to take command of the battle.

Buller's brigade had also been attacked but they were further from the ravine and had time to rake the oncoming Ansar with rifle and Gatling fire; thus the full force of the Ansar attack on Buller's brigade never struck home and many warriors soon broke off to join in the wild fight ahead with the men of Davis's brigade. This was fortunate, for Buller's men were then able to open aimed fire on the Ansar tribesmen swarming around Davis's crumbling flanks. Then Stewart's cavalry came surging up on the flank where the troopers dismounted and began to rake the Ansar with their carbines. Caught in a crossfire the Dervish warriors were finally forced to flee, but it was a very close-run thing.

After about half an hour of hand-to-hand fighting, the Ansar drew off and Graham was able to re-muster his men and restore Davis's brigade to order. The brigade reformed, with the Royal Marines now on the right flank, the Yorks and Lancs in the centre, the Black Watch on the left and the naval brigade's bluejackets making up the rear. Supported by cavalry and fire from the Gatling machine-guns, the entire force of two brigades then advanced through the scrub, shooting or bayoneting any warriors they found, enduring rifle fire from wounded Ansar warriors hidden in the broken ground until they, too, could be flushed out and silenced. By early afternoon Davis's brigade had taken the ridge above the village of Tamai and were able to rake the ground round about with Gatling and artillery fire. After an hour of such pounding the Ansar bands slowly and finally drew off.

Casualties in this violent brawl at Tamai were much higher than at El Teb. The British lost five officers and about one hundred men killed, with seven officers and over three hundred men wounded, many bearing ghastly, disfiguring wounds from the razor-sharp Hadendowa swords.

Graham reported: 'Our losses were grievous, many brave men of the Royal Highlanders [the Black Watch] and the York and Lancaster Regt, devoting their lives to save the honour of their regiments.'

Ansar losses totalled about four thousand. Over half of these had been killed but, as before, the Sudanese had withdrawn slowly and in good order, having given a good account of themselves, and were clearly willing to fight again. These Sudanese warriors had succeeded where French and Russian infantry had failed: they had broken a British square, a fact that their immediate opponents in the battle of Tamai, the Black Watch, have remembered to this day.

Graham's force had fought well and British honour had been satisfied but very little of use had been achieved. It was now mid-March and had Graham been allowed to follow up on this success and clear the route across the desert to Berber, Gordon's prospects in Khartoum might have been much brighter. Such an advance was not however covered by Graham's orders.

The Queen and the British public were delighted to hear of these victories. British military prestige had been sufficiently re-established for Kipling to immortalize the stout-hearted 'Fuzzy-Wuzzies' in verse but that was about all. The Mahdi, Osman Digna and his Ansars had not been cowed. Osman Digna held on to his gains at Sinkat and Tokar and the vital caravan route from Suakin to Berber on the Nile remained closed, though General Graham pleaded for permission to press on to the river and open it. His plea fell on deaf ears; Gladstone was quite adamant that no further commitment in the Sudan was permissible.

By April 1884, Graham's force had been withdrawn to Cairo and the Nile Delta and broken up. Osman Digna then swiftly re-occupied the territory outside Suakin and away to the west in Kordofan the Mahdi resumed his conquest of the Sudan. Nothing of any significance had been achieved by Baker's rout and Graham's victories. Graham's campaign had been satisfying but ultimately pointless, for the crux of the Sudan situation lay not along the Red Sea coast but on the Nile. In April 1884 all eyes therefore turned back to the city of Khartoum, where General Charles Gordon had now been in residence for six weeks and showed little sign of leaving.

9

Gordon in Khartoum

February–August 1884

'I feel quite happy, for if I stay and God is with me, who can hurt me?'

Major-General C. G. Gordon,
Khartoum, 1884

WHILE GENERAL GRAHAM and his men were moving up to fight Osman Digna and his forces around Suakin in the early months of 1884, General Charles Gordon and his small staff were making their way south down the Nile to Khartoum. After arriving in Egypt, Gordon had spent a short but busy time in Cairo, a city he consented to visit only with the greatest reluctance. He had intended to sail right through the Suez Canal to Suakin and head inland from there to Berber and Khartoum but Osman Digna barred the road to Berber and Gordon was eventually prevailed upon to pass through Cairo.

Had Gordon kept to his original intention and tried the Berber route the famous and tragic siege of Khartoum might never have occurred. Gordon originally hoped to avoid Baring, a man he had elected to dislike, but he was obliged by Lord Granville to disembark at Alexandria and go to Cairo for a meeting with Baring and the Khedive Tewfik. Gordon's instructions effectively put him under Baring's orders and this attempt to avoid his superior was an indication of trouble to come.

The meeting in Cairo was also urged upon Gordon by various old friends from Crimea days. One of these was General Graham, who had not yet left Cairo to take up his command in the Eastern

Sudan. Another was the Sirdar of the Egyptian army, Sir Evelyn Wood. Both were anxious to talk to Gordon before he vanished to the south. For all his strange ways, Gordon had a gift for friendship; the opportunity to see these old comrades was not one to miss.

While Gordon was on the train from Alexandria to Cairo he thought of another advantage that might be obtained in Cairo. His current role in the Sudan, whether as adviser or executor, must lead to the abandonment of that country to the Mahdi. Gordon already felt that there must be another solution, for the Sudanese people could not be abandoned to an uncertain fate. Some local leader must be found who could oppose the Mahdi and maintain the Sudan for the Khedive. On the train ride to Cairo, Gordon thought of just the man.

Zobeir Pasha, formerly the most active of slavers, once the *de facto* ruler of Darfur, and Gordon's old and most bitter enemy from his time as Governor-General, must be the new ruler of the entire Sudan, and take on the burden of command after Gordon and the Egyptian garrisons had left. The idea was – to say the least – ingenious.

Zobeir was now a prisoner in Cairo and Gordon's chief lieutenant, Romolo Gessi, had hunted Zobeir's son Suleiman down and put him to death. Those long-ago matters did not concern Gordon now and he saw no reason why they should trouble anyone else. The solution to the problem of succession in the Sudan was now obvious. Zobeir must go with him to Khartoum and rule the country for the Khedive after he had left.

This proposal stunned everyone in Cairo, including Baring, the Khedive . . . and Zobeir himself. When they got to hear of it, it also stunned – even appalled – the British government, for Zobeir was best known in Britain as an unrepentant slaver. On reflection, Baring began to see that the suggestion had some merit. Zobeir had once ruled a large province of the Sudan and Gordon's proposal amounted to no more than setting up a political Sudanese leader to oppose a spiritual one. The problem lay less with the idea than with the central character. Zobeir had been sentenced to death in 1879 but escaped execution by paying a heavy bribe to Ismail, and had spent the last five years under house arrest in Cairo. He was a notorious rogue and the whole world knew it. Could the British government be seen to do business with such a man?

That apart, Zobeir hated Gordon. Gordon had destroyed Zobeir's slave-hunting army. He had sent Romolo Gessi into

Darfur to harry his followers, a campaign followed by Gessi's execution of his son Suleiman and a dozen of Zobeir's followers. Zobeir had neither forgotten nor forgiven any of this. Their meeting was not a happy encounter. Zobeir refused to shake Gordon's hand and reproached Gordon loudly and at length for all the wrongs done to him. Gordon promptly forgot his new scheme and reminded Zobeir of his numerous crimes, adding that the execution of Suleiman by Gessi had been both richly deserved and long overdue.

After this encounter Baring intervened to point out that Gordon's idea was obviously impractical on two counts. Firstly, Zobeir was not interested and was anyway Gordon's bitter enemy. Secondly, the British government would not, and indeed could not, permit a notorious slaver like Zobeir to return to his old territory, let alone with the support and encouragement of their chosen emissary, General Gordon. The Anti-Slavery Society and the British press and public would explode with anger at the merest hint of the idea.

Given Zobeir's background it is hard to understand why Gordon ever proposed such a scheme; he himself said that the idea came to him as a 'mystic feeling', a statement that can hardly have altered Baring's personal opinion that Gordon was not the man for the Sudan. However, it is equally hard to understand the British government's insistence that Gordon was only going to the Sudan to 'report and advise' on the feasibility of an evacuation.

Baring and the British government had already received plenty of advice on the situation in Khartoum from some authoritative sources, most recently from Abd-el-Kadar, formerly Governor in Khartoum, now the Egyptian Minister of War. His words should have been considered, for Abd-el-Kadar had been the commander of Baker's 'Forty Thieves' and was therefore both a good soldier and a man with long experience of the Sudan.

El-Kadar had already made a survey of the Sudan situation and reported that since there were tens of thousands of soldiers and civilians desperate to leave the Sudan the evacuation would require several thousand camels, the services of everything that could float on the Nile, and from nine months to a year to complete. The infrastructure of the Sudan did not permit a swift withdrawal and there was no point in pretending otherwise. There were no railways, desert tracks in place of roads, poor telegraphic links, and hostile Dervishes everywhere. Anyone with the slightest knowledge of the Sudan would have seen the difficulties of a withdrawal, so why send General Gordon at all? What report could he deliver that would override the known facts?

Abd-el-Kadar had been willing to take on the task of evacuation some months before, until he heard that the Khedive had been 'advised' – or ordered – by the British government to issue a proclamation announcing the abandonment of the Sudan. Rightly declaring that such an announcement would make his task impossible, for all the friendly or uncommitted tribes would promptly join the Mahdi, el-Kadar then flatly refused to go. The British government must have known all this since it was only after Abd-el-Kadar's refusal to conduct an evacuation that Baring had asked the British government to '. . . send a qualified British officer with full powers, military and civil, to conduct the retreat.'

The only reasonable conclusion that can be drawn is that the British government had no intention of getting further enmeshed in the Sudan débâcle but were obliged to go through the motions of assistance for reasons not entirely detached from a wish to remain in office in Britain. Sending Gordon in response to public demand in Britain may have seemed a shrewd move at the time, a way to demonstrate official concern for the benighted people of the Sudan, but it reckoned without the character of General Gordon. Even without that volatile factor, there were soon other matters on hand to muddy the waters and create confusion over Gordon's precise role.

During a meeting with Tewfik, Baring and Nuba Pasha, the Egyptian Prime Minister, the emphasis of Gordon's instructions changed again from that of 'adviser and reporter' to that of 'organizer and executor'. He was now charged with actually evacuating the Sudan. Nineteenth-century historians made much of this alteration but it seems less relevant now. Whatever his instructions from London or Cairo, Gordon would be on his own in Khartoum and would go his own way, as always.

Throughout his career Gordon had always taken a relaxed approach to orders; those he gave to others were written on tablets of stone, to be obeyed at all costs; those he received were a basis for negotiation, and could be altered at will. The delicate phrasing or the variations in his instructions would bother him not at all; he would do what he thought best. That evening Gordon set off by train for Aswan and the Sudan. He left Zobeir behind but took another problem with him instead.

In the short time since Gordon had proposed taking Zobeir to Khartoum, Nuba Pasha and the Khedive Tewfik had considered the basic idea and decided that it had a certain merit. Gordon should have a deputy who would rule in the Sudan after he left, and to fill this role they chose a Sudanese emir, Abd-el-Shakur, a portly young man now happily residing in Cairo. He was plucked from obscurity, given a smart uniform hung about with medals and pushed on to Gordon's train accompanied by his four brothers, twenty-three wives, a harem full of concubines and a great quantity of liquor.

The Emir-el-Shakur was horrified at the thought of going to Khartoum and spent most of the journey from Cairo to Aswan in either a drunken stupor or a blind panic. At Aswan he fled; he and his entire court vanished from Gordon's train to reappear in Cairo some weeks later by which time the Khedive Tewfik had forgotten all about his mission.

By train and river-steamer Gordon made his way south to Korosko, accompanied by his friend, General Graham, and his aide, Colonel J. H. D. Stewart, a most useful man for the Sudan. Colonel Stewart, a Scot, was a senior regimental officer of the 11th Hussars, a distinguished regiment, and a man with considerable experience of the Sudan. Gordon was wary of his aide, who was a calm, sensible man, not given to impulsive actions. He would have been even more wary had he been aware that Baring had instructed Stewart to report to him directly, even if – particularly if – his judgement of any situation differed from that of General Gordon.

Like most of those who came to know Gordon well, Stewart grew to admire the General's personal qualities but learned to doubt his judgement. In his turn Gordon came to like Stewart and even came to rely on him, but somewhere in his personality lurked the urge to be alone. Whenever he had a reasonable excuse, he would rid himself of Colonel Stewart and stay as he wished to – alone but for his God.

At Korosko Gordon hired camels for the perilous three-hundred-mile journey across the Nubian desert to Khartoum. Gordon was not worried about the dangers on this journey from sun or thirst or the Mahdi. He had discovered that the Mahdi was the nephew of one of his former guides from his last time in the Sudan and still thought that all the tales of Dervish success and Ansar ferocity had been greatly exaggerated. He even proposed riding past

Khartoum and going into Kordofan to meet the Mahdi in person, a suggestion that led to a direct order from Baring forbidding him to do so.

General Graham accompanied Gordon as he left Korosko, climbing a small hill to watch the little party with his field-glasses as they headed out across the desert, '. . . hoping that he would turn so I might wave to him, but he rode on without turning, until I could see him no more.'

*

It took Gordon eighteen days to reach Khartoum from Korosko, and the journey was not completed without more controversy. At Berber, on 11 February, he summoned a meeting of the local chiefs and issued the proclamation urged on the Khedive by Baring informing the chiefs that the British had advised the Khedive to withdraw from the Sudan and had no intention of becoming involved themselves. As el-Kadar had predicted, this announcement proved most unwise, as Gordon instantly lost the support of all those Sudanese who were not yet committed to the Mahdi.

Having upset the loyal Sudanese, Gordon's next move infuriated the public in Britain. After heralding the withdrawal the sheiks asked if the terms of the 1878 Anglo-Egyptian Convention, abolishing domestic slavery in the Sudan, would therefore take effect, as arranged, at the end of 1889. In the circumstances, stated Gordon, this Convention was void in the Sudan. When they heard of this, the British press and public, and above all the Anti-Slavery Society, erupted. Another storm of protest arrived from Britain to descend on the long-suffering Sir Evelyn Baring.

In recent decades the world in general and Great Britain in particular has become very familiar with well-meaning organizations who have but one point of view and press it relentlessly on anyone who will listen, but Baring's views on just such an organization are still worth recording:

> Every Englishman is proud of the part his country has borne in the suppression of the slave trade; few will deny the distinguished part played by the Anti-Slavery Society in this work.
>
> The Society, however, is not without its defects. Concentration of thought and action on one subject, together with a certain lack of imagination which occasionally characterises the conduct

of Englishmen in dealing with foreign affairs, due perhaps to their insular habits of thought, produce their natural effect.

The members of the Anti-Slavery Society appear sometimes to be unable to look at any questions except from an Anti-Slavery point of view. Even from that point of view they are often liable to error through a failure to judge accurately the relative importance of events . . . the main question, whether from the general or anti-slavery point of view was to quieten the Sudan. It was in deference to the Society that it was decided not to send Zobeir to the Sudan.

That decision had far-reaching effects. Baring had finally decided to support Gordon's wish for Zobeir and the British government's refusal to countenance such a move was a major contributor to the fact that since there was no one to rule the Sudan and oppose the Mahdi after he left, Gordon decided to stay in Khartoum.

On the particular issue of the evacuation proclamation, Baring pointed out to the government and public that if the Sudan was to be abandoned the Convention must lapse anyway, since the Anglo-Egyptians would not be in a position to enforce it. While that argument was still in progress, Gordon embarked on the river-steamer *Tewfik* and sailed south for Khartoum.

Gordon arrived in Khartoum on 18 February 1884. He found the city much as he had left it five years before, but with all the instruments of oppression back in place and the expatriate citizens and most of the garrison on the verge of panic. In Sudanese terms, Khartoum was still prosperous; the fact that in a total population of about fifty thousand some thirty thousand were slaves only served to confirm this prosperity for slaves were an indication of wealth. Those expatriates who were doing well were reluctant to leave the city unless they had to, and they were mightily afraid of the Mahdi. Gordon was therefore greeted as a saviour and he began well, by opening the prison, making a bonfire of all the tax records and ordering that the wooden stocks and all the *courbash* – hippopotamus-hide whips – should be thrown on to the flames. 'I have come without troops,' he told the crowd, 'but with God's help we shall address the evils of the Sudan.'

In February 1884, the free citizens of Khartoum were a mixture of races and nationalities, the sort of expatriate community that could then be found – and is still to be found – all over the Middle

East and the Levant. There were a few British merchants, some of them wanderers or remittance men. The rest was composed of Armenians, Algerians, Indians, Italians, Jews, Syrians and a quantity of rich Arabs, most of the latter deeply involved in the slave trade. These made up the middle and trading classes within the city and were at risk of their lives and fortunes when the Mahdi turned his attention to their continued existence in his domain.

The safety of these people from the Mahdi's wrath and the evacuation of those who wished to leave was Gordon's prime task. He had begun this task even before reaching Khartoum by sending a messenger to the Mahdi at El Obeid bearing a red ceremonial robe, a Pasha's fez, and Gordon's greetings, offering the Mahdi his friendship and the Sultanate of Kordofan, if his campaign against the Turko-Egyptians would cease.

The Mahdi sent back the robe and the fez, sending in return a patched Mahdist jibbah and a terse note inviting Gordon to convert to Islam and join his army. From Gordon's subsequent actions it would appear that this sharp exchange of presents altered his opinion of the Mahdi. Until then, Gordon had considered the Mahdi to be just another fanatic; now he began to understand that the Mahdi was a Muslim prophet and a national leader, a charismatic man with a large army at his back and the will to use it. As that realization dawned, Gordon began to consider what steps would be necessary to counter the Mahdi's power.

Gordon possessed two sets of orders, one from London, one from Cairo, requiring him either to round up the garrisons of the Sudan and evacuate the country or report on how this aim might be achieved, leaving the question of Egyptian suzerainty for another time. Gordon now began to grasp that the evacuation of the Sudan would not be an easy task and the thought of leaving the bulk of the population to the Mahdi's mercy was not attractive, even if the thought of doing so ever entered his head, which is most unlikely. He therefore began to consider abandoning both sets of instructions and staying on to fight it out.

The telegraph line between Khartoum and Cairo was still intact and ever since leaving the Delta, Gordon had been bombarding Baring with telegrams. He now sent a message to Baring and the Khedive repeating the proposal that Zobeir should be offered the Governorship of the Sudan. For reasons already explained, while Baring supported this proposal, he had no option but to reject it. Gordon also suggested that the Egyptian army, supported by elements of the British army in Egypt, should advance into the Sudan via Wadi Halfa and Berber and do battle with the Mahdi, pointing out that if the Mahdi continued to gain strength he would have to be fought sooner or later, either in the Sudan or inside Egypt, so why not now? This suggestion too was rejected. The Egyptian army was in no state to engage the Ansar and Gladstone flatly forbade any further deployment of British troops inside the Sudan.

Gordon continued to rake Foreign Secretary Lord Granville and Baring with a daily volley of telegrams and cables. After a while, Baring adopted the sensible habit of allowing Gordon's messages to collect on his desk for a day or two. Only when he had a dozen or more would he lay them out in some coherent order – not necessarily the order in which they had been received – work out the gist of Gordon's meaning and forward that to Granville with his comments and recommendations. A rather long telegram arrived in Cairo soon after Gordon reached Khartoum.

'You must remember,' Gordon telegraphed to Baring and London on 26 February, 'when evacuation is carried out, Mahdi will come here and will not let Egypt quiet. My duty is evacuation and to establish a quiet government. The first I can do, the second is difficult. If Egypt is to be quiet, Mahdi must be smashed up. Once Khartoum belongs to Mahdi the task will be far more difficult, yet you intend, for safety of Egypt, to evacuate it. I repeat, evacuation is possible but you will feel the effect in Egypt and will be forced to enter into a far more serious affair in order to guard Egypt. At present it will be comparatively easy to destroy Mahdi.'

Baring and the British Government were not so sure of that. Gladstone had already decided to abandon the Sudan at once and leave Egypt as soon as possible thereafter and he found Gordon's new belligerence alarming. Neither of Gordon's suggestions met with much favour in Cairo or London but if Gordon felt he could evacuate the Sudan they only wished he would hurry up and do it.

Then, on 13 March 1884, before the discussion could go any further, the Mahdi's forces closed in on Berber and the telegraph line was cut. From then on communication with Khartoum was to be by river-steamer or secret messenger only, although the close siege of Khartoum had not yet begun.

Over the next six weeks the Mahdi's forces began to close in on Khartoum. First he sent a messenger to rouse the local river tribes, ordering them to invest the city closely before he arrived with the bulk of his army. If he had ever seriously considered a withdrawal, Gordon had now left the evacuation too late. As the Mahdi's men settled down to starve the garrison out, Gordon was faced with three stark choices: he could follow his original instructions from London, deliver a report and leave the city, abandoning the citizens and the garrison to their fate while he escaped across the desert to the North. His spies and messengers were crossing the desert each night and he could probably have slipped away quite easily. The second choice – a slim one – was to take the garrison and those who wanted to leave, and attempt a break-out to the north. Gordon began this task by sending about six hundred sick soldiers and two thousand civilians, men, women and children, away down the Nile to Berber on steamers.

The third choice – at the moment more of a forlorn hope – was to hold the city with local forces until the British were forced to mount an expedition and get him out. The third option would clearly take time and was not part of his orders. Gordon had not been forbidden to defend Khartoum because it was never envisaged that he would attempt to do so. If he did elect to do so the question was would – or could – the British get him out?

Either way it would take time: time to put personal pressure on the British government, time for his situation to become critical, time for public pressure to mount on Baring and Gladstone, time for Wolseley to mount a relief. Until all that could happen, having resolved to stay and lead the fight against the Mahdi, Gordon began to improve the defences of Khartoum. It is at this point that the story, the legend, of 'Gordon in Khartoum' really begins.

*

The British have a curious taste for celebrating their military disasters and last stands. This predilection seems to date back to their earliest days as a nation. From Harold the Saxon and his housecarls going down before the Normans on Senlac Hill to Richard III spurring to the ruck at Bosworth, to the Scottish spearmen standing firm on Flodden Field and Sir Richard Grenville fighting the *Revenge* until she sank under him, tales like these are the very stuff of British history.

It hardly seems to matter if the outcome of the last stand is victory or defeat. Both can be worthy of record if the gallantry of the defenders is in adequate supply. The Victorian era had already added to the score of gallant defeats in this ancient collection with the last stand of the 44th Foot at Gandamack in the retreat from Kabul during the First Afghan War and the recent gallant fight of the 24th Foot, the South Wales Borderers, at Isandhlwana and Rorke's Drift during the Zulu War of 1879. Both these incidents, one a victory and one a defeat, were still proudly remembered in Britain.

The plight of General Gordon in Khartoum offered all that Rorke's Drift and Gandamack could offer and more. Of course, Gordon was not yet alone. He had a few British officers and Frank Powers, a correspondent from *The Times*, who was also the British Consul in Khartoum. There was a garrison of about seven thousand men drawn from Egyptian regiments and commanded by Egyptian officers, but it was their leader, the famous 'Chinese' Gordon of the Ever-Victorious Army, who caught the public's imagination in Britain and America.

It was gradually becoming clear, in Britain and Egypt, that Gordon intended to stay at his post and fight it out in Khartoum as a Christian gentleman and a British officer should, ready to do his duty though surrounded by hordes of Muslim savages. Gladstone, Baring and many members of the British government may have been quietly furious or thought him an insubordinate lunatic, but to the British public Gordon was the man of the hour. Her Majesty the Queen had the whole nation with her when she called General Gordon a hero.

All Britain was concerned about his fate and news of his plight soon spread. Within weeks the whole world knew of 'Gordon in Khartoum' and prayed for his deliverance. His image is still with us, familiar from old prints and history books. There is Gordon on the roof of his palace in Khartoum, peering north through his telescope, looking in vain for the smoke from the steamers of a relief force darkening the sky above Tutti Island. There is Gordon at the last, sword in hand on the steps of his palace, daring the maddened Dervishes to rush upon him with their spears. Even after the lapse of a hundred years he stands defiantly on that bloody flight of steps.

The questions that have to be asked are: did Gordon ever intend to evacuate Khartoum and is there any truth in the suggestion that he went there seeking his death? These thoughts are not attractive and the last point can be rejected. Gordon would not have wished fifty thousand people to share his martyrdom. What is rather less certain is the call of honour.

Honour was no empty word to a Victorian officer or to any English gentleman a hundred years ago; as this story reveals, many British Ministers referred to their honour when the matter of assisting Gordon was raised in the press or the Houses of Parliament; their honour must not be called into question. The English gentleman of today might not understand the compulsions of honour but to anyone living at the end of the last century, its demands were compelling.

Gordon arrived in Khartoum with two sets of instructions. When he examined the situation he realized that the first set, to 'examine and report' was pointless, and the second, to 'organize and evacuate', was impossible, certainly without help from a British force sent from Egypt, which he had already been denied. What was he to do now?

Gladstone and Baring would have preferred that he leave Khartoum and return at once to Cairo. He might have done that, bringing with him a few thousand expatriates and soldiers but many thousands more would have been left behind, leaderless and defenceless. Gordon had asked for a leader, Zobeir, and this request too had been denied. What would people have said if he returned to Cairo and safety, and the next news from Khartoum was of the fall of the city and the slaughter of forty thousand people? Gordon's decision to stay is understandable: it was, quite simply, a point of honour.

There has been speculation over Gordon's reasons for staying in Khartoum for over a hundred years and no one has yet come to a definite conclusion. There is one small incident, however, which indicates that the matter of his personal honour might have motivated Gordon's decision to stay.

Some months into the siege, Gordon ordered his aide, Colonel Stewart, downstream in a steamer with messages for Baring. When he was ordered to leave, Stewart refused to go. In the end Stewart did leave, accompanied by Frank Powers and the French Consul, but not before asking Gordon to put his orders and the reason for them in writing. Colonel Stewart was careful of his honour and he wanted no man to accuse him of wishing to leave a post of danger in Khartoum. If this point exercised Colonel Stewart, a very sensible soldier, how much more would it engage the mind of General Gordon?

No one could order Gordon to leave. He had no one to turn to and no one had ordered him to remain. Staying put was entirely his own decision and having made it he could not recant. Every time he looked out of his windows in Khartoum, every stroll he took along the streets must have made it clear that he could not, in honour, abandon these people. It is also interesting that although Baring and Gladstone were angry and anxious about Gordon in Khartoum, they never at any time ordered him to leave.

As to why he agreed to go to Khartoum in the first place the simplest answer is the obvious one: he went there expecting to reason with the Mahdi – as indeed he tried to do – and if not successful in that aim, to extricate the people or hold the town until relieved. One by one he tried to do all these things. That his decision to stay would infuriate Gladstone and must lead to a full-scale British relief expedition would not have bothered Gordon in the slightest. If the British government sent relief they did it for their own sake, not for his. Gordon stood, or so he thought, for the honour of Britain, and the British public agreed with him. Besides, it had not yet come to that in the spring of 1884.

As the siege began, Gordon and the garrison enjoyed certain tactical advantages. Khartoum occupies a good defensive position at the junction of the Blue and White Niles and an adequate number of defensive walls and outlying forts had been established by his soldierly predecessor, Abd-el-Kadar. He had adequate stores of food if the siege did not last too long, and the Dervish forces around the city were not yet so close or so numerous that foraging parties could not go out and gather more.

On the other hand, large Dervish forces were already converging on the town and more, possibly commanded by the Mahdi himself, were sure to follow. Within a few weeks a full-scale withdrawal would be no longer possible, and as Gordon was determined to stay in Khartoum, the crux of the matter, and for the rest of the siege, was *time*.

Whatever the declarations of Mr Gladstone, the British would – must – sooner or later send a force to Khartoum. Public opinion and Queen Victoria would eventually drive the government to it, so it all came down to this: would a relief force arrive before the Dervishes either assaulted the town or starved the defenders into submission? With his mind clear on that point, General Gordon mustered his forces, calculated his resources and settled down to wait.

10

The Defences of Khartoum

March–August 1884

'It is impossible to leave Khartoum without leaving a
regular government established by some power.'

General C. G. Gordon,
September 1884

IN MARCH 1884, Gordon must have been well aware that the
British government had no intention of sending an expedition to
challenge the Mahdi. Without the assistance of a British army,
from where was help to come, either to cover the withdrawal or
lift a Mahdist siege of Khartoum? The Egyptian army was in no
state to take on the Mahdist forces. When it had done so in recent
times, either under Hicks Pasha or Valentine Baker, it had been
soundly and bloodily defeated. The British army in Egypt was not
currently strong enough, in fighting units or logistical support, to
mount a relief expedition, had no orders to do so and – certainly
if Gladstone had anything to do with it – would not be reinforced
and ordered to move south of Wadi Halfa.

Prime Minister Gladstone was a Liberal, not a glory-seeking,
empire-building Tory. He felt that the British Empire was already
big enough and but for the Suez Canal would have ordered an
immediate evacuation of Egypt. If any more territory were added
to the Empire it would definitely not be a wilderness of fanatic-
haunted swamp and desert like the Sudan. Besides, his personal
sympathies in the matter of the Mahdist revolt tended to be with
the Sudanese people and therefore, implicitly, with the Mahdi.
When the matter of assisting Gordon was raised in Parliament,

Gladstone affirmed that '. . . to send troops would be a war of conquest against a people struggling to be free – and struggling rightly to be free.'

Gladstone's view of the Mahdist rising was shared by a man on the spot in Khartoum, the journalist and British Consul Frank Powers. Even after the massacres at El Obeid and elsewhere, Powers wrote: 'The rebels are in the right and I hope they will hunt the Egyptians neck and crop out of the Sudan.'

This liberal, sympathetic view was not widely shared by the British public or the Queen. In their opinion Gordon should be strongly supported and if necessary rescued, but Gladstone was determined to avoid further involvement and refused to budge. Gordon must have known Gladstone's views on this matter but he nonetheless still elected to stay and fight the Mahdi. Within days of arriving in Khartoum he had began to put the city into a state of defence.

Khartoum stands on a spit of land, the Gaziera, at the confluence of the White and Blue Niles. The city itself stands on the left bank of the Blue Nile, which is divided into two channels here by the flat sprawl of Tutti Island. Khartoum is therefore bounded by water on two sides. At the time of the siege, south of the city lay a number of outlying fortifications and trenches built by Abd-el-Kadar while he was Governor. These defences Gordon proceeded to restore and improve. A deep ditch was dug and flooded between the two rivers and defences, including staked fences and home-made mines, constructed with all the ingenuity an officer of the Royal Engineers could devise, were put in place around the mud walls of the city.

There was also a number of scattered outworks and forts. On the south bank of the Blue Nile were two forts, Fort Mohgren and Fort Burri. Another, the North Fort, lay on the north bank of the river. These were quite small and could hold no more than a platoon of men. Occupying a position on a ridge above the left bank of the White Nile stood a much larger fortress, Fort Omdurman. This last Gordon proceeded to occupy in some strength, for the ridge it commanded offered both a viewpoint and a site for artillery positions looking right down into the centre of Khartoum.

Before the land defences Gordon laid a thick carpet of broken bottles, up-ended in the sand. He buried old Krupp 20-pounder shells in the sand, fused to serve as land mines. He transformed four outlying houses into small forts, laid barbed-wire entanglements, planted a forest of sharpened stakes and set out dynamite charges in wooden boxes filled with scrap iron and rusty nails.

This created a thin but adequate defence system as long as the Nile waters remained high, for Gordon did not have enough men to man these defences in depth. At the moment, in early summer, the waters of the Nile lapped the banks at either end of his defence line. As the river fell during the summer, these defences would be exposed at either end and the defenders of Khartoum would be gradually more vulnerable to assault.

Gordon's main problems at the moment however were a shortage of food and fighting men. The garrison consisted of just two and a half thousand Egyptian regulars and about five thousand Sudanese militia, all armed with .45 calibre Remington single-shot rifles. For support he had a few Gardner and Nordenfeld machine-guns, two Krupp 20-pounder cannon and about twenty smaller guns and howitzers. Fortunately, he had ample supplies of ammunition and an arsenal in the town that could produce more. If time permitted he could train enough men to man the guns. However these men were of poor quality and had no wish to stay in Khartoum, let alone fight the Mahdi and his fifty thousand fanatical followers.

The question of food was rather more pressing, for a city full of people can consume a lot of food each day and there were few reserve stocks in the granaries and warehouses. To encourage the local peasants to send in fresh food Gordon organized a daily market. He left the city gates open, though heavily guarded, and sent expeditions by boat up the two branches of the Nile to show the flag and gather supplies. This brought in a certain amount of produce during the first few weeks but as the Ansar closed in, so supplies from the surrounding countryside gradually dried up. Gordon eventually took charge of all the food in Khartoum, stored it in guarded warehouses and imposed rationing.

What he did not do was start implementing or even planning an evacuation; quite the contrary. From the moment he arrived in Khartoum Gordon seems to have assumed that if he stayed there and hung on long enough then somehow a relief expedition would be sent after him. He even elected for a 'forward' defence and on 26 February, just a week after arriving, he telegraphed Baring: 'Expedition starts at once to attack rebels in vicinity.'

At this Baring immediately became seriously concerned. Gordon had no business attacking the Dervishes at all, let alone sending out punitive expeditions. Baring would have been even more concerned if he had known what Gordon had done on the same day. After sending the cable to Baring, he issued a proclamation to the citizens of Khartoum telling them that 'Troops of the British Government are now on their way and will be in Khartoum in a few days.'

This was simply not true. Gordon may have assumed that when General Graham had thrashed Osman Digna on the Red Sea coast he would advance down the caravan road to Berber and press on down the Nile to Khartoum. He may even have discussed that course of action with Graham before they parted at Korosko. However there is no evidence of this and at this time Graham had yet to fight Osman Digna – the engagement at El Teb took place on 29 February and at Tamai on 10 March – and there is no evidence that Graham's orders would then have permitted him to advance on Berber. The sole intention of the British government was to evacuate the Sudan or demonstrate their firm intention to do so but it was already beginning to dawn on Baring and Gladstone that Gordon had other ideas. Gordon was putting Khartoum into a state of defence; that done, he settled down to wait for relief. The Prime Minister, on the other hand, was quite determined that no relief would be sent.

The government in London was preparing for the worst, the fall of the city and Gordon's death. Lord Granville, the Foreign Secretary, already suspected that Gordon was developing his own policy regarding the Sudan and, in a statement to the House of Lords on 17 February 1884, he pointed out that Gordon had accepted the assignment in Khartoum quite willingly and that, 'When a number of men volunteer for a forlorn hope there is no obligation in honour on the Commander of the Army to risk more lives in saving that forlorn hope.' This comment, especially on the point of honour, and the government's subsequent reluctance to send immediate aid to Gordon, were not well received by Members of the Lords, the House of Commons, or the country at large.

As the weeks passed, people in Cairo and Britain began to wonder what was happening inside Khartoum. They began to ask questions and write letters to the newspapers. Once again the press became involved and so did Queen Victoria. She began to bombard Gladstone and Granville with notes and telegrams, demanding news of the situation in Khartoum, expressing concern for the fate of General Gordon and enquiring, with growing acerbity, what they proposed to do about it.

Her Majesty's concern for the Sudan was not new. As early as 9 February 1884, she was harassing her Prime Minister on these points: 'She feels very strongly about the Soudan [*sic*] and Egypt, and She must say She thinks a blow should be struck to convince the Mahomaduns [*sic*] that they have not beaten us. They are wild Arabs and will not stand against regular good troops . . . The Queen trembles for General Gordon's safety. If anything befalls him the result will be awful.'

This was before Gordon had even arrived in Khartoum and the Queen was only marginally reassured by Graham's victories at Tamai and El Teb a few weeks later. Throughout the summer she continued to press the government to mount a relief expedition.

Since Gordon clearly seemed determined to stay in Khartoum unless someone was sent to replace him, Baring again telegraphed Gladstone suggesting that the Zobeir proposal might be reconsidered. Zobeir could succeed Gordon and be offered an annual cash subsidy by the Khedive if he would refrain from slaving. Lord Granville again turned this proposal down flat. Instead he enquired what progress was being made with the evacuation and how many garrisons had already been sent back from the Sudan? Since the government seemed determined to cling to Gordon's earlier conviction – that an evacuation was possible – in spite of all advice and subsequent evidence, Baring then made another proposal.

General Graham had now fought two successful engagements in the Eastern Sudan and was on the coast with a strong force of fighting men. Although Osman Digna was still in the field with a considerable army, it was evident that Graham's men could probably march the two hundred and thirty miles from the coast to Berber, beating off any Dervish force on the way. Apart from reinforcing the threatened Berber garrison, Graham would then be ideally placed to aid an evacuation down the Nile or over the desert from Khartoum.

Of course there were many weaknesses in this proposal. Two hundred and thirty miles across the open desert was further than a British army had ever marched in the Sudan, and with the approach of summer the sun was very hot. There was a great shortage of transport camels and the wells on the Suakin–Berber route might have been poisoned, but Baring and the Sirdar, Sir Evelyn Wood, still thought it could be done.

The British government thought otherwise and sent a note to that effect on 25 March 1884: 'In view of the climate and the extraordinary military risk, Her Majesty's Government do not think it justifiable to send an expedition to Berber. Full discretion is given to General Gordon to stay in Khartoum if he considers it necessary or withdraw to the South or by any other route which might be found available.'

The government were clearly attempting to distance themselves from the probable outcome of Gordon's actions. It had finally dawned on Baring and Gladstone that their worst fears had come true. Gordon had decided to stay with the people of Khartoum, and die with them if need be. That left the stark choice between sending an expedition to rescue him or facing a storm of protest from Queen and country if he suffered the fate of Hicks Pasha.

The sight of politicians caught in a trap of their own devising is always enjoyable. The truth of the matter was that the Gladstone government, in sending General Gordon to Khartoum, had been attempting to placate public disquiet over their neglect of the Sudan and evade the blame for whatever subsequently happened there. Gordon had been sent to the Sudan purely in response to public pressure, to demonstrate that, in spite of all the evidence, the government were anxious to help the beleaguered Sudanese. It never entered their heads for a moment that, if he could not evacuate Khartoum, Gordon would elect to stay there.

Now the worst had happened: a British general, and not just any British general but Gordon, the famous and popular 'Chinese' Gordon, had decided to defy the government's wishes and fight it out with the Mahdi. Had the risk of his death not been so real, the government's immense discomfort might have been amusing.

In Gladstone's eyes Gordon's actions amounted to blackmail; hence the telegram to Baring on 25 March. Gladstone was furious with Gordon, and with reason. Gordon's orders were to report on or conduct an evacuation of Khartoum. If he could not do that he should have left at once. Neither Baring nor the government had ordered him to take command of the Egyptian garrison and make a stand at Khartoum; that had been Gordon's own decision. To put it bluntly, the government was damned if it was going to let one insubordinate sapper general drag Britain into an all-out war in the Sudan.

Gladstone was prepared to face Gordon and his supporters down on this matter. On 3 April he made a statement in the House of Commons declaring: 'According to the latest reports, General Gordon believes himself safe in Khartoum and has no anticipation of danger.' Gladstone went on to add: 'The debates thus constantly renewed [on this matter] are out of all proportion to the pressure and urgency of the question.'

Baring, as ever logical and reasonable, was less adamant over the matter of a relief expedition and could see where Gordon's stand might lead. Around 26 March he telegraphed to Lord Granville laying out the Sudan situation in plain terms:

Let the Government consider the position of Gordon and Colonel Stewart. They have been sent by the Government on a difficult and dangerous mission. Their proposal to send Zobeir, which would have altered the situation, could have been acted on weeks ago and the consequences which they foresaw have now occurred. If they receive the instructions contained in the telegram of 25 March they will realize that they, and all with them, have been abandoned. No one regrets more than I the necessity of sending British or Indian troops to the Sudan, but having sent Gordon to Khartoum it appears to me that it is our duty, both as a matter of humanity and policy, not to abandon him.

Baring's telegram provoked an immediate message of support from the Queen who told Gladstone, 'For the honour of the Government and the nation, Gordon must not be abandoned.' Gladstone however remained adamant and on 28 March a further telegram was sent out to Baring, slamming the door on his proposal:

We have considered the proposals in your telegram. With the greatest wish to help General Gordon we do not see how we can alter our decision. Communicate our instructions to General Gordon as soon as possible. We are not prepared to alter them until we hear what is General Gordon's actual condition and prospects as to security, his plans for proceeding and what he desires under the present circumstances.

The government was determined to defy the Queen, Gordon and the British public on this issue, hoping thereby to convince Gordon that there was no hope of relief and that his best course was to leave Khartoum, with or without the troops of the garrison and the civilian refugees. Yet the cutting of the telegraph line at Berber on 12 March had put a stop to the swift exchange of messages between Gordon and Baring and so the waiting game dragged on in London, Cairo and Khartoum.

On 1 April a despatch from Frank Powers in Khartoum, sent out before the telegraph line was cut, was finally published in *The Times*: 'We are expecting the arrival of British troops,' he wrote, 'and cannot believe that we are to be abandoned by the Government.'

Gordon might have been out of contact but he was not out of the newspapers. Throughout the spring and summer the debate went on in the local and national press: to relieve Gordon or not, with Gladstone, Granville and some of the government ranged on one side of the argument and the Queen and most of the country on the other. There were furious editorials in the press, public meetings and petitions to Parliament. A Vote of Censure in the House of Commons on 12 May condemning the Government's delays was only diffused when Lord Hartington, the Minister for War, promised a relief expedition in the autumn if Gordon was still besieged in Khartoum.

Gradually, as spring moved into summer, Gladstone's position crumbled. The government's resistance to a relief expedition was fatally undermined on 25 July 1884 when Lord Hartington was reminded in the House that he had promised a relief expedition in the autumn and, given the current situation and the time necessary to mount such an expedition, preparations should now be put in hand.

Hartington told Gladstone that his 'personal honour and good faith was being called into question,' and said he would resign if no action was taken to assist General Gordon. Hartington's resignation would have brought the government down and so, weary with the argument, on 5 August 1884 Gladstone gave in and asked the House to grant a subsidy of £300,000 'to undertake operations for the relief of General Gordon should they become necessary.'

The matter was now urgent. Apart from a few scraps of information smuggled north by camel drivers, there had been little word from Khartoum for several months, but everyone knew that

Mahdist armies were surrounding the city and that Gordon was somehow holding on. The question was, for how long? The Arabists informed the government that the main Mahdist assault on the city would probably begin in a few weeks, after the end of the Muslim fast of Ramadan, so if a relief expedition was to be sent, it must be sent soon.

Fortunately, the British army had already drawn up contingency plans, laid in stores, issued kit and mustered shipping. On 26 August, an expeditionary force – known as the Gordon Relief Expedition – under the command of General Lord Wolseley was ordered to assemble in Egypt, cover the sixteen hundred miles of country between Cairo and Khartoum with all despatch and extract General Gordon. With the news of this expedition a surge of relief and enthusiasm swept the nation.

Within days the marching regiments of the British army were parading through streets lined by cheering crowds, heading for the railway stations, the ports and the waiting transports. At the same time, far away on the dry plains of Kordofan, the Mahdi was ordering his emirs to summon their men and march for the junction of the two Niles. The race for Khartoum had begun.

11

The Gordon Relief Expedition

September 1884–January 1885

'I ought to shake hands with Gordon in Khartoum, about 31st January next.'

General Lord Wolseley,
September 1884

THE FIRST PROBLEM facing General Lord Wolseley when he arrived in Cairo in September 1884 was how to get his army to Khartoum. There were three main routes to Khartoum: from the east via the Red Sea, Suakin and Berber; directly south across the desert from Wadi Halfa via Abu Hamed and Shendi, following the camel trails and touching the Nile at various points; or all the way by the Nile. Each of these routes presented difficulties.

The shortest, via the Red Sea and Berber, would first involve a combined naval and military operation to shift the entire expedition, with its camels and stores, ammunition, cannon and cavalry to Suakin. The Expedition must then cross two hundred and fifty miles of Dervish-occupied desert to Berber. The wells would certainly have been destroyed or fouled, the way was barred by the formidable Osman Digna and the Nile port of Berber was already in Dervish hands. The Expedition would have a fight on its hands from the moment it stepped ashore.

The desert route via the camel trails from Wadi Halfa or Korosko to Abu Hamed or Korti and then to Berber or Shendi might be less complicated and offer fewer logistical problems but it too promised a shortage of water. This was the deciding factor; both desert routes were impractical because there was no way large numbers of troops, with their horses and camels, could be kept supplied with water under those circumstances.

The most obvious approach to Khartoum was up the Nile. There was a well-established river route from Cairo to Khartoum but it was far from easy. The distance is some 1,600 miles and upriver from Aswan the Nile is barred by many sets of rapids and six major cataracts. The Nile 'cataracts' are in fact gorges, most of them several miles long, strewn with rocks, and steamers advancing through them would meet the full force of the downstream current.

These physical difficulties would make the Nile ascent extremely difficult even without opposition from Mahdist forces. In addition, the Nile route was by no means direct and Wolseley was constantly aware that time was pressing. The river makes a great sweep to the east at Dongola between the Third and Fourth Cataracts, and swings west again in a great arc south of Berber and the Atbara confluence. Whichever route Wolseley opted for, the problems were daunting.

Khartoum lies 800 miles from Wadi Halfa, the border town of Egypt and the Sudan. It was soon clear that the infantry in Wolseley's seven-thousand-strong army would have to march every step of the way from Wadi Halfa unless some means could be found of transporting the men and their supplies at least part of the way by river. Wolseley was clearly confronted with a vast logistical problem; the possibility of reaching Khartoum in time now depended on how the relief force could be ferried up the Nile.

The climate and height of the Nile waters were two of the chief factors influencing campaigning in the Sudan. The summer months, from April to September, are intensely hot and far from ideal for campaigning but in those months the river is high and the cataracts therefore much easier to pass. On the other hand, the best campaigning season is in the cooler months, from October to March, but at that time the river is low and the exposed rocks make navigation hazardous. It was already September, six months into the siege of Khartoum, and time was not on Wolseley's side. He had to press on up the river, solve the problems and surmount the cataracts as best he could.

Wolseley arrived in Cairo on 9 September 1884. While his forces assembled in the desert the general began his preparations with a careful study of the map. Wolseley knew Egypt and he had prepared an outline plan for the relief of Khartoum as long ago as

April 1884; this now led him to propose an advance on two routes.

First, he would send a large, powerful 'River Column' commanded by General Earle up the Nile to force a passage through the cataracts from Korti via Berber. This column would contain most of the infantry, the 1st battalions of the Black Watch, the Cameron Highlanders, the Gordon Highlanders, the South Staffordshire Regiment, the Royal West Kents, the Royal Irish Regiment, the Duke of Cambridge's Light Infantry – to please the C-in-C – and the 2nd battalion of the Essex Regiment, eight battalions in all, plus engineers, artillery, three hundred and fifty men of the 19th Hussars, some Egyptian transport and an Egyptian artillery battery. This force would be carried up the Nile in boats.

Wolseley would also send a smaller, more mobile 'Desert Column' under General Sir Herbert Stewart, another of his 'Ring' which would march from Korti to Shendi, a distance, with diversions to the wells at Gakdul and Abu Klea, of about two hundred miles. This column would contain an infantry battalion, the 1st battalion the Royal Sussex Regiment, a small amount of artillery and machine guns and all the cavalry except a few troops of the 19th Hussars retained for scouting with the River Column. If time permitted and Khartoum was not in immediate danger of falling, both columns would join up at Shendi and advance on the city. If not, the first column to reach Shendi must press on to Khartoum and raise the siege. Although this plan meant splitting his force, it would offer the vital advantage of speed and reduce the logistical problems.

As an aid to this end, Wolseley decided to form a 'camel corps' for the Desert Column, assembling a great quantity of camels and drawing men from a number of crack British regiments to ride them. The soldiers would also have to learn how to care for these truculent beasts which with a number of transport camels and all the cavalry would make up a large part of the Desert Column. The thought of guardsmen, riflemen and Royal Marines on camels is said to have reduced the Duke of Cambridge to fury, but Wolseley had his way.

Wolseley was not to command either column of his force in person, a fact he was always to regret. He could not be with the Desert Column, the River Column and at his advance headquarters at Korti all at once, so he elected to stay at his headquarters and follow the troops south towards Dongola as they advanced.

By the end of September 1884, Wolseley commanded a considerable army. The main part of his force was composed of several battalions of the British army in Egypt. There were no Egyptian or Sudanese battalions, though some officers from the Sirdar's army were attached to the Relief Expedition as advisers. One of these was a Major Herbert Kitchener who, heavily disguised as an Arab, was operating as a freelance intelligence officer in the desert to the south. Kitchener had devised a means of getting messages in and out of Khartoum and his information would be useful.

Wolseley now had more than ten thousand men under command and was quite confident that Khartoum could be relieved. This confidence was unshaken by the news that on 12 September, Colonel Stewart, Frank Powers and the French Consul in Khartoum, sent downriver by Gordon, had been set upon and murdered by Dervishes when they went ashore north of Berber.

To handle the vast quantity of supplies, the most immediate requirement was for boats and camels: hundreds of boats and thousands of camels. For the first leg of the journey from Wadi Halfa Wolseley relied on the railway which ran to Sarras, where the Expedition was to assemble. This railway was single track, in a poor state of maintenance and unable to handle the sudden rush of traffic without constant attention from the Royal Engineers. The Expedition moved south, by route march and on river steamers provided by the travel company, Thomas Cook, but it was on this single creaking railway track that most of Wolseley's army, horse, foot and guns, reached their advance base at Sarras and began to organize themselves for the march on Khartoum.

From Sarras the River Column would have to force its way upstream against the current. Some of the river steamers had the necessary shallow draught and powerful engines to beat their way upstream, but there were not enough of them to handle the number of troops or the quantity of stores envisaged. Fortunately, Wolseley had previous experience of river expeditions, and the experienced officers of his 'Ring' to call on. As soon as word of the Relief Expedition got out, all Wolseley's old comrades hastened to the scene, anxious to be of service. Some of them, like Sir Evelyn Wood, the Sirdar of the Egyptian army, were already on post and the rest came in off every boat.

Sir Herbert Stewart KCB was to command the Desert Column. Stewart had served in the campaign against Arabi and before that in the Zulu War of 1879. His comrade on that campaign, Redvers Buller VC, was serving here as Wolseley's Chief-of-Staff. Buller was a blunt, gallant, fighting soldier and had not shone as Chief of Intelligence during the Arabi campaign. That post now went to Sir Charles Wilson, another Royal Engineers officer, not a member of the 'Ring' but a man who knew the country. Buller was principally responsible for the vital task of getting stores and supplies up the river and Sir Charles Beresford RN, another crony of Wolseley, was there to assist him as Naval ADC.

After one look at the river, Wolseley recalled his experience on the Red River Expedition. He decided that the answer to his difficulties here lay in those hard-paddling, expert canoeists, the Canadian *voyageurs*, who had conveyed his troops across Canada in 1870. A call for volunteers was sent to Canada and swiftly produced more than four hundred 'boatmen', though it soon transpired that the fur-trading *voyageurs* so common fifteen years before were now a dying breed. The volunteers this time included a number of lawyers, a city alderman from Toronto and several Ojibway Indians; while willing to be of service, most of these men were less than adequately qualified to tackle the turbulent waters of the Nile.

Meanwhile, Wolseley had placed orders with a number of English boatbuilders for what were described in the specification as 'whaling gigs'. These were oared river-craft, thirty feet long, six feet in the beam, capable of carrying a large quantity of stores and up to twelve passengers plus a Canadian *voyageur* as steersman and adviser. These boats were produced within weeks and on arrival in Egypt were towed up to Wadi Halfa by Thomas Cook steamers.

The next stage was to get the entire force up the river to Korti where the Desert and Nile Columns would go their separate ways. The 'gigs' could be sailed, or rowed by six of the soldiers, and with his eye on the clock, Wolseley offered a prize of £100 to the first battalion to reach Korti. Buller was placed in charge of the competition and the money was won by the Royal Irish Regiment. The award attracted a tart rebuke from the Queen who, ever critical of Wolseley, said that *Her* soldiers did not have to be bribed to give their best efforts. Wolseley sighed wearily and returned to his affairs; whatever he did, the Queen would find fault with it.

Other problems were affecting the organization of the Desert Column, most notably a shortage of camels. Wolseley's camel corps was made up of volunteers drawn from a number of famous regiments and corps, including the Household Cavalry, the Royal Marines, the Rifle Brigade and the Guards. Back in Egypt was Lieutenant-Colonel Frederick Burnaby of the Blues who, again forbidden by the War Office to attend this campaign, had taken 'sick leave' to join Wolseley. He became Second-in-Command of the Desert Column under Stewart. Wolseley eventually formed four camel regiments: the Guards Camel Regiment and the Light Camel Regiment, Heavy Camel Regiment and Mounted Infantry. They were to prove invaluable in the desert crossing to Shendi and Metemmeh.

However, forming a camel corps meant finding an extra two thousand camels in addition to the many thousands of transport camels already purchased or taken over from the Egyptian army. Saddles and harnesses had to be made, fodder provided and the men taught the business of camel riding and camel care. All this ate up more precious time.

It was not until 6 November 1884, nearly two months after he arrived in Egypt, that the first of Wolseley's troops, the 1st Battalion the South Staffordshire Regiment, set out from Sarras for Korti to be followed by the hard-rowing 1st Battalion the Royal Irish Regiment. Wolseley had meanwhile moved south to Dongola with his staff. There, on 17 November, he received a message from Gordon sent from Khartoum two weeks previously. In it Gordon stated that he had sent five of his remaining steamers down to Metemmeh to await Wolseley's force, adding ominously, 'We can hold out for forty days but after that it will be difficult.' By 12 December, the day Gordon's forty-day guarantee expired, the first of Wolseley's troops had only reached Korti.

Wolseley intended to divide his force at Korti, which lay below the Fourth Cataract. The Desert Column, commanded by Sir Herbert Stewart and consisting of about three thousand men, would march south-east across the Bayuda Desert, occupying the wells at Abu Klea and Gakdul *en route*, and meet up at Metemmeh with the steamers sent by Gordon from Khartoum. This was a small force on a dangerous mission but Stewart was an experienced, hard-fighting cavalry officer and Wolseley had every faith in him.

Stewart had been commissioned into the 3rd Dragoon Guards and was a long-time member of the Wolseley 'Ring'. He had served with Wolseley in Arabi's war, fought in the Transvaal against the Boers and in Natal during the Zulu War of 1879. He had also commanded the cavalry brigade for Graham at the battles of El Teb and Tamai earlier in the year. If anyone could force a passage to Shendi-el-Metemmeh it was Sir Herbert Stewart.

Wolseley knew that the secret of overcoming the Mahdist forces was discipline and firepower. Graham had demonstrated that much at Tamai and El Teb, where his small, disciplined force had shot Osman Digna's much larger Dervish army to pieces. The problem was not so much the risk of attack as time, distance and the difficulties of the terrain.

While the Desert Column was crossing the Bayuda wastes, the River Column, consisting of the infantry battalions under Major-General William Earle, would force a passage upriver via Kirbekan, re-occupy Berber and meet up with the Desert Column at Metemmeh. Earle was another sound officer, a Grenadier Guardsman who had fought in the Crimea. When the Expedition was being organized he was the garrison commander at Alexandria, so he had some experience of local conditions. The River Column set out upstream from Korti on 28 December 1884, followed two days later by Stewart's Desert Column, which struck directly south across the desert for Metemmeh and Shendi.

*

The situation in Khartoum was now desperate. On 30 December, the day the Desert Column set out, a crumpled message from Gordon arrived at Korti. Dated more than two weeks before, 12 December 1884, it stated simply, 'Khartoum all right. C. G. Gordon'.

This was misleading; the situation in Khartoum was anything but all right. Food stocks were very low, the people were hungry and the river level was falling steadily, threatening to expose the flanks of the exterior fortifications. The ever-increasing Mahdist forces around the city now had the defences under attack by day and night and the Egyptian troops of the garrison were starting to despair.

The advance party of the Desert Column, one thousand men mounted on the finest horses and camels, made good time across the firm, flat sand and gravel of the Bayuda Desert. With fresh camels they managed thirty miles a day and by 2 January were at the Gakdul oasis, about halfway to Metemmeh. Stewart secured the oasis with the Heavy Camel Regiment and returned to Korti to bring up more supplies and the rest of the Column. He left Korti again on 8 January and by 12 January was back at Gakdul with his entire force of three thousand men, ready for the next goal of his advance, the oasis at Abu Klea. Stewart's force left Gakdul on 14 January and by the evening of 16 January 1885, the Desert Column was encamped in the desert three miles south of the wells at Abu Klea.

During their advance, Ansar activity had been slight, just the occasional horseman or camel-mounted scout on a distant rise. Even so, Stewart was in no doubt that the Mahdi and his local emirs were well aware of his numbers and position and equally aware that the pugnacious Ansar would be mustering for an attack. That attack came on the morning of 17 January.

On arriving at Abu Klea on the previous evening, Stewart's force had constructed a stout, mimosa-wood zareba. During the hours of darkness this came under heavy and ever-increasing rifle fire from the surrounding wadis. This, plus the throbbing of drums, kept the soldiers up and on guard for most of the night. After the dawn 'stand-to', when all the soldiers were on guard around the zareba, the men were told to strip their Martini-Henry rifles by platoons, remove the oil and rub the moving parts with graphite to stop them becoming clogged with sand. That done, Stewart left a strong party to guard the baggage and moved the rest of his force out of the zareba on to the open desert. There they formed up in the usual 'hollow square' formation and began to advance across the desert towards Abu Klea.

For this advance Stewart kept his cavalry and some of his camel regiments well in hand, using dismounted men of the Guards Heavy Camel Regiment and the Mounted Infantry Camel Regiment as the front face of the square and the forward halves of the flanks. More of the camel regiments made up the rear of the left face and men of the Royal Scots Greys, the Royal Dragoon Guards, the 5th and 4th Dragoon Guards, the Royal Horse Guards, the Life Guards and the Bays, all on foot, made up the right face, with the infantry companies of the Royal Sussex Regiment and the Royal Marine Light Infantry making up the rear. These men, totalling about 2,500 in all, were formed up in four ranks. There were three 7-pounder field pieces, guarded by men of the naval brigade, a 'brigade' containing just 58 men and a Gardner machine-gun. All the camels and spare horses were mustered in the centre of the square.

The British square was a large and unwieldy formation and the forming-up was not completed easily. This large target was already under rifle fire from Dervishes, entrenched or concealed in the scrub nearby, but Stewart was determined not to move until he was ready. It was nearly mid-morning and the sun was blazing hot when the square began to march across the desert towards Abu Klea.

The advance went slowly. The square had to be halted time and again to retrieve the wounded, who could not be left behind. The square had therefore not gone very far before, on cresting a ridge, the leading ranks suddenly saw before them a sprawling mass of banners and spear-tips, indicating a large Dervish army. The surprise may have been mutual for with a great shout and a beating of drums the Dervish force suddenly surged forward in a mass charge against the British square. This attack was greeted with a great blast of rifle fire from the British soldiers, who were ordered to 'fire at will' into the seething mass of Ansar warriors coming in at the run against the front face of the square.

Close-range rifle and machine-gun fire did terrible execution among the advancing Ansar but it failed to stop the charge. The enemy had closed to within fifty yards of the square before the hail of bullets had any real effect. At this point, while some of the Ansar halted and began to fire back, a body of sword- and spearmen swerved away from the front face and swung round to their right flank to come in hard against the left-hand corner of the square.

Here, standing as usual just outside the square, stood Lieutenant-Colonel Frederick Burnaby, armed with his 12-bore shotgun. Burnaby was attempting to bring men forward to aid the bluejackets of the naval brigade, who had brought their Gardner machine-gun out of the square to obtain a better field of fire to the front. These sailors were totally exposed to this new attack . . . and then their Gardner jammed.

Burnaby gave the Ansar both barrels, threw down his shotgun and drew his sword. Surrounded by the enemy, he fought on but the flooding Ansar soon cut him down, overran the naval gunners, closed with the British line and began hacking their way into the square. The leading Dervish emir rode his horse across a wall of bodies and had galloped into the middle of the square before he was shot down. The soldiers' Martini-Henrys were overheating, the soft brass Martini cartridges jamming in the breech. It turned into hand-to-hand combat as sword clashed against bayonet, spear hafts were swept aside by rifle butts. The fight inside the square became a swirling mêlée of struggling men and plunging camels. Rifles and revolvers were fired directly into the yelling faces of the Ansar warriors but still they came on. For a few desperate minutes everything hung in the balance.

Fortunately, at this critical moment, the dismounted cavalry of the Royals and Scots Greys in the rear rank of the square were able to turn about and fire on the Dervishes inside the square. The camels, pressed into the centre by the closing faces of the square, acted like a breakwater, stemming the onrush of the Ansar spearmen, but it was a close-run thing.

Even General Stewart was in action, fighting on foot with sword and revolver against the Dervish warriors . . . there was a hard five minutes of close-quarter fighting and then, suddenly, it was over. The Ansar were running out from the square, the British lines were hurriedly reforming as the pressure relaxed, the yelling and roaring of hastily fired weapons gave way to steady, aimed shots as the Dervishes withdrew into the scrub.

The Battle of Abu Klea was one of the shortest battles in military history. It lasted about fifteen minutes from start to finish but that violent quarter of an hour saw a huge amount of fighting and killing. Over a thousand Ansar, about ten per cent of the Dervish force, now lay dead or seriously wounded in or around the square. British casualties in that violent exchange totalled nine officers and seventy-two other ranks killed and eight officers and ninety-nine other ranks wounded.

This is the fight that Henry Newbolt wrote about, when '. . . the sand of the desert was sodden red, the Gatling jammed and the Colonel dead', the colonel in question being the gallant Fred Burnaby of the 'Blues'. Once again the formidable Dervish warriors had broken a British square.

As soon as the firing died down, the 19th Hussars, who had been skirmishing around the square, were ordered forward to capture the Abu Klea wells, for the British soldiers were now in desperate need of water. That done, the rest of the square came slowly forward and by mid-afternoon the force was in a defensive position around the wells in a scraped-together zareba, with the undaunted Ansar moving back once again to snipe at the sentries.

Stewart was now very anxious to press on to the Nile at Metemmeh and on the following morning the Column moved out again, still in square but moving more quickly now behind a strong cavalry screen provided by the 19th Hussars and the Camel Regiments. Water for men and animals was the sole priority now and this day's march went on for a full twenty-four hours. During the hours of darkness on 18/19 January the Desert Column gradually lost cohesion as tired, thirsty men and camels began to straggle. The situation became critical soon after dawn when the leading cavalry scouts were alarmed to discover that a large Ansar army was coming out of Metemmeh and preparing to advance against them.

Stewart's Column had now reached the village of Abu Kru, only four miles from the river. Here, close to the river, the desert was covered with thorn-scrub so, halting his leading troops, Stewart ordered them to pull together a zareba. The rest of his troops poured into this as they came up but the position was soon under steady and accurate fire from Ansar riflemen. This caused a number of casualties and among those hit was General Sir Herbert Stewart. Shot in the groin and mortally wounded, he did not die for several days, but he was not able to remain in command.

With Burnaby dead, Colonel Sir Charles Wilson now took command of the beleaguered Desert Column. Wilson was a Royal Engineer officer like Gordon though he had spent most of his career in Intelligence work and on the Staff. He had little experience of action or field command but since the men, camels and horses were now desperately short of water, he took the risk of leaving the zareba and making a dash for the Nile, leaving his artillery within the zareba, with a body of infantry for local protection.

Covered by artillery fire from the zareba until they were out of range, the desert column marched out, formed up into square again and began to march towards the Nile, harassed all the way by rifle fire and sporadic attacks from small groups of Ansar. Gaining confidence, the Dervishes, reinforced by the garrison of Metemmeh, then put in a major attack, sword- and spearmen sweeping forward in force against the square. This attack was beaten off with rifle fire but the Ansar put in attack after attack throughout that afternoon as the square plodded slowly on towards the Nile.

At nightfall the Desert Column finally reached the river at the village of Gumbat, having lost a further twenty-four men killed and a hundred more wounded in a long day of marching and fighting. The artillery and infantry left behind in the zareba came up and rejoined that night. Two days later, on 21 January 1885, Wilson led the Column out again on the last four miles to Metemmeh, only to find that the Ansar were inside the town and prepar-

ing to make a stand. With his wounded to think of – and as yet
no sign of the River Column – Wilson prudently decided to pull
back to Gumbat and set up a defensive position there. He had
several hundred wounded, had expended a great deal of ammunition, and seen both his superiors killed. Until the River Column
arrived, Wilson felt he could do no more.

*

The River Column, in boats or on foot, had set out from Korti on
28 December 1884, meeting little opposition from the Ansar but
plenty of problems on the river. Earle's force, totalling six and a
half thousand men, travelled in two hundred whaling gigs, rowed
by the soldiers, steered by the *voyageurs*, and towed when necessary
by four hundred Egyptian fellahin on the bank.

As Wolseley had anticipated, travelling by river took time; it
took the Column four full days to cover the first seven miles and
Earle only reached the Fourth Cataract above Korti on 4 February.
He halted there to let the rest of his force catch up. While they
were waiting the news arrived that Khartoum had fallen.

To say that this dreadful news shocked and depressed Earle's
battalions is to understate the facts. The entire army was thrown
into mourning by the news but apart from his personal distress,
this put General Earle in a severe quandary. With the loss of
Khartoum and the probable death of General Gordon, the sole
reason for the Relief Expedition had gone. Earle therefore waited
four days before fresh orders arrived from Wolseley: to move
upriver to make a junction with Wilson's Desert Column over two
hundred miles away. No one knew what the Dervishes might do
after overwhelming Khartoum but the Desert Column was clearly
in danger.

*

The troops of Sir Charles Wilson's Desert Column had just reoccu-
pied Gumbat on 22 January and were busy knocking loopholes in
the walls of the houses when four small steamers were seen coming
down the river. These had been sent from Khartoum by General
Gordon and the crews brought graphic, eye-witness accounts of
the state of affairs within the city. The sum of these accounts was
that the city would fall unless help arrived soon.

Wilson was later to be accused of undue delay in sending help to Khartoum; all the evidence however is that although certainly no firebrand, he acted as quickly as he could in the circumstances. The Desert Column was not large, totally isolated, burdened with a quantity of wounded and close to a large force of unsubdued Dervishes. The steamers had been severely shelled on their way downstream and would clearly need some form of armoured protection before they could make their way back to Khartoum. Wilson's naval aide, Sir Charles Beresford, who might otherwise have taken charge of this work, was sick with boils and desert sores.

It was necessary to cannibalize two of the vessels before the other two, the *Bordein* and the *Talahawiyeh*, were ready to make the return journey. To strip the first two vessels down, remove the necessary parts and build bulwarks on the two destined for the return to Khartoum, nail sheet-iron over the vulnerable parts of the vessels and overhaul the engines took three full days. Many of the Desert Column's naval ratings had been killed or wounded in the fighting around the Gardner gun at Abu Klea, so the crews had to be augmented with volunteers from the infantry. Wilson did the best he could but it all took time.

A relief force of just two hundred and forty men, including Wilson, all that could be squeezed on board the two steamers, finally sailed from Gumbat on 24 January. This force included twenty-four men of the Royal Sussex Regiment clad in their red British infantry coats, for it was thought that the very sight of these red coats would cause the Dervishes around Khartoum to pull back.

The Nile was now unusually and ominously low. The steamers continually ran aground, and were under constant rifle fire from the banks. Wilson was forced to deploy troops ashore whenever it was necessary to stop for fuel and so more time was lost.

As a result, it was 28 January before the rooftops of Khartoum finally appeared above the palm trees on Tutti Island. As the steamers coasted in towards the city, the crews could see that the headland of the Gaziera was swarming with Ansar. Hearts sank. Wilson had no need of his field glasses to tell him that the Dervish army now held Khartoum. The city had fallen two days before, but the story of the final days of the siege and fate of General Gordon had yet to be made known.

12

The Fall of Khartoum

August 1884–January 1885

'We can hold out for forty days; after that it will be difficult.'

> General C. G. Gordon, in a
> message to Lord Wolseley,
> 14 November 1884

'TOO LATE!' THE cry rang around the Empire and no one needed to ask what it meant. The Gordon Relief Expedition had failed. Khartoum had fallen and Gordon was dead, and it only remained to discover how this disaster had happened and apportion the blame. In the immediate aftermath of the news most of the blame fell on Colonel Sir Charles Wilson, the unfortunate commander of the tardy Desert Column. Before long, however, there was blame to spare, in the desert, in Cairo, in London, and in Khartoum.

To review the events leading up to the fall of Khartoum and the death of General Gordon in January 1885, it is necessary to go back to August 1884, when the Relief Expedition and the means to finance it were finally approved by the British Parliament. By then Gordon had been in Khartoum for six months and in that time had achieved a great deal.

He had improved the defences of the town, conserved and even increased the stocks of food and ammunition and worked wonders with the garrison troops, restoring their morale and improving their weapon training and discipline. He had evacuated at least some of the 'useless mouths' and raised the spirits of the remaining citizens. What he had *not* done was obey his orders. This fact is crucial because in the end Gordon's fate was Gordon's fault. That may have been the way he wished it.

Gordon's orders, whichever version is accepted as the definitive final set of instructions, required him either to report on the situation in Khartoum, or evacuate the garrison and the expatriate community. Nowhere was he instructed to stay in the town, defy the Mahdi and wait for relief, yet that is what he proceeded to do. This fact is worth repeating because as the weeks became months, to stay and fight clearly remained his intention, in spite of his bland remark in early August 1884 when he declared in a message to Baring, 'I am staying in Khartoum because the Arabs have shut us up and will not let us out.'

As early as 9 April 1884, five weeks after arriving in Khartoum and on learning that Gladstone would not authorize an expedition, Gordon wrote to Baring, 'You state the intention not to send a Relief Force up here or to Berber, or to send me Zobeir. I consider myself free to act according to circumstances. I shall hold on as long as I can and if I can suppress the rebellion I shall do so. If I cannot, I shall retire to the Equator and leave you the indelible disgrace of abandoning the garrisons of Sennor, Kassaba, Berber and Dongola.'

This is a curious message for Baring had never proposed sending a relief column to Khartoum or Berber and did not have the authority or resources to do so. Gordon's decision to stay put and hang on as long as possible was entirely his own and his resolve did not change as the months passed. He never showed any signs of fleeing to the south, as suggested by Gladstone, but remained determined to stay at his post.

As late as 24 August 1884, he wrote in his journal: 'We are going to hold out here for ever.' Unless relief came, this was unlikely. The town was already surrounded by the Dervishes and two days previously, on 22 August, at the end of the fast of Ramadan, the Mahdi left his camp in the Kordofan desert south of El Obeid and headed north towards Khartoum with the main, sixty-thousand-strong Dervish army.

Gordon fatally miscalculated the resolve of Prime Minister Gladstone. As early as March 1884, Gordon had anticipated that if he sat tight in Khartoum, the British government would – must – send forces to his relief. What he had not anticipated was that, even with immense public pressure, it would take so long to change the Prime Minister's mind. Gordon thought, or professed to think, that any Relief Expedition sent into the Sudan was to aid the Egyptian garrisons, not simply for himself. On 20 September 1884 he wrote in his journal: 'I decline the imputation that the projected expedition has come to relieve me. It has come to save our NATIONAL honour in extricating the garrisons from a position our action in Egypt has placed these garrisons in . . . I was Relief Expedition No. 1; they are Relief Expedition No. 2 and we are equally engaged for the honour of England . . . I am NOT the rescued lamb and I will not be.'

Gordon was not a stupid man but this surely was too ingenuous. Even in the Victorian age, when honour was more than a word, no one seriously suggested or supposed that Great Britain was sending an expedition to the Sudan in order to help the Egyptians or save the Sudanese. The expedition went in to save General Gordon and for no other reason. Gladstone's government would not have done that much had not the Queen, the press and the British public finally shamed them into it.

*

Having made his preparations and put the city into a state of defence, Gordon settled down to wait. Weeks passed and the relief did not come. As summer faded into autumn he spent a great deal of time on the roof of the Governor-General's palace, telescope in hand, staring down the river, waiting for the relief that never came. The Dervishes were pressing ever closer to the city and communications were becoming increasingly difficult, but from time to time messages went in or out.

Some of these passed through the hands of Major Herbert Kitchener, who had got himself attached to the Desert Column for intelligence duties and was operating in the desert somewhere to the north, acting as a precarious link between Gordon and the outside world. As the months rolled by, Kitchener's messages became less clear, for they were written in cypher and Gordon's cypher codes were long out of date. Gordon's attitude to Kitchener varied: at times he was irritated by Kitchener's questions and requests for information. At other times he regarded Kitchener's messages as indispensable, even remarking, with strange prescience, that Kitchener should one day follow him as ruler of the Sudan.

Meanwhile, the Mahdist forces had tightened their grip around the city, closing in until the patrols that had gone out almost daily to seek food in the surrounding countryside had to be stopped. Steamers still made their way north along the Nile, though often under fire from the banks, but when the city of Berber fell on 28 May, its fall followed by the usual bloody massacre of the defenders, the last hope of any large-scale evacuation from Khartoum was gone.

In Berber the Dervishes captured Gordon's agent, an Austrian, Giuseppe Cuzzi, who to save his own life was obliged to become a Muslim. A few weeks later, wearing patched Dervish robes and carrying a flag of truce, Cuzzi turned up at the gates of Khartoum bearing messages from the Mahdi and a summons to surrender. Gordon flatly refused to see him. Gordon, a devout Christian, believed that Slatin and Cuzzi and the other Christian prisoners of the Mahdi should have died rather than abandon their faith and sent back the Mahdi's summons without reply.

Time was clearly running out for the defenders of Khartoum, and when the Dervishes moved artillery on to the east bank of the river at the end of September, the movements of Gordon's few remaining river steamers were greatly curtailed. Parts of the Nile remained open to steamers if they were able to survive the shelling and rifle fire from Mahdist-held villages along the shore, but their range was limited by a shortage of fuel and putting in to cut wood for fuel was a risky enterprise with the Dervishes controlling the banks.

Gordon was still not entirely isolated or alone. He had the company of Colonel Stewart and Frank Powers, and the expatriate community contained a number of other Europeans. Yet they found the General ever more withdrawn. When he was not working to improve the defences or encourage the troops, Gordon spent an increasing amount of time with his Bible and sometimes with the Bible and a bottle of brandy. Lack of food freed him from the obligation of inviting anyone to dinner and for this relief at least Gordon was glad. Gordon had always detested dinner parties and whole pages of his journal were taken up with rambling protestations against this deplorable form of social intercourse.

Gordon was not relying entirely on the arrival of a relief expedition or simply on passive defence. He was one of the masters of irregular warfare and had a force of seven thousand Egyptian soldiers, a force which far exceeded that which Graham had used to such effect against Osman Digna. The difference was that these were Egyptian soldiers of very poor quality, most of whom had no wish to be in the Sudan at all, let alone fight the Mahdi. Some however were still keen to fight and with such men Gordon continued to harry the Ansar whenever he could. For much of the summer he believed he could repel the Dervishes or at least make the cost of taking Khartoum high enough to be unacceptable to the Mahdi.

In August Gordon sent one of his more capable subordinates, Muhammed Ali Hussein Bey on a series of raids along the river, with orders to harass the Ansar and bring back vital supplies of food. Hussein Bey managed several of these expeditions with great skill and success but in September he over-reached himself. Pursuing an Ansar force inland from the river, he was ambushed at Al Aylafuh, twenty miles from Khartoum, losing his entire force of eight hundred men, more than a thousand Remington rifles and a great quantity of ammunition. After that reverse, Gordon sent no more raiding parties from the city.

By the end of September there was still no sign of relief. If Gordon remained in the city he would surely suffer the fate of the other Europeans who had recently fallen into the hands of the Mahdi. The Austrian Rudolf Slatin, once Gordon's Governor-General of Darfur in the western Sudan, and an Englishman, Frank Lupton, who had succeeded Romolo Gessi as Governor of the Bahr-el-Ghazal province, had already been taken by the Mahdi. Both of them only escaped death, like Cuzzi, by converting to Islam. A deeply committed Christian, Charles Gordon would never become a Muslim but even if he was not killed the thought of a British Major-General being dragged about the Sudan in chains sent shudders through the British government.

By September, after six months in the city, Gordon's position, though critical, was not yet desperate. He still had about six thousand Egyptian and Sudanese soldiers and his constant training and their deep fear of the Ansar should have made them formidable fighters – provided they could be fed. He had two million rounds of rifle ammunition in the magazines and the city arsenal was capable of producing another forty thousand cartridges every week. With the Nile at the door there was no shortage of water, but the big problem was food. As the Dervishes tightened their grip about the city this crisis grew acute and rationing was imposed on the citizens. Gordon also decided to make one final plea for assistance to his superiors in Cairo and London, unaware that the Relief Expedition was already mustering in the Delta.

Cut off from the outside world, Gordon did not believe that the seriousness of the situation was appreciated. He was not worried for himself; fear was completely unknown to General Charles Gordon. His concern was for the people of Khartoum and the honour of his country. If the former were massacred, the latter would be besmirched. It was then that he decided to send a delegation to Cairo consisting of Colonel Stewart, Frank Powers and the French Consul. They would go downstream in the steamer *Abbas*, with despatches for Baring and London. If those three well-regarded men could not stir the world into action, then he really was alone. It may also be that Gordon deliberately sought isolation and only sent these three away in order to achieve that end.

Stewart was most reluctant to leave, fearing that his departure might be seen as a desertion of his post, and only agreed to go after receiving a written order from Gordon. Stewart prepared the *Abbas* carefully for the dangerous voyage and took two other vessels with him in the hope that one at least would survive the journey. He piled the craft high with firewood, partly to offer protection from snipers on shore, partly to avoid the necessity of landing in search of fuel, and had metal sheeting nailed up over the vulnerable steering house and the engine compartment.

The party left Khartoum on 6 September 1884, and at first all went well. The steamers made it downriver and past Berber with only occasional sniping from the shore, and then, believing themselves almost out of danger, Stewart sent the two support vessels back. Two days short of Dongola their steamer ran aground.

Stewart, Powers and the French Consul, Monsieur Herbin, went ashore for help and were lured into the house of a sheik, Suliman Na'man. While plying them with coffee and supposedly sending for camels, the sheik sent instead for the local Ansar who fell on the three Europeans and murdered them. Stewart's head and Gordon's despatches and cypher keys were sent upstream to the Mahdi, but it was another month before Gordon learned what had happened to his men. Before that, however, he had learned that Wolseley was in the Delta with a British army and that a Relief Expedition was at last on the way.

*

By early October Gordon was effectively alone in the palace of Khartoum. The main problem now was a collapse in morale among the citizens. In spite of their hunger, the major cause of their depression was a chronic shortage of news. The inhabitants of Khartoum were a riverine people, used to the bustling life of a trading port and the absence of shipping on the river depressed them sorely. This curtailing of river traffic and the non-arrival of desert caravans from the outside world created the feeling that the city and its citizens had been abandoned to their fate.

Gordon was well aware of this. Therefore, at the end of September, when a message from Major Kitchener brought the news that the Relief Expedition was assembling at Wadi Halfa, he ordered a celebration, with the firing of heavy guns and the putting out of flags and bunting. Posters were prepared and plastered on walls throughout the city showing redcoat British infantry on the march. There was also an extra issue of food and for a few days spirits rose.

However fleeting, this celebration had a good effect on the population; the news had come only just in time. In the same month, Gordon heard that a group of citizens were planning to open the gates to the Mahdi; he placed these traitors under arrest, a move which was accompanied by a declaration of loyalty and resistance from the city council, but matters were clearly coming to a head. Ramadan was over and the campaigning season had begun.

By mid-October the Mahdi had come north and was now camped with his army just across the Nile from Khartoum. He ordered his prisoner Rudolf Slatin to start writing to Gordon, renewing the demand for surrender. Slatin did so, using German or French in the hope that Gordon could read his letters and the Mahdi could not. In these he apologized for his apostasy, explained his position and told Gordon of the death of Stewart. This terrible news was confirmed by a message sent directly to Gordon from the Mahdi, telling him also that his old protégé, the former merchant seaman Frank Lupton, had surrendered in the Bahr-el-Ghazal and become a Muslim. Quoting from the messages carried by Stewart the Mahdi again demanded that Gordon surrender Khartoum and adopt the Muslim religion:

> In the name of Allah the merciful and compassionate, the bountiful ruler and blessing of our Lord Mohammed, Greetings to Gordon Pasha of Khartoum. Know that the steamer 'Abbas',

which you sent to Cairo with Stewart Pasha and others has been captured by the will of God. Those who believed in us, the Mahdi, have been spared and those who did not have been destroyed, as was your representative and the consuls with him and God has condemned their souls to the fire and misery. See here all the papers and the messages which you, Gordon Pasha, have sent and know that we have understood it all.

Surrender to us now, before it is too late, for if you surrender after the battle has begun that will be from fear and not willingly and we will not accept it.

Gordon's reply was brief but firm:

We have a letter from Mohammed Ahmed [the Mahdi] informing us that Lupton Bey has surrendered to him and that Stewart Pasha's steamer has been captured. He demands that we should surrender. It is all one to me if Lupton Bey has surrendered or not. And whether Mohammed Ahmed has captured 20,000 steamers like the 'Abbas' or killed 20,000 men like Stewart Pasha; it is all one to me. I am here like iron and I hope to see the arrival of the English and if Mohammed Ahmed says the English will die, it is still all one to me. It is impossible to have any more words with Mohammed Ahmed.

By November 1884, though the bulk of the Mahdi's forces were in the North, preparing to engage Wolseley's Expedition, there were still some thirty thousand Ansar warriors around the city. The Dervishes were now keeping the town under sporadic fire by day and night, their patrols always ready to swoop down on any parties straying far beyond the walls. During October, the Dervishes had brought up artillery and shells now began to fall on the city and around the palace. The morale of the citizens and their hopes of survival at this time depended entirely on General Gordon, who was seen everywhere about the city, in the streets, in the store-houses, in the gun-pits and trenches. Dispensing justice, sharing out food, organizing the digging of defences, visiting the sentries and briefing the raiding parties, praising, encouraging, setting an example, Gordon's courage alone kept the soldiers of the garrison at their posts and the citizens from despair.

When the Mahdi sent in another demand for surrender, Gordon took the citizens into his confidence, reading out the demand to the Council of Notables. They rejected it unhesitatingly. Surrender was anyway unthinkable. Even if the city surrendered without a fight, the Ansar would put it to the sack, the officers and soldiers would be massacred or pressed into the Mahdist army, the male civilians would be sold as slaves, their wives and daughters distributed among the harems of the Mahdi's emirs. Better to fight, or hang on in hope of relief, than tamely surrender to such a fate as this.

On 12 November, the Mahdi's warriors delivered a series of sharp attacks against Fort Omdurman, the outpost on the west bank of the Nile. The garrison held on and fought back manfully, aided by artillery fire from Khartoum and Gatling fire from the last two river steamers. Even so, the outer defences of the fort were soon over-run and it was doubtful how long the garrison could continue to resist.

On the same day, with the Nile falling fast, Gordon sent the steamers *Bordein* and *Talahawiyeh* downriver to Shendi, hoping that the Relief Expedition would find a use for them. It might still have been possible for Gordon, his officers and a good number of the garrison to escape but the bulk of the citizens could not now be evacuated and that settled the matter. The garrison would not abandon the city, the officers would not desert their men, and Gordon was determined to stay in Khartoum and fight it out. Nothing would budge him.

At the end of the month, there was a brief moment of excitement when the steamer *Bordein* came back, battling around Tutti Island under a storm of rifle and shell fire. However, she brought not the expected redcoat soldiers but a few sacks of corn and letters, including messages from Prime Minister Gladstone, some dating back to July, which Gordon could not transcribe, having sent his cypher keys out with Stewart. This was a terrible disappointment and as morale sagged yet again, Gordon found it necessary to issue a further proclamation, assuring the citizens that he had, in fact, received good news on the *Bordein*: the Relief Expedition was on its way and 'If God wills, in the next few days the siege will be raised and the danger pass away.'

On 14 December a final message came out of the city: 'We are besieged on three sides. Fighting goes on day and night. Enemy cannot take us except by starving us out. Do not scatter your troops. Enemy are numerous.'

The city was now so short of food and ammunition that it could hold out for only ten more days, though in fact it held out for another six weeks. During the daylight hours, when he was not busy with his duties or touring the defences, Gordon spent much of his time on the roof of the palace, leaning on the flagpole where the Khedival flag still flapped defiantly, scanning the river and the surrounding desert through his telescope. At night the light in his study was always burning; he spent those nights reading his Bible, writing letters to his beloved sister Augusta, or making entries in his journal. Apart from his servants and the soldiers of his guard Gordon was living alone in the Governor-General's palace. Perhaps that is what he wanted, to wait and pray in solitude, to prepare himself for death and martyrdom; with Gordon it is never easy to tell.

Throughout December and early January, as the level of the Nile steadily fell, so the defensive position worsened. The falling waters left a widening gap between the landward defences and the Blue and White Nile on either side. On 5 January Gordon permitted the garrison of Fort Omdurman to surrender, since they were totally isolated and running out of supplies and ammunition. The garrison were led away into slavery and the loss of Fort Omdurman enabled the Mahdists to mount heavy guns on the hills on the west bank of the White Nile. They then brought Khartoum under plunging artillery fire to which Gordon had no means of replying.

On 14 January, Gordon sent the *Bordein* and three other small steamers back downstream. With them went his journals and some letters addressed to the commanders of the Relief Expedition, stating: 'I think the game is up unless we receive help in ten days time.' These steamers reached Gumbat on 19 January where, as already related, Colonel Wilson and the Desert Column were waiting, uncertain what to do. In fact, Wilson's indecision at Gumbat was matched by that of the Mahdi outside Khartoum.

Khartoum was no longer defensible. The walls still held and there were adequate supplies of ammunition, but the garrison was exhausted by weeks of constant fighting and lack of sleep and the entire population was starving. The granaries were empty, children were dying of hunger, the soldiers growing too weak even to hold their weapons.

On 20 January the Mahdi received news of their defeat at Abu Klea. That night he held a Council of War with his kalifas and emirs, debating the advisability of lifting the siege and withdrawing into the wastes of Kordofan. The arguments swayed to and fro but in the end the decision was put off until more news came in from the north. It then became evident that while the British soldiers of the Desert Column had triumphed again at Abu Kru and reached the river, they had now halted on the banks of the Nile and showed no signs of advancing. Thus encouraged, the Dervish forces prepared for a major assault on Khartoum.

Soon after dusk on 25 January 1885, large parties of Ansar began to cross the Nile. By midnight more than fifty thousand warriors were waiting in the open desert of the Gaziera, massed before the defences of the city, their presence undetected by the weary soldiers of the garrison. The assault began at 3 a.m. on 26 January when, swarming silently forward, the Ansar penetrated the first fortified line. Other warriors poured in on either flank through the gaps between the defences and the river. Attacking from front and flank they were able swiftly to roll up the defenders' positions and rush on into the city. This assault was supported by artillery fire from the heavy guns around Fort Omdurman.

The soldiers of the garrison were swiftly overwhelmed and those citizens who came into the streets were ruthlessly cut down. A general massacre then began. Throats were cut, house doors stove in, houses set ablaze, women dragged out screaming into the streets to be raped and murdered or carried off. Those men who were not immediately killed were stripped and hustled away into captivity and slavery.

According to an account left by Bordini Bey, a merchant living in the city at this time, Gordon had been writing in his journal until midnight and then taken a few hours sleep. He was still asleep when the attack began. It was about three miles from the outer defences of the city to the Governor's palace and some time before the heavy firing aroused him. Once awake, General Gordon heard the approaching commotion in the streets outside and went up on to the palace roof to see what was going on.

In the growing light of the burning houses he could see the massacres in the street below and spot sword- and spear-armed Dervishes capering in the streets. There was a gun mounted on the roof of the palace, probably a Gatling or a Gardner machine-gun, and Gordon began firing at the enemy swarming towards the palace through the streets below. When the mob of spear-waving Ansar got too close to the walls for him to tilt the muzzle sufficiently, he went back to his bedroom, pulled on his white uniform,

1. Portrait of General Gordon in the governor's palace, Khartoum, 1884, by J. Faed after A. Melville

2. Mohammed Ahmed-Ibn-el-Sayed-Abdullah, the Mahdi

3. Landing troops at the Khedive's Palace after the bombardment of Alexandria by British warships, July 1882

4. General Sir Gerald Graham VC, the first British commander to defeat the Ansar

5. Major-General William Earle CB, CSI, commander of the River Column during the Gordon Relief Expedition

6. General Sir Redvers Buller VC

7. Major-General Sir Herbert Stewart KCB, commander of the Desert Column during the Gordon Relief Expedition

8. Khedive Tewfik of Egypt

9. The Desert Column at Korti, December 1884

10. Lieutenant-Colonel Fred Burnaby, commanding officer of the Royal Horse Guards, the 'Blues', who lost his life at the Battle of Abu Klea

11. The Battle of Abu Klea, 17 January 1885

12. Gunboat with troop-carrying barges lashed to the sides

13. Teaching the bagpipes to men of the Egyptian army, c. 1890

14. Hauling the gunboat *El Teb* up the 2nd Cataract at the start of the reconquest, March 1896

15. The emir Mahmud in blood-stained jibbah with Colonel Wingate, Kitchener's intelligence chief, after Mahmud's capture at the Battle of the Atbara, 8 April 1898

16. Advance of 1st Brigade from Wadi Hamed, 25 August 1898

17. Grenadier Guards at rest prior to the Battle of Omdurman, 2 September 1898

18. Awaiting the Dervish advance behind the zareba, dawn, 2 September 1898

19. Major-General Gatacre giving final instructions before the battle, with Gatling guns in the foreground

20. An artist's impression of the Battle of Omdurman, drawn as it was happening. In the right foreground is the Egyptian cavalry returning from their fight in the Kerreri Hills

21. The Sirdar directing the battle

22. The 21st Lancers at rest prior to the Battle of Omdurman

23. The Charge of the 21st Lancers, 9 a.m. 2 September 1898, by E.M.Hale

24. A unique shot of Macdonald's 1st Sudanese brigade resisting the main Ansar attack, late morning, 2 September 1898

25. Macdonald's brigade pouring fire at Osman el-Din's forces

26. Troops resting after the battle, 12.30 p.m. 2 September 1898

27. Cameron Highlanders burying their dead

28. After Omdurman: a Dervish breech-loading gun with the bodies of its gunners beneath it

29. Captured Hadendowa warriors with an Egyptian military policeman in the foreground

30. The Sirdar flies the Black Flag of the Kalifa after its capture at Omdurman

31. Riding into Omdurman after the battle with the Mahdi's tomb
showing the effect of shelling

32. The Rifle Brigade entering Omdurman after the battle

33. Dervish prisoners passing in front of the ruined prayer house, Khartoum

34. The raising of the British and Khedival flags on the walls of the governor's palace, Khartoum, 4 September 1898

35. British troops investigating the steps of the governor's palace where Gordon was killed

36. Karl Neufeld (*right*) in chains and a fellow prisoner shortly after their discovery in the House of Stone, September 1898

37. A souvenir of Omdurman published in the *Navy and Army Illustrated*, December 1898

took his sword and revolver and went out to meet them. By the time he reached the upper terrace of the palace the Dervishes had beaten in the outer gates and cut down his guards.

Gordon was waiting quietly on the top of the steps leading up to the terrace when the first of the Dervishes burst into the garden. No one really knows what happened then. The best reports state that Gordon made no attempt to defend himself but stood looking down at the Ansar '. . . in a calm and dignified manner.' Other reports say that he fired his revolver until it was empty and then went down against the Ansar with his sword. The most reliable accounts seem to agree that the mob paused at the foot of the steps, almost in awe at the sight of Gordon Pasha, until one warrior, crying out 'Accursed One, your time has come,' ran up the steps and hurled a heavy spear into General Gordon's chest.

Gordon fell forward and came tumbling down the steps to the ground. The spell now broken, the Ansar swarmed towards him, stabbing and slashing, plunging their swords and spears repeatedly into his body. Within a few minutes Gordon's body had been cut to ribbons. Someone then cut off his head and impaled it on a spear and a shrieking mob carried it back through the streets of Khartoum to the Dervish encampment.

The Mahdi had ordered that Gordon should be taken alive but he took no action against the men who had killed him. Early next morning Gordon's head was shown to Slatin and later that day it was fixed in the fork of a tree where small boys spent the afternoon throwing stones at it.

What happened to the body of Gordon was never known and hardly matters. He had died and passed into legend, and the legend of Gordon in Khartoum still endures. Charles Gordon had held Khartoum against all odds for three hundred and seventeen days, and he fell, sword in hand and facing the enemy. 'He was a brave soldier, who died at his post,' said the Mahdi's prisoner Rudolf Slatin, when the Dervishes showed him Gordon's head. 'Happy is he to have fallen, for his sufferings are over.'

13

The British Withdraw

February–November 1885

'It is now for the Government to tell me what course they wish me to pursue. The fall of Khartoum leaves me without instruction, the object of my mission in this country being no longer possible.'

General Lord Wolseley,
March 1885

WILSON'S STEAMERS REACHED Khartoum some sixty hours after the town had fallen. Seeing the Dervishes swarming on the banks of the Nile, and knowing that Gordon must be dead, they withdrew under heavy fire and returned to Metemmeh. The soldiers of the Desert Column were immediately plunged into grief by the news from Khartoum. Everywhere, when the news arrived, people went into mourning.

A few weeks later Lord Ponsonby, the Queen's Private Secretary, wrote to Baring and told him of Her Majesty's reaction to the news. 'The Queen was in a terrible state about the fall of Khartoum and indeed it has made Her ill. She was just going out when She got the telegram and sent for me. She then walked to my cottage, came in pale and trembling and said to my wife, who was terrified at her appearance, "Too late."'

The Queen was not alone. When the news of Gordon's death reached London, the entire country went into mourning. Flags were lowered, blinds drawn and a public day of mourning declared. This grief, though still abundant, was soon replaced by fury, the particular object of which was the Prime Minister, Mr Gladstone.

Gladstone was almost submerged in a tidal wave of outrage at the fall of Khartoum. Public wrath was increased by reports that on the night the news of Gordon's death reached Downing Street, Mr Gladstone and his wife had gone to the theatre. Gladstone's usual soubriquet of GOM – Grand Old Man – was changed to MOG – Murderer of Gordon. Excoriated by press and public, Gladstone was even less popular with the Queen.

Victoria was quite distraught at the fall of Khartoum and the death of Gordon. On 5 February 1885 she opened her attack on the government with a telegram to Gladstone: 'The news from Khartoum are frightful and to think that all this might have been prevented and many precious lives saved by earlier action is too fearful.'

Gladstone's letter to the Queen of the same date, spelling out the circumstances of the disaster and attributing it to the harsh climate, the long distances and the lack of firm information, was swiftly brushed aside: 'It is absolutely necessary that we must ascertain Gordon's fate. Trust Cabinet will promptly agree to a bold and decisive course: hesitation and half measures will be disastrous. What is Lord Wolseley's and Baring's advice? What is the military situation?'

On 6 February the Queen wrote Mr Gladstone a note: 'The Queen will write later to Mr Gladstone about the deplorable event, the fall of Khartoum and the uncertain fate of that gallant man Colonel Gordon, as soon as She can trust Herself to write about it – Her feelings are too strong.'

In the circumstances the Government considered it unwise to order a precipitate withdrawal from the Sudan though Gladstone insisted that no further advances were to be made towards Khartoum. In spite of Gladstone's wishes, however, action in the Sudan continued, for the exultant Dervishes were now trying to force the invading British columns back up the Nile. The River Column had now been in action at Kirbekan where yet another British general had been killed by the enemy.

In the fury over Gordon, the death of General Earle and the fortunes of the River Column went almost unnoticed. After leaving Korti, General Earle had found progress along the Nile painfully slow. On 8 February, he elected to leave the river for a while and march the bulk of his force across the desert to Abu Hamed for this would cut off a corner of the river and lighten the boats for a swifter passage upstream. Both courses of action seemed desirable, for Earle was now desperate to join up with the Desert Column and move swiftly on Khartoum.

Two days later he encountered a large Dervish force drawn up on a ridge beside the Nile near the village of Kirbekan. Earle studied this position for a while and then elected to feint a frontal attack on the Ansar position with the Egyptian camel corps and two companies of the South Staffordshire Regiment, supported by two field guns, while he took the rest of his force off to the right and came in on the flank of the Dervish position.

At first all went well. Artillery fire, the manoeuvring of the camel corps and the steady advance of the 'South Staffs' distracted the Ansar until the Black Watch were on their ridge and sweeping along it to winkle the Dervishes out of their sangars and trenches with rifle fire and the bayonet. Then came a tragic reverse. General Earle who, like many Victorian generals, preferred leading his troops from the front, was struck in the head by a single shot from a hidden Dervish rifleman and killed outright.

This did not halt the British advance for the attack was now in full swing from the front and flank. British infantry came swarming along the Kirbekan ridge, killing hundreds of Ansar, including the two emirs who commanded the Dervish force. As usual when matched by discipline and fire-power, the Ansars' courage proved their downfall. Hundreds were shot down or bayoneted before the rest pulled back and British losses were slight.

Apart from General Earle only twelve men were killed and fifty more wounded at Kirbekan. Yet it is notable that in the course of this campaign the Dervishes had already killed three British generals – Gordon, Stewart and Earle – the senior commanders of Khartoum, the Desert Column and the River Column – all in the course of a few days, as well as some highly regarded soldiers like Colonel Frederick Burnaby.

The Nile Column still had its second-in-command, Colonel Henry Brackenbury, another member of the Wolseley 'Ring', and under his command the advance upriver towards the Desert Column continued. A week later they reached El Habba on the Nile where the wreck of the steamer *Abbas* still lay canted up on a rock. The bloodstained possessions of Stewart and Powers lay in the hut where they had fallen.

The Column now moved on cautiously towards Abu Hamed, their patrols searching ahead for news of the Desert Column. Then, on 24 February, they received a message from Wolseley: they were to halt and withdraw, first to Merowe and then back to Korti. Gordon was dead; Khartoum had fallen; there was no point now in continuing the advance. The campaign was over. Sick at heart, for they wanted to re-take Khartoum and avenge Gordon, the Nile Column trailed into Korti on 8 March. There they were met by the men of the Desert Column, which had fought its way back down the river bank from Metemmeh and was now commanded by Sir Redvers Buller. He alone seemed indifferent to the fate of General Gordon. 'The man was not worth the camels,' he declared bluntly.

Buller's view was not widely shared. To most of the officers and men of the Relief Expedition, rescuing General Gordon and marching into Khartoum behind their bands and pipes had been a crusade, for the man himself was a hero if not a saint . . . and now he was dead and cut to pieces. After a few days in Korti, the expedition withdrew down the Nile to Wadi Halfa, with deep depression in every heart.

Any statements or beliefs that the Expedition had been sent to save anyone other than General Gordon are discredited by the fact that after the fall of Khartoum, no efforts were made to save the Egyptian garrisons remaining in the Sudan. They were either swiftly massacred by the Mahdist armies or surrendered and vanished into captivity.

Urged on by the Queen and with the country still simmering with rage, Gladstone was soon obliged to order Wolseley to proceed against the Mahdi, while on the east coast General Graham was ordered to advance with his forces on Berber, laying a railway line as he went. Had this been done six months earlier, the outcome in Khartoum might have been very different. These orders were soon changed however. The British ceased the campaign and the remaining Egyptian garrisons in the Sudan were swiftly overwhelmed.

The two-hundred-strong garrison of Gadieri surrendered to the Mahdi in April. The town of Sennar fell in August 1885, after a six-month siege, during which two-thirds of the garrison died of wounds or starvation. Kassala, on the Abyssinian frontier, the principal town of the eastern Sudan, also fell in August and after the surrender the Egyptian commander of the garrison was publicly beheaded. By the end of the summer of 1885, the only Sudanese province still free of the Dervishes was Equatoria, far beyond the Sudd marshes, where Emin Pasha still hung on, and would continue to hang on for many years, until he was eventually brought out to the coast of Tanganyika – now Tanzania – by Henry Morton Stanley.

*

Short-term political considerations aside, Gladstone's views on Egypt and the Sudan had not changed. In his opinion, Great Britain had no interest whatsoever in the Sudan. The country offered no strategic or commercial benefits to Britain and if the truth were told, Britain had no business there, fighting a people who wished only to be free of an intolerable and corrupt outside power, even if that power, Egypt, was currently a British responsibility.

Gladstone was only too well aware that the fundamental problems of the Sudan, poverty, ignorance, corruption and slavery, could only be eliminated if Britain was to conquer the country and take on the entire burden of the administration, at great cost. On those grounds alone, further adventures in the Sudan were unthinkable. Egypt had no spare forces or money for the Sudan wars and Britain had no intention of funding further campaigns with either men or money.

However sound the cost argument seemed to Gladstone, it was not likely to appeal to the British people in the immediate aftermath of Gordon's death. Lord Wolseley was now ill, but was instructed to hold his ground around Wadi Halfa and if possible teach the Dervishes a sharp lesson and restore Britain's dented prestige, but to go not an inch further south into the Sudan. When British passions cooled – and Gladstone was aware that they soon would cool – then the Sudan could be abandoned and with any luck forgotten.

Wolseley had remained at Korti while his two Columns advanced on Khartoum. He received the news of Gordon's death on 4 February and spoke of it thereafter as 'The saddest day of my life.' It was also the day when his career, so successful up to now, went into decline. Although he was still only 52 he was never offered another field command. Nearly thirty years later, in 1913, the year of his death, he could say, 'The sun of my luck set when Stewart was wounded.'

Wolseley personally blamed Wilson for the fall of Khartoum. He believed that had Stewart lived or Burnaby replaced him, the gunboats would have been loaded with men at Metemmeh and pushed upriver at once against all hazards. Wolseley never forgave Wilson or indeed the Prime Minister, declining to attend Gladstone's funeral in 1898 as he 'could not go to the funeral of a man who preferred office to the honour and good of England.'

Wolseley's immediate reaction when he heard of Gordon's death was to resume the advance on Khartoum, but his force was in no condition for further adventures. The Desert Column was worn out, its boots and camels in no state for more service and the River Column had been harassed and shot at all the way back to Korti. Even Buller was reluctant to take the field again until fresh men and camels could be provided. The Expedition pulled back to Dongola to await further orders, and on 11 May 1885 they were ordered to evacuate the Sudan entirely and retire behind the Egyptian frontier. While they were doing so, news came in of General Graham's activities west of Suakin.

While the River and Desert Columns were retiring to Wadi Halfa another expedition had been setting out from Suakin under the command of General Graham. His task was to protect the men building a new military railroad west from Suakin to Berber on the Nile. This had always been considered a far quicker and easier way to Khartoum than the perilous routes up the Nile or over the Nubian Desert, provided the supply problem could be overcome; also, a railway would be very useful in the event that the British elected to continue the fight against the Mahdi after Khartoum had been relieved.

Graham's force was far larger than anything previously deployed on the Red Sea Coast. The harbour at Suakin was crammed with transports and warships and men poured ashore from the Indian and British armies; the troops landing here included the Guards Brigade, two battalions of the Coldstream and a battalion of the Scots Guards, who had been seen off from Windsor Castle by Queen Victoria herself.

The Guards were reinforced at Suakin by the arrival from Australia of a five-hundred-strong battalion of the New South Wales Regiment, the first Australian unit ever to serve with the British army, an indication of the Empire-wide concern for General Gordon and a foretaste of support to come in future conflicts. The Australians arrived in March 1885 in the traditional red infantry coats but soon changed into khaki. Graham's force eventually totalled some thirteen thousand men in four brigades, three infantry and one cavalry, plus a considerable amount of artillery and three companies of the Royal Engineers.

Strong and well balanced though it was, Graham's force did not greatly deter the ever-combative Osman Digna who sent men to raid the railway line, harass the construction teams and shoot up supply parties. Had Osman Digna's tactics been applied against Wolseley's Desert and River Columns, they might have proved highly effective.

In order to protect the construction parties, Graham's first task was to subdue Osman Digna. To do this he marched out of Suakin early on the morning of 20 March 1885, two full months after Gordon had fallen at Khartoum. Graham's force marched west and that evening camped twenty miles inland at the deserted village of Tamai on the old caravan route to Berber. The village was rapidly surrounded with a stout thornbush zareba, for Dervish scouts had shadowed the column for most of the day and they continued to snipe at the camp throughout the night. When the force moved out at dawn next morning the troops were deployed in the usual hollow-square formation, the sides made up of infantry, with the baggage, medical and engineers in the centre and the cavalry and mounted infantry scouting ahead. The 1st Battalion of the Shropshire Regiment remained in the zareba at Tamai as camp guards.

As the morning wore on the day became immensely hot and the ground increasingly rough, littered with boulders and covered with acacia and mimosa thorn. Maintaining the square formation over this terrain became difficult and progress slowed. The Dervish army was finally encountered at mid-morning, dug-in in trenches or in stone-built sangars on the slopes of Dihilbat Hill, which was attacked by the Berkshire Regiment and the Royal Marines. The 'battle' of Tamai then developed into a day-long series of skirmishes while the British square advanced slowly west over difficult country.

Hodson's Horse (3rd Bengal Cavalry) a regiment from the Indian army, charged a Dervish force skirmishing south of the advancing square and suffered many casualties from Dervish sword- and spearmen lying prone in the scrub. After a little of this the cavalry and mounted infantry found it wiser to dismount and proceed on foot, or advance slowly on horseback through the scrub, engaging the Dervishes with their carbines and revolvers.

Meanwhile, the main square was kept busy repelling assaults

from clumps of Osman's Hadendowa warriors, tall, bushy-haired 'Fuzzy Wuzzies', who repeatedly swept out of the undergrowth and had to be beaten off with rifle fire and bayonet. The outcome of the day was inconclusive. Although the Hadendowa lost more than five hundred men they were still in the field that evening when Graham's force withdrew back to the Tamai zareba, having sustained twenty-two men killed and a further forty wounded.

Next day, 22 March 1885, Graham's men marched out again with their leader sending a force from his 2nd Infantry Brigade under Major General Sir John McNeill VC to build zarebas as staging posts between the two villages of Hashin and Tamai. The zareba was to be built at the village of Tofrik, but having arrived there McNeill elected to build three, set out in echelon, a large central one for the stores, flanked on its top right-hand and bottom left-hand corners by two smaller zarebas which were to be manned on completion by the Royal Marines and the Berkshire Regiment respectively.

These zarebas had not been completed by the early afternoon when the cavalry vedettes from the 5th Royal Irish Lancers came galloping in with the warning that a large Dervish force was coming up fast through the scrub. Before the infantry could seize their weapons and man the half-completed zareba walls, the Dervishes rushed out of the scrub and were upon them. There was no time for the infantry to form square or even a firing line, and swarming hand-to-hand action began all over the area.

Thousands of Hadendowa came screaming out of the bush and swept straight into the zareba. The Bengal Light Infantry, who had recently arrived in the Sudan and had never encountered this sort of thing before, fired one volley and fled. It might all have gone badly for the defending forces had not a company of the Berkshire Regiment managed to form square in the central zareba and engage the rushing tribesmen with volleys of aimed fire. When they failed to stop the 'Fuzzy-Wuzzies', the British used the bayonet.

Some fifty Hadendowa warriors had simultaneously burst into the Royal Marines' zareba on the north-eastern corner of the camp, where there was another violent outbreak of stabbing and hacking before they were shot down. In the main zareba meanwhile was a maelstrom of fighting men, British, Indian and Hadendowa, mixed up with screaming camels and plunging horses. Deafened by the roar of rifle fire, blinded by clouds of dust, men fought alone or in small groups, stabbing or shooting at any enemy in view or within reach.

The central zareba was mainly occupied by the men of the 15th Sikhs and the 28th Bombay Infantry and these men, aided by volleys from the Royal Marines and the Berkshires, finally drove the Hadendowa off. The battle of Tofrik only lasted about half an hour but in that time the British lost eight officers and one hundred and fifty-three men killed; five officers and one hundred and seventeen men were wounded. Dervish losses were estimated at over a thousand yet even so the Hadendowa drew off slowly and refused to be routed. Tofrik was a very stiff fight, later recognized as such by Queen Victoria, who awarded the title 'Royal' to the Berkshire Regiment in honour of their courage in this engagement.

Graham's force stayed at Tofrik for some days after the battle, looking after their wounded and patrolling in the surrounding countryside, which was still swarming with aggressive groups of Hadendowa. On 2 April Graham marched again to Tamai, which he found deserted, and most of the Dervish tribes now began to melt away into the desert. In spite of, or largely because of, their bravery, the Hadendowa losses had been considerable. Osman Digna's statement, before the battle at Tofrik, that the British bullets could not harm them, was now seen to be false, but his prestige among the Beja and Hadendowa people did not suffer.

At the end of April 1885, news arrived in London that was to save Prime Minister Gladstone from further duplicity over the Sudan. Far away on the North-West Frontier of India the Pathan and Afghan tribes were on the march again, stirred up by Russian agents who believed that Britain's attention was fully engaged in the Sudan.

This news was all the excuse Gladstone needed. Orders went to Wolseley, instructing him to discontinue actions in the Sudan and return the Indian regiments to the sub-continent without delay; Graham's Indian infantry brigade and the Indian cavalry were the first to sail. The news that the British forces were departing from Suakin delighted Osman Digna who wrote at once to the Mahdi, saying: 'God struck fear into the hearts of the English and they went away.'

The British departure actually took a little longer to complete. On 2 May 1885, Lord Wolseley informed Graham at Suakin that the remains of his force were to be broken up. Graham left Suakin on 17 May. On that day the last British troops left Korti on the

Nile, and by the end of the month the entire British army was north of the Sudan-Egypt frontier. Wolseley and Graham were back in England on 8 June.

The failure of the Gordon Relief Expedition, though it was hardly his fault, badly damaged Wolseley's reputation. Nor did Gladstone escape unscathed. In June 1885, six months after Gordon's death, Gladstone's Liberal government fell from office, but not over the recent disaster at Khartoum. It was the old matter of Irish Home Rule that finally brought his administration down. Even so, but for Khartoum he might have survived the vote of confidence; as other, later, Prime Ministers have found, a successful war almost guarantees electoral victory but a defeat in the field is usually followed by another at the polls.

In the Sudan, the news that the British had left the country should have been a cause for rejoicing amongst the people but that news had hardly been digested in Khartoum when there was a new and unexpected reason for mourning.

14

The Mahdiya

1885–1896

The days of the Mahdiya are slipping away into legend
and it would be a mistake to gild those years, for they
were years of violence and insecurity, but from the
gloom stand out great men and great deeds.

A. B. Theobald, *The Mahdiya*, 1951

MOHAMMED AHMED, CALLED the Mahdi, died in his capital of
Omdurman on 20 June 1885, probably of typhus. He had outlived
his most famous opponent by less than four months and since the
fall of Khartoum he had gone into a steep physical decline. On
the other hand, he died in the knowledge that he had probably
achieved all that he could in the Sudan and left a lasting mark on
his people.

Few leaders of any nation have achieved as much as the Mahdi
in such a short space of time. In four years he had freed his country
from the Egyptians and defeated the British. He had returned his
people to what he saw to be the true path of the Muslim religion
and demonstrated how effective and inspiring this doctrine could
be. After seventy years of foreign domination, the Sudan was free.
The Mahdi was, and remains today a hundred years after his
death, a hero to his people, and his creation, the Mahdiya, is still
remembered as a golden age.

His military triumphs and political achievements must have
given him pleasure, but his death was certainly hastened by the
mode of life he adopted after the fall of Khartoum. He abandoned
his desert existence and settled in a palace at Omdurman, just

across the White Nile from Khartoum. There he gave himself over to a life of indolence and luxury, surrounded by sycophants and a great quantity of concubines, many of them the wives or daughters of the recently slaughtered garrison soldiers of Khartoum.

There is a strange dichotomy in the life of the desert-dwelling Arab. The harsh climate and terrain of the desert enforces an existence that is never less than brutally hard, but it remains a life that seems to suit those who lean towards the mystic and the ascetic. This harshness may be part of the attraction of the desert and the culture of the people who live there to those who dwell in less demanding places. Nevertheless, it is also true that these hard-living desert Arabs will indulge to the full in luxury and sensuality if given the chance to do so. So it has often been, and so it was with the Mahdi.

The Mahdi had just defied the might of the British Empire, overthrown the Egyptian garrisons in the Sudan, defeated armies, won many battles, killed one of Britain's national heroes, several British generals and a large number of British and Egyptian soldiers and established a stern rule over the Sudan. To do all this he had employed the harshest of measures, flinging his heroic sword- and spear-armed followers into battle again and again, against modern weapons, cannon, machine-guns and rifle fire, where they took terrible casualties without counting the cost. In spite of their losses he remained a hero, even a saint, to his people and his version of Islam now dominated the Sudan. Then, following the fall of Khartoum, his grip began to slip.

On the morning after the fall of Khartoum, the Mahdi, his Kalifas and the principal emirs made their way to the market place where the women of Khartoum had been assembled. Stripped of their clothing, these women were divided up among the Mahdist leaders, the Mahdi himself choosing the youngest and fairest for his harem before his followers made their choice. The captured men were also examined, some enlisted in the Madhist army, others loaded with chains, the majority being sold off as slaves to the highest bidder. Khartoum had been badly damaged by months of shelling before and during the final assault, but much of the city was still habitable and the city markets, including the slave market, were soon back in business.

Many of the Mahdist emirs swiftly took over abandoned houses and set up home in Khartoum, but the Mahdi himself decided to build a new capital at Omdurman, on the far side of the White

Nile. This work was put in hand and slaves were sent to demolish the houses in Khartoum; within days all that was left standing were some buildings and warehouses in the dockyard, and the Governor-General's palace. From time to time the Mahdi would cross the Nile and stay in the palace for a few days while his quarters in Omdurman were cleaned, but for the most part he stayed in Omdurman, enjoying his victory and the spoils it had brought him.

Most of the accounts covering life at the Mahdi's court, or that of his successor, the Kalifa Abdulla, come from books subsequently written by his prisoners, men like Rudolf Slatin and the Austrian priest, Father Ohrwalder, and a German trader, Karl Neufeld, all of whom spent years in Mahdist captivity. Slatin and Ohrwalder record that after the fall of Khartoum the Mahdi became very fat and much addicted to the life of the harem. His harem was now full of women sent in tribute from all over his widening domains and beyond, glistening Negro women from Equatoria, slim Danakil girls from the mountains of Abyssinia, buxom Turkish dancers from Anatolia and the Hataye, slim, pale Circassian women sent from Syria.

The Mahdi would now spend most of the day in the harem, attended by droves of concubines who would massage his body with sandalwood oil and paint his eyelids with antimony. Some of these attendants were just little girls, no more than eleven or twelve years old. Within the privacy of the harem, the patched cotton jibbah enforced amongst his Ansar soldiers and worn by the Mahdi in public, was replaced by silken garments.

Thus arrayed and attended, the Mahdi would hold court, waiting out the heat of the day until it was time to attend the mosque. Then a worn, patched jibbah would be slipped over his silken robes and he would be escorted to his prayers through streets thronged by an adoring multitude. These people came to celebrate the Mahdi's triumph, hoping for a share in the spoils and the wages due for work in rebuilding the Sudan as a Mahdist state. This work had hardly begun when in early June 1885, the Mahdi fell ill. In six days he was dead and his people were in despair.

Over the last hundred years British history and popular Western accounts of this time have depicted the Mahdi as a savage and a tyrant, and Mahdism as a barbaric creed. His people and most Sudanese historians did not see it like that. To this day, more than a hundred years after his death, the Muslims of the Sudan revere the Mahdi as a saint and prophet. Even while he was alive there were many people in the West, Gladstone and the journalist Frank Powers among them, who saw the Mahdist revolt as a liberation movement, a natural, even a praiseworthy reaction to decades of neglect, exploitation and cruelty by the Egyptians.

In the case of Gladstone, any support for Sudanese national aspirations must be related to the Prime Minister's desire that Britain should stay clear of the Sudan. In Frank Powers' case such motives are not so evident. He was in Khartoum throughout the early years of the Mahdist revolt, saw it develop and was aware of what it might mean to him personally should the city fall. He went in danger of his life if the Mahdist revolt succeeded and in the end he died under Mahdist swords. Even so, he continued to support Mahdist aspirations, if not the Mahdi's methods, until his death.

To maintain an accurate perspective, the Mahdi must be seen as the Sudanese saw him. When he died, so soon after his great triumph, the people were inconsolable. According to the mullahs, the Mahdi was now in paradise and there was still much to do on earth to continue his mission, a task taken on by his nominated successor the Kalifa Abdulla, a sterner, more ruthless figure. The Mahdist Sudan was not a total tyranny, however, in spite of British attempts to present it as such. The Kalifa Abdulla ruled firmly but fairly according to his lights and the Sudanese people were perfectly content under his rule, certainly far happier than they had been under the Egyptians, and but for the return of the British army in the 1890s, the Mahdist state would in all likelihood have continued and prospered.

Having installed the Mahdi's body in a handsome domed tomb in Omdurman, a tomb which soon became a place of pilgrimage, the new ruler of the Sudan, the Kalifa Abdulla Abd Allah, set about securing all power in the Sudan, while ordering fresh operations by the Ansar armies against the retreating British and Egyptian forces.

The Kalifa Abdulla was one of the Taa'isha, a branch of the Baggara tribe, a nomadic people who roamed the deserts of the Western Sudan, south of Khartoum. Abdulla had been one of the Mahdi's first supporters on Abba Island in 1881, and became the man who supplied the military edge to the Mahdi's aspirations. He continued to do this after the capture of Khartoum, pressing forward with the campaign to expel the British and Egyptians from the Sudan while his idol, the Mahdi, fell into sensual lethargy.

The Kalifa resembled the Western ideal of a desert warrior: a tall, hawk-like man, swathed in flowing robes, his dark face scarred by smallpox, his gaze fierce and searching. According to his prisoners, Abdullah's nature reflected his appearance. The Kalifa was suspicious, despotic, cruel and quick-tempered. Anyone who fell foul of the Kalifa was not long for this world, and his reaction to any hint of revolt was always ruthless and frequently cruel. It was also acknowledged, even by his detractors, that the Kalifa had a quick intelligence, a great deal of common sense and was uncommonly shrewd.

When Abdulla's succession was contested by two other Kalifas, he moved against them swiftly. The Kalifa Sharif, a relative of the Mahdi and therefore a distinct threat to the new ruler's ambitions, was foolish enough to ride about Khartoum accompanied by a large bodyguard and a group of musicians beating war drums. There was an immediate confrontation with the new ruler and a show of force by the Kalifa Abdulla's followers. Sharif was forced to back down, disperse his men throughout the Ansar armies and content himself with a small bodyguard of just fifty men.

Another potential rival, the emir of Darfur, was chased right across Kordofan by Abdulla's forces. The emir wisely surrendered without a fight but was forced to give up both his fighting men and a great quantity of treasure in exchange for his life. Another sheik, Salah-Was-Selim of the Kababish tribe in Northern Kordofan, was not so lucky.

Not all the tribes of the Sudan were Mahdist. Selim and his tribe had resisted Mahdism and even sent to the Egyptians for arms and ammunition. Karl Neufeld, a German trader, was captured by the Kalifa's men while attempting to negotiate the hand-over of these rifles and spent years in chains or in the dreadful confines of the 'Umm Hagar' or 'House of Stone' in Omdurman. He was lucky to escape execution. For Selim there was no such mercy: he was hunted down, captured and beheaded, his head placed on a spear in Omdurman and his tribe extirpated.

An even harsher fate befell seventy captured members of the Batahin tribe, who were slaughtered for no other crime than refusing to move to land allotted to them by the Kalifa. They were taken to the market place in Khartoum and divided into three groups. One third were hanged, one third decapitated, one third mutilated, each man losing a hand and a foot. When Slatin arrived in the market place with the Kalifa that morning, 'the ground was littered with severed heads, hands and feet.' The chief of the Batahin was then summoned to the scene by the Kalifa and told, 'You may now take what is left of your tribe to your allotted home'. Anyone defying the Kalifa risked terrible punishment and many were decapitated, hanged or flogged to death or loaded with chains simply for displaying opposition to his rule.

The Kalifa's first task on taking power was to order the liquidation of the remaining Egyptian garrisons in the Sudan. Meanwhile, the seat of the Kalifa's power was transferred across the river to Omdurman, close to the newly built 80-foot-high dome that sheltered the perfumed remains of the Mahdi.

Whether from personal conviction or political wisdom, Abdulla was careful to continue in the strict Mahdist tradition. He avoided luxury in food or dress. He insisted on observance of the Koran and the strict Sharia laws, inflicting gruesome punishments, hangings and floggings, on those who fell short of the highest Mahdist ideals. Thieves lost a hand for their first offence, a foot for the second offence. Adulterous women were beheaded or stoned to death. This did not stop Abdulla himself from indulging fully in the pleasures of his harem, which was soon enlarged by the contents of the Mahdi's seraglio.

The Kalifa's rule in the Sudan, though far from democratic where it was not thoroughly brutal, was highly effective. The two main planks of the Kalifa's policy were to suppress even a hint of revolt and, while enforcing the tenets of the Faithful, to reduce any residual power claimed by the Ashraf, the family of the Mahdi.

Within months of the Mahdi's death all posts of power and influence were held by members of the Kalifa's family or his tribe. Life in the Sudan gradually returned to the way it had been before Gordon and his adherents had burst on to the Sudanese scene in the 1870s. Not all Gordon's appointees had been wise enough to flee, and there were some eighty European captives in Omdurman kept in various degrees of subjection by the Kalifa and his leading emirs. The Kalifa seems to have particularly enjoyed tormenting Rudolf Slatin, who was kept at the Kalifa's court as an interpreter but was in and out of chains as he rose and fell in favour.

Most of these Europeans found some means of employment and all except Karl Neufeld and the priest Ohrwalder deemed it advisable to adopt the Muslim religion. Some of those who refused to do so, like the nuns captured at the fall of Father Ohrwalder's mission, were brutally tortured and beaten. The nuns were forced to marry and then kept as slaves, sewing jibbahs for the Ansar soldiers.

Slavery rapidly returned to Omdurman, although never reaching the heights of horror achieved under Egyptian rule. The slave raids south into Central Africa began again with renewed ferocity and the slave market in Omdurman was soon in business, with up to a hundred slaves offered for sale every day. These slaves were generally well treated and the sale of slaves to Egypt was forbidden for fear they would return as soldiers. The slave trade had been crippled by the loss of the Red Sea ports and patrolling British warships caught anyone ferrying slaves across from Arabia, yet slavery in the Sudan did not finally die out until the 1940s.

Under the Kalifa's rule, Omdurman became a thriving merchant city, though of a somewhat medieval kind. The population rapidly doubled and then trebled to reach one hundred and fifty thousand by 1887. Added to the residents were the thousands of Arabs who came on pilgrimage to the Mahdi's tomb. The Kalifa himself prayed five times a day and made a daily visit to the Mahdi's shrine, accompanied by most of his resident emirs, who usually found it advisable to attend and risked being considered disloyal if they stayed away.

Unlike the Mahdi, the Kalifa did not allow the available advantages and privileges of his position to affect his daily life, at least to outward appearances. He remained in Omdurman, living in a small palace by the river, dressed in simple desert garments or a patched Mahdist jibbah, publicly preaching and displaying the virtues of austerity.

Behind the scenes his life was rather different. The Kalifa maintained a bodyguard of five hundred well-armed men drawn from his own Taa'isha tribe. These men went with him everywhere. He was remorseless in claiming his share of any spoils, imposed taxes, seized fertile lands and soon became very rich. He also devoted a lot of time to the women in his harem. More than four hundred women of every available age and race were kept there for his personal pleasure. He also became imperious and obliged anyone approaching him to crawl up to his chair on all fours. Without the rigours of constant campaigning to keep him in condition he soon began to put on weight, and before long he required the assistance of a strong negro slave in order to mount his horse.

Although the Kalifa was a total despot and his country was

without liberal or democratic institutions of any kind, the leader himself was popular with the people. Under his rule they prospered, after a fashion, and were certainly no worse off than they had been under Egyptian rule. The Sudanese displayed no evident desire to alter their condition and they were – or at least felt themselves to be – their own masters at last.

For all their faults the Mahdi and the Kalifa were at least Sudanese. By Sudanese standards the Kalifa's rule was not unduly oppressive and by 1886 the Kalifa felt himself secure enough to begin thinking of expanding the Mahdiya. In 1887 he even sent personal letters to Queen Victoria, the Sultan of Turkey, and the Khedive of Egypt, inviting them to submit to his rule, and in the case of the Queen, to become a Muslim. Her Majesty's envoys in Egypt returned the summons without deigning to reply, as did the Sultan and the Khedive, but while Queen and Sultan could afford to dismiss the Kalifa's pretensions, the Khedive and Sir Evelyn Baring were alive to the continuing Mahdist threat.

The Kalifa still wanted to make his mark against the British and an opportunity for a strike against them existed, for the British army were still maintaining outposts near Kosha and Mograka on the northern border. In the months after the death of the Mahdi, the Dervishes had pushed north down the Nile and along the desert caravan routes. The Kalifa's intention was first to clear the British out of the Sudan and then invade Egypt. The Ansar had reached Merowe when the Mahdi died but after a month of mourning they continued advancing and by November 1885 they had retaken Dongola and the Sudanese villages of Kosha and Gennis, a few miles south of the forts along the Egyptian frontier.

Unknown to the Dervishes these forts had been reinforced with several battalions of the newly trained Egyptian army, in need of blooding in some brisk, successful action. Evelyn Wood had now returned to England and been replaced as Sirdar by Major General Sir Francis Grenfell. A member of the large and well-connected Grenfell family and a good soldier, he rose to be a Field Marshal with a chestful of decorations. Grenfell was now anxious to get his troops into action against the Ansar and build up their confidence with a decisive victory. On 30 December 1885 the Kalifa marched on these outposts with a large army of riflemen and was brought to battle at Gennis by General Sir Frederick Stephenson, the officer commanding the British troops in Egypt, who had six thousand men of the Anglo-Egyptian army under his command, all well-equipped with Martini-Henry or Remington rifles and Gatling guns.

Gennis was a small, scrambling affair. Losses on either side were small, less than fifty in Stephenson's force, a few hundred among the Ansar, but by mid-morning the Kalifa's forces were in full retreat. Gennis is mainly remembered as the last battle in which the British infantry wore their scarlet coats in battle. It is some indication of the fighting ability now reached by the Egyptian army that the 9th Cameron Highlanders, a battalion not easily impressed, presented their comrades-in-arms in the 9th Sudanese Battalion with a special Colour after this battle.

Gennis can also be regarded as the last engagement of the Khartoum campaign. By New Year's Day 1886, the British had withdrawn totally from the Sudan and the Egyptian-Sudanese frontier became fixed at Wadi Halfa. The British were not to return in force for another ten years, and while they were otherwise occupied rebuilding Egypt and the Egyptian army, the Kalifa established his state and made war on Abyssinia.

The Mahdiya, the Kalifa's state, was a simple, pastoral nation. The Kalifa Abdulla was the overall ruler, the ultimate court of appeal in any matter, lay or religious. Muslim law prevailed, based on the Koran. As for commerce, the tribes of the Sudan traded among themselves, for external trade was at a standstill. The mullahs looked after the religious life of the people, and since all the people really wanted was to be left alone, their life, if hard, was a comparatively happy one.

The Kalifa's war with Abyssinia lasted for three years, from early 1887 to the end of 1889, and it is hard to see exactly what the two countries were fighting about. There were no territorial or political disputes and although one country was radically Muslim and the other fanatically Christian, neither side attempted to convert the other. Conflict could and should have been avoided and the most simple explanation may be that both rulers, the Kalifa Abdulla and King John of Abyssinia, were anxious to 'busy giddy minds with foreign quarrels', diverting their internal enemies with a struggle abroad.

This war falls outside the scope of this book, but should still be covered briefly because Abyssinia later became the indirect cause of the British returning to the Sudan. It began in January 1887, a week or two after the engagement at Gennis, when the Abyssinians sacked and destroyed the Sudanese village of Gallabat, massacring the garrison and beheading the resident emir. The Kalifa sent one of his family, the Emir Yunes, to rebuild and reoccupy Gallabat and once cross-border trade had been restored, Yunes fell on the village one market day, killed any Abyssinians who resisted capture and sent about one thousand back to Omdurman as slaves.

Both sides then prepared for all-out war. King John raised a large army in the mountains while the Kalifa entrusted the struggle to his best general, Hamdan Abu Anja, a warrior from Kordofan and a former slave. Abu Anja came up to Omdurman with a well-equipped army of thirty thousand men, half of them armed with rifles. He then doubled the size of this force with another thirty thousand Ansar and in July 1887 led his army into Abyssinia and defeated King John on the plains of Debra Sin, where the Baggara horsemen and the Ansar riflemen made short work of the sword- and spear-armed Abyssinians. This victory was announced to the Kalifa in Omdurman by the return of Abu Anja's entire force, laden with booty and thousands of slaves.

Abu Anja died in 1889, but the war continued, with another emir, Zaki Tamal, now in command of the Mahdist armies. This army stood on the defensive around Gallabat, where it was attacked on 9 March 1889 by a huge Abyssinian army commanded by King John in person. The Abyssinians overran the Mahdist zareba and were on the point of victory when a bullet killed King John. His death took all the heart out of the Abyssinian soldiers and they withdrew, only to be followed and massacred by the Dervish army. The body of King John was among the booty and his severed head sent to dangle from the public gallows in Omdurman.

The battle at Gallabat in March 1889 is notable as the last major battle ever fought with edged weapons. Apart from a few rifles on the Dervish side, both armies fought hand-to-hand with sword, spear and dagger, as in medieval times. This battle also marked the apogee of the Kalifa's power. Four years after the fall of Khartoum he was now the undisputed ruler of the Sudan. The people accepted his rule, his enemies were dead or quiescent, his country was mildly prosperous and obedient to his rule. What danger there was lay in the north, where the Egyptians and their British allies were beginning to stir.

Flushed with his victories in Abyssinia, the Kalifa elected to invade Egypt and in June 1889 the Emir Wad-el-Najumi, the general who had led the final assault on Khartoum, took a force of eight thousand warriors across the northern frontier. Considering the numbers of Ansar available, this seems a pitifully small force. The only explanation seems to be that El Najumi was a fervent Muslim who believed that with Allah on his side this force was more than adequate.

He was also convinced that the riverine tribes of Southern Egypt would rise and join him, but in this belief he was woefully mistaken. The riverine tribes lived by trade along the Nile and since the Mahdists had taken the Sudan, this trade – and their livelihoods – had declined dramatically. Even without their assistance though, El Najumi remained convinced he could shatter the Egyptian army.

El Najumi left Dongola on 1 July 1889, first marching west into the desert, intending to swing north and east behind the frontier forts and strike the Nile somewhere north of Aswan. The Egyptian army, commanded by Grenfell, with Colonel Herbert Kitchener commanding the Cavalry Brigade, met Najumi's eight-thousand-strong force at Toski on 3 August 1889. The result was a slaughter.

The Egyptian army had changed out of all recognition in the years since 1882. It was now a confident, well-trained fighting force and anxious to get to grips with the Mahdists. Grenfell had a well-balanced and mobile army, able to move up and down the river on a fleet of Nile steamers equipped with cannon and machine guns, virtually floating forts. As always, the Dervishes came on with courage and dash, but they never got to grips with their opponents. Artillery concentrations, Gatling and rifle fire halted the Dervish charge and cut the Ansar down in swathes. From a Dervish force of eight thousand, some twelve hundred were killed and most of the survivors were taken prisoner. Less than one thousand returned to the Sudan and among the dead was El Najumi, the conqueror of Khartoum.

*

The defeat at Toski was only the first of several setbacks for the Mahdiya. In 1888 the rains had failed and the crops withered. The rains failed again in 1889 when the grain stocks were already low. Famine began to lay waste the population of the Sudan. Now surrounded by enemies on every side, there was no one to help the Kalifa's stricken people, even had he unbent enough to ask for it. The horrors of an African famine have become all too familiar in recent years and were no less horrible at the end of the nineteenth century.

Father Joseph Ohrwalder, the captive priest, was in Omdurman in 1889 and saw the effects of the famine at first hand:

> The scenes in the market place at Omdurman are beyond description . . . As one walked along, one could count fifty dead bodies lying in the street, and this quite irrespective of the dead in the houses. In the market the dealers stood with big sticks in their hands to beat off the poor wretched skeletons with deep-sunk eyes, casting glares at the food which was denied them. One could see hundreds of starving people wandering about, bags of skin and bone . . . even the decaying carcases of donkeys were consumed in this terrible struggle for food.

There was no help for the starving Sudanese and their sufferings were terrible. Some of the citizens resorted to cannibalism and children had to be carefully guarded lest they be snatched away and eaten. These sufferings continued for months without relief. No food was sent in; no aid was offered. Eventually the rains came, but in the years after 1889 the Kalifa's rule gradually came apart.

There were constant small rebellions as one tribe after another came out against the Mahdist creed or the Kalifa's edicts. The frontiers also remained active: Osman Digna was still raiding along the Red Sea coast around Suakin, keeping enmity with Egypt alive up there, and the French were gradually pushing into the Sudan from Equatorial Africa to the west, coming down the Bahr-el-Ghazal. Internally, there were problems with the Mahdi's family and their supporters – the Ashraf – who were constantly intriguing against the Kalifa. Ever suspicious, he acted ruthlessly to repress dissent and so made more enemies.

Then two of his European prisoners escaped. Frank Lupton had died of typhus in Omdurman and Karl Neufeld hung on to life as a prisoner in the House of Stone, but in 1891 Father Ohrwalder escaped into Egypt. Four years later, in March 1895, Rudolf Slatin got away after twelve years in captivity, providing the British in Egypt with useful intelligence as well as joining the British army.

Slatin and Ohrwalder both wrote harrowing accounts of their imprisonment in the Sudan which, by carrying the news of the Kalifa's 'brutal' rule to the attention of the British public, reminded them of Gordon and inflamed the desire for reconquest. In 1896, eleven years after Gordon's death, the move back into the Sudan began.

15

Egypt

1885–1896

'The care which has been taken in selecting native
officers has borne good fruit; for their conduct has been
very satisfactory and there have been many instances
of personal gallantry.'

Lieutenant-Colonel Parr, Adjutant General in
the Egyptian army, 1886

F ROM 1882, WHEN he returned from India as British Resident,
until he retired to Britain in 1907, Egypt was effectively ruled by
Sir Evelyn Baring, who in 1892 had become Lord Cromer. Baring
and the British government paid a certain amount of deference to
the Khedive and ran their proposals through the Egyptian government, but no one was in any doubt where the real power lay.
Throughout this period, Baring's principal concerns were to
rebuild the shattered Egyptian economy, pay off the foreign debt,
introduce sensible economic procedures and install the elements
of democracy.

The combination of tasks might have engaged the lifetime efforts
of a whole cabinet of politicians but, while he was not without
help, the bulk of the work and the entire responsibility for success
or failure rested on the broad shoulders of Evelyn Baring. In all
these tasks he succeeded admirably, thanks to a combination of
common sense, great intelligence and an iron will. Egypt recovered
and even flourished under his benign despotism; few countries had
ever had such an efficient and devoted servant.

For more than twenty years all decisions arrived at by the Egyptian government were subject to Baring's personal approval. He enjoyed the confidence of the British government, who therefore left him largely alone and Baring had no interest whatsoever in restoring Egyptian rule to the Sudan.

As for the British, both government and people, they gradually forgot about Gordon and the entire Sudan débâcle. There were many other matters much closer to home in need of attention, such as the extension of the franchise and the question of Home Rule for Ireland. In the event therefore, Egyptian affairs were handled almost entirely by Baring – and he handled them exceptionally well.

Apart from maintaining patrols along the Sudanese border and a fortified base at Suakin, the British army in Egypt lost all interest in fighting the Dervishes. Their task now was to provide help for the Resident should he ever need it, and protect the Suez Canal. Military camps were established in a zone along the banks of the Canal in the 1880s and remained there until the British left Egypt for ever in the 1950s.

The Egyptian army, which contained Sudanese as well as Egyptian battalions, continued to recruit and train under its Sirdar and his team of British officers. Gradually it expanded. Here lay the military muscle for any future campaign, for in the British or Egyptian armies the Sudan had not been entirely forgotten; the Gordon Relief Expedition had been a failure, and the British army in particular was not used to accepting failure. When times changed, the followers of the Mahdi, the 'murderers of Gordon', would have to be seen to. When that time came, in 1896, it was European intervention in Africa rather than British intentions or Dervish incursions that provided the reason for war.

This is not to say that the Sudan was ever very far from the thoughts of those in power in Cairo. Ever since the withdrawal of Wolseley's troops in 1885, the Egyptians had been wondering if or when the Mahdist tide would come lapping over their southern border. The Dervishes continued to creep forward to Wadi Halfa, and by the summer of 1888 they had established outposts nearly a hundred miles inside Egyptian territory. These outposts were commercially useful to the Mahdiya and the Kalifa allowed them to trade with the north and so provide him and his people with those necessities his barren realm could not provide.

The Dervish garrisons in these outposts were faced by the new Egyptian army which, with a small force of British infantry acting as a back-stop at Aswan, had the task of stopping any Dervish advance. The British contingent was gradually withdrawn as the Dervishes crept on down the river, but if Egypt was to be kept secure from the Kalifa, by 1890 it was clearly time for Baring and the Khedive to look to their defences. In the absence of a strong British military presence on the frontier, these defences depended upon the untested fighting ability of the Egyptian army. In the event, the new, British-trained Egyptian army proved itself more than up to the task.

After the fall of Arabi in 1882, the Egyptian army fell on hard times. A large number of fellah officers were dismissed or allowed to resign. Others were jailed or, like Arabi, sent into exile. Prior to 1881 the Egyptian army had recruited Americans as their overseas instructors, but after Arabi fell these American soldiers were swiftly dismissed. Those Egyptian troops who had been too forward in supporting Arabi found themselves transported in chains to the Sudan, where a good many were slaughtered by the Ansar in the defeat of Hicks Pasha.

By the time of the Gordon Expedition, after the series of defeats at the hands of Osman Digna in the eastern Sudan, it was clear that if the Egyptian army was ever to be the kind of fighting force the country required, it needed to be rebuilt and retrained from the ground up. The task was given to that tough old soldier, Sir Evelyn Wood VC, who became Sirdar of the Egyptian army in 1883. With a cadre of British officers and NCOs, Sir Evelyn fell on the Egyptian army like a thunderbolt.

The British have a talent for training native armies. At the start of the nineteenth century, the once-ramshackle, demoralized Portuguese army had been taken in hand by General Beresford and a cadre of drill-sergeants from the Brigade of Guards and swiftly transformed into a formidable fighting force, able to march and soldier with the British infantry of the Peninsular army and shatter the veteran regiments of France. It cannot be claimed that British skill in training armies is based on an undue love of other nations, but as in Portugal, so in Egypt: the British officers and NCOs seconded to the Sirdar's staff were competent and fair and they came to the task equipped with long experience in handling soldiers, a great deal of patience and a strong sense of humour. The result was little short of a miracle.

The way in which British sergeants trained soldiers had not changed much in the eighty years since the Peninsular War and their methods proved equally effective in Egypt. The Egyptian recruits were given smart uniforms, large amounts of close-order drill and chivvied to within an inch of their lives. They spent hour after hour on the drill square and rifle range, they went on long route marches and endured countless inspections. Together with all this military harassment though, came a care and concern for their welfare: for the first time the Egyptian soldiers met officers and NCOs who knew their business, who treated them harshly but fairly, who attended to their comfort and health, who provided them with decent food and clean barracks and saw to it that their pay, if small, was paid on the due date. For the first time they were treated like men and, rather more than men, like soldiers.

Their families were taken care of and the soldiers were allowed leave to visit them. If a soldier fell sick the officers saw to his treatment and visited him in hospital. This care was clearly demonstrated during a cholera outbreak in 1884. The Egyptian officers fled; the British officers stayed to nurse their sick soldiers, washing and feeding them, carrying bedpans, burying the dead. More than all that though, the soldiers were respected by their commanders and their instructors. As a result the men began to develop self-respect; they grew proud of their regiments and loyal to their comrades.

It has long been a tenet of British military life that there are no bad soldiers, only bad officers. A military academy was therefore established in Cairo, organized on Sandhurst or Woolwich lines, a place where the Egyptian officer corps was also taken apart and rebuilt. Those officers who had left their sick soldiers to die during the cholera outbreak were dismissed. Those who were simply stupid or useless were swiftly hounded out; those officers who stayed were trained in their duties and inculcated with the necessity and the simple common sense of taking care of their men.

All this actively underpinned the purely military side of training, the endless hours of drill, the musketry courses, the instruction in heavy weapons and engineering, in problems of attack and defence. Then came days of fieldcraft and weeks of large-scale exercises where horse, foot and gun began to work together and gel into a cohesive force. Before long good treatment and hard training began to take effect. The Egyptian army became a respected, professional force, an army in which men were eager to serve.

The army expanded from the small post-Arabi establishment to eighteen battalions of infantry, two regiments of cavalry, five batteries of artillery, various supporting arms and a camel corps, prior to the campaign of 1895. The bulk of the troops were peasant fellahin but there were also six battalions of black Sudanese infantry, including the 9th Battalion, the first Sudanese battalion to join the Egyptian army, which did so well at Gennis in 1885. The growing power and fighting spirit of the Egyptian army was demonstrated again at Toski in 1889. Many of the Sudanese troops were deserters from the Ansar or came from the non-Mahdist tribes along the Nile, in Darfur or Kordofan. The fellahin were recruited for six years but these Sudanese warriors enlisted for life and became the crack troops of the Egyptian army.

In 1889, Sir Evelyn Wood was followed as Sirdar by General Sir Francis Grenfell, who secured the southern border and commanded the Egyptian army at Toski. Grenfell was succeeded in 1892 by Major-General Horatio Herbert Kitchener, who was to command the Egyptian armies for another six years until the battle at Omdurman marked the end of the Mahdiya.

*

Kitchener is still a dominating presence in British military history. His face stares out from old photographs and contemporary portraits, the eyes piercing, the gaze fixed and almost menacing, that heavy moustache copied by a generation of drill-sergeants curving above a grimly-set mouth, the be-starred and be-medalled uniform snug on broad shoulders. Everything in Kitchener's appearance speaks of the stern disciplinarian, the fighting soldier; his burning ambition was rather less in evidence, and his leadership qualities in battle or the field were sometimes found wanting. Kitchener got on in military life mainly because he looked the part.

A study of Kitchener's personality reveals a hollow man. He seems to have been able to stand outside himself, observing the archetypal soldier that the world admired or detested, dictating what it did and said, without his soul or his feelings – other than burning ambition – becoming in any way involved.

Kitchener was a complex, contradictory character. He took pains to appear a competent general and a fighting soldier. He looked the part and he played the part, but some people, Baring for one, saw through Kitchener's well-built façade. Baring kept Kitchener because he could control him and make him do his bidding and because they shared – or at least Kitchener appeared to share – a strong interest in economy. There were occasions when Kitchener's actions matched his intentions, and he did have some useful qualities. He was an able administrator and he had the ability to plan ahead. Only on the battlefield did the image slip.

Like his hero, Charles Gordon, Kitchener was an officer of the Royal Engineers. Like Gordon, Kitchener was a man with an obsession, but while Gordon's was mysticism and religion, Kitchener was concerned solely with his own advancement and the prosecution of a distinguished career. He was, from his youth, a hard, driven man who spared nothing and no one to get ahead and gain wealth, titles and glory.

This is not to say that Kitchener was a total sham. He studied the elements of his profession carefully, was a competent officer and an adequate commander. His problems lay at the sharp end, when his forces were in the field and facing the enemy, but his personal courage cannot be questioned. Like all successful Victorian officers he was relentlessly brave and constantly on the look-out for action. While still a cadet at Woolwich, Kitchener took part in the Franco-Prussian War, an act for which he was later officially reprimanded – and then privately praised – by his Commander-in-Chief, the Duke of Cambridge.

Throughout his life Kitchener made a point of shining in the eyes of the Queen, the aristocracy and the senior members of the military establishment. He cannot fairly be described as obsequious – he was too clever for that – but his superiors, military and social, were carefully cultivated. His inferiors or those people who were no longer of service to him, he simply ignored. People like Garnet Wolseley, who sensed Kitchener's cold ambition, disliked him intensely. However he gave Kitchener unstinting praise for his intelligence work during the Gordon Expedition and acknowledged his abilities.

As for the men, Kitchener ignored them. He never spoke to a private soldier if he could help it and took no interest whatsoever in their welfare. His popularity with the men – a popularity not widespread among civilians or his brother officers – was due to the fact that he was a highly professional soldier who knew his business, and kept casualties to a minimum.

Like Gordon, Kitchener was a lifelong bachelor. The two men shared other traits. Both formed strong, but to all appearances strictly platonic, friendships with young and handsome men who became their constant companions. Neither showed the slightest interest in women. Indeed, when he became Sirdar, Kitchener flatly refused to employ officers who were married, claiming that marriage would be a distraction from more serious matters, like war. It is probable that both men were sexually neuter and may even have lived and died as virgins, though Kitchener did have a softer side. He was interested in *objets d'art* and interior decor, he collected porcelain, and furnished his quarters in Cairo in a lavish, even exotic style. He also had a pet poodle on whom he doted.

Kitchener joined the Egyptian army in 1883, serving under the first Sirdar, Sir Evelyn Wood, with the rank of 'bimbashi' or major, as second-in-command of a cavalry regiment. He performed well as an intelligence officer in the Gordon relief expedition of 1884–5, and in his journals Gordon even suggested that Major Kitchener might one day make a good ruler of the Sudan. Kitchener was well thought of by Sir Evelyn Wood and in 1886 he was appointed Governor of Suakin. He immediately commenced operations against that wily old fox, Osman Digna, who had continued to harry the coastal garrisons since Graham had left the eastern Sudan in 1885. In January 1888, after a few months of forays and cavalry patrols, denied the help of British or Egyptian regulars, Kitchener put together a scratch force of irregular Sudanese troops and attacked Osman Digna's base at Handub.

Kitchener was not a good tactical general and his attack was not successful. Osman Digna was a warrior who knew the terrain and had no fear whatsoever of British troops. The Dervishes far outnumbered Kitchener's five hundred irregulars and were armed with plenty of Remington rifles. Osman's Hadendowa swiftly over-awed the Egyptian and Sudanese levies and then a Dervish bullet smashed Kitchener's jaw. Though in great pain, Kitchener remained in command and conducted a fighting withdrawal to Suakin. His enterprise and courage, if not his tactical ability, attracted much favourable comment and led to his appointment as Adjutant-General of the Egyptian army under the new Sirdar, Sir Francis Grenfell. This elevation was not popular with his peers and fellow officers.

Having driven Kitchener back to Suakin, Osman Digna was now on the rampage across the eastern Sudan. He still had the port under siege when Kitchener returned to his command in December 1888 and drove the besieging Ansar off. On 3 August 1889 Kitchener commanded a brigade at the battle of Toski, and on this occasion the Dervishes were totally routed. In 1892 Sir Francis Grenfell retired and Kitchener was appointed Sirdar in his place, much to the chagrin of the other senior officers in the Egyptian army and most of the British community in Cairo, where Kitchener was cordially detested.

Fortunately, Kitchener was popular with Baring – or, as he should now be called, Lord Cromer – who regarded him as 'a good man of business', and that was all that mattered. Kitchener was less tactful and far less successful with the Khedive Abbas II, who succeeded his father Tewfik in the same year Kitchener took over as Sirdar. Abbas disliked the British intensely and Kitchener was, in theory, his subordinate. There was constant friction between Abbas and Cromer but his disputes with Kitchener culminated in a two-day public row at Wadi Halfa in 1894.

The young Khedive, Abbas Hilmi II, who was just twenty when he mounted the viceregal throne and lacked maturity, accepted his subordinate position and the necessary business of getting on with his European overlords. Tact, however, was not one of Kitchener's qualities and their mutual antipathy came to a head at an army review, an event which demonstrated just what a grip the British, and Cromer, had on Egyptian affairs.

The army review and inspection took place over several days out on the desert between Aswan and Wadi Halfa. Abbas was critical of the army from the moment he arrived, no detail was too small for him to find fault and carp about. In the 10th Sudanese Battalion, he found the men were of an unequal height and did not hold their rifles properly. The Khedive also declared that he did not approve of Negro officers commanding Egyptian troops.

Kitchener and his staff endured all this in stiff silence. On the following day, warming to the task, the young Khedive declared that Kitchener Pasha did not understand the basic elements of foot-drill. He then stated that the British officer in charge of the military hospital at Aswan was 'incompetent and excessively ignorant'. At a reception that night the Khedive declared that an obviously sober Negro officer was offensively drunk . . . and so it went on for six days. Finally, on the last day of his visit, the Khedive told Kitchener, 'I consider it a disgrace that Egypt is served by such an Army.' Kitchener's reply was devastating: 'In that case, I beg to tender Your Highness my resignation.'

The young Khedive was aghast. Hurriedly backing down, he offered his hand and tried to mend the breach but Kitchener would not be mollified. No apology, no excuses would make him withdraw his resignation. The matter soon reached Cromer's ears and, while feeling that Kitchener had acted impulsively, he had no hesitation in supporting the Sirdar and bringing his full weight to bear on the unfortunate and thoroughly alarmed young Khedive.

An ultimatum was presented. The Khedive must make a public apology to the Sirdar and the British officers. This apology was to be in writing and, as an added humiliation, would be published in the Egyptian Official Journal. His Minister of War, who was blamed for leading the Khedive into error, was to be dismissed. If Abbas declined or failed to do any of this, the British would assume full control of the Egyptian army and the Khedive would be forced to abdicate. The Khedive duly complied, but if he had disliked the British before, he hated them now.

Kitchener was therefore firmly in command of the Egyptian army when the decision was taken to re-occupy the Sudan. Various causes, most of them having only tenuous connections with the Sudan, led to a renewal of hostilities in 1896. Gladstone had returned to office in 1886 and finally retired in 1895. Lord Salisbury and the Conservatives took office and the Tories had always been far more interested in expanding the Empire than the Liberals.

By 1895 Cromer had so far restored the Egyptian economy that he was able to contemplate, if not actually encourage, Egypt regaining her lost territory of the Sudan. He was even able to urge Britain to support such a move. Meanwhile, public opinion against the Kalifa and the Dervishes had been fanned into flame by Rudolf Slatin, who had escaped from Omdurman in 1895 and written a best-selling book, *Fire and Sword in the Sudan*, which detailed – and exaggerated – the tyranny and cruelty of the Mahdi and the Kalifa.

All this added some weight to the re-occupation movement, but there were some fresh political factors. The French Republic had recovered from the political and economic effects of the Franco-Prussian War of 1870–1 and paid off the indemnities demanded by the Kaiser. The French expansionists were now on the march again, heading east for the Nile from their bases in Equatorial Africa. It was known that a French expedition under a Major Jean-Baptiste Marchand had entered the Bahr-el-Ghazal from Equatorial Africa and was *en route* for the Central African lakes. If the French established a band of settlements or colonies running west to east across Central Africa, then Britain's idea of a group of colonies running south from the Mediterranean to the Cape would clearly be threatened.

As the nineteenth century drew to a close all the European powers, Britain, France, Italy, Germany and Belgium, were snapping up territory in East and Central Africa. By 1895 the Sudan was surrounded by new-found colonies and unless Britain and Egypt re-occupied the Sudan, some other power would do so instead.

There was no political restraint on the other European powers, for the Sudan was currently outside any 'zone of influence'. The Egyptians might lay claim to the suzerainty of the Sudan but it was well known that they could not enforce it. Egypt was virtually a colony of Great Britain, while the Sudan, if savagely ruled and primitive, was at least wholly independent. The Egyptians and the British had been driven out in 1885 and as far as the French were concerned any power which could defeat the Dervishes and occupy the Sudan was perfectly free to do so. The French would then incorporate the country – the largest in Africa – into the French Empire.

Until 1895 the British did not openly contest this view because they were in no position to do so, but they left the world in no doubt that they did not agree with it. The British view was that the Egyptian claim to the Sudan had merely been suspended, not renounced. They had no intention of letting that vast tract of Africa between their colony in Uganda and the Egyptian border fall into the grasp of any other European power, let alone the French.

The British had always found it advisable to keep an eye on the French but the final catalyst for a renewed invasion of the Sudan in 1886 came through a tangle of alliances and from a surprising quarter: Italy.

In the nineteenth-century drive for African colonies the Italians had elected to take over Abyssinia. Italy had no mandate for this role other than its imperial pretensions and the fact that Abyssinia was there for the taking. This decision did not meet with the approval of the Abyssinian people or their emperor, who were quite content managing their own affairs. The Abyssinians therefore fought back fiercely against this intrusion and in 1896 routed an Italian army at Adowa. After this victory the Abyssinian warriors massacred the Italian wounded and castrated their Italian prisoners.

This defeat, apart from horrifying the continent of Europe, had some strategic consequences. Italy was a member of the Triple Alliance, a European grouping formed with Germany and Austria and much concerned with containing the actions and advances of France and Russia, two countries which were regarded as having expansionist imperial ambitions in the Balkans and along the North African shore.

France and Russia were also being watched carefully by Great Britain which, though not a member of the Triple Alliance, was determined to maintain the balance of power in Europe. Lord Salisbury, the new Prime Minister, felt that the defeat at Adowa, by weakening Italy, also weakened the Triple Alliance. Therefore, when Italy asked for some action in the Sudan to divert the Kalifa from joining the Abyssinians in their struggle with Italy, he was not unwilling to provide it, not least because the Kalifa, forgetting his previous war with King John, had already proposed an alliance with the Abyssinians prior to a joint attack on the Italians and the British.

The Italian government requested the British to make a diversion up the Nile into the Sudan to take possession of the town of Kassala, a border fortress some distance south of Adowa. This move was calculated to thwart any Dervish moves designed to take advantage of the Italian defeat and was backed with the promise to hand Kassala over to Egypt as soon as it was in Anglo-British hands. Agreement for this advance was swiftly reached in London and Cairo and in April 1896 Cromer instructed his Sirdar, Major-General Herbert Kitchener, to prepare his forces for an advance up the Nile on the city of Dongola. The reconquest of the Sudan had begun.

16

The Reconquest Begins

1896–1897

'The decision to advance was inspired by a desire to help the Italians at Kassala. In addition we desired to kill two birds with one stone and use the same effort to plant the foot of Egypt further up the Nile.'

Marquis of Salisbury, Prime Minister,
in a letter to Lord Cromer, March 1896

THE RECONQUEST OF the Sudan was a three-year campaign fought in annual phases. In 1896 Kitchener retook the province of Dongola. In 1897 the Anglo-Egyptian army advanced to Berber and the Atbara river. Finally, in 1898, the Dervishes were defeated at the Atbara and overwhelmed outside the city of Omdurman. During this final phase the British army returned in force to Egypt and the Sudan.

The Dongola phase in 1896 was a 'political war' ordered by the British Foreign Office concerned for the Triple Alliance. It was approved by Cromer and executed by Kitchener and his Egyptian army without any aid from British troops, apart from a few hundred men of the North Staffordshire Regiment and some Maxim machine-gunners. The Ministry of War in London had very little to do with it. Only in 1897, twelve years after the fall of Khartoum, did the British army re-enter the Sudan. This army was very different from the one that had trailed north from Metemmeh and Korti over a decade before.

The Dervish Wars of 1881–5 and 1896–8 bridge the gap between a British army that would have been familiar to the Duke of Wellington and the army of the present day. The army of 1881–5 was a Victorian army; the army that marched into the Sudan in 1897 belonged to the modern world.

Two generals provide the most striking example of this change. General Lord Wolseley, who commanded in Egypt during Arabi's war and the Gordon Relief Expedition, got his commission through the good offices of the Duke of Wellington himself. Wolseley spent his early years in an army that was not all that different from the one the Duke himself had commanded; he was also a prime mover in changing that army into a modern one. General Kitchener, who commanded the armies advancing on Dongola, the Atbara and Khartoum, was to command the entire British army at the outbreak of the Great War in 1914.

Wolseley was now a Field-Marshal and Commander-in-Chief of the British army but the authority of that post had been greatly reduced when the Duke of Cambridge finally retired in 1895. The Commander-in-Chief was now firmly under the thumb of the Secretary of State for War.

Wolseley's star was fading and Kitchener, who now begins to occupy a central role in this story, was on his steady rise through the ranks of the British army until, in 1915, exactly one hundred years after the Great Duke's victory at Waterloo, he became Secretary-of-State for War. Kitchener always knew where the real power lay and took steps to obtain it.

Kitchener was not the only officer present in the Sudan who would rise to senior command in the First World War. Among the cavalry officers now serving with the Sirdar's forces was a Captain Douglas Haig of the 7th Hussars, a man who was to command the British armies in France for most of the Great War. Among the Royal Navy officers commanding gunboats on the Nile was Lieutenant David Beatty, who was to command the battle cruiser squadron at the Battle of Jutland twenty years later.

Another naval officer serving in the Nile gunboats, Lieutenant Walter Cowan, had an even longer career. Fifty years later, in August 1941, Admiral Sir Walter Cowan, KCB, DSO, was captured by the Italians in the Western Desert while engaging enemy tanks with his service revolver. Admiral Cowan was then seventy-four years of age. The Italians politely returned this pensioner to the British lines judging him, 'of no further use to the British war effort'.

They could not have been more wrong. Admiral Cowan then attached himself to No. 8 Commando and took part in several commando raids on the enemy coast, and remained in – largely unofficial – service until the end of the war. They were a tough, hard-fighting crew, those Victorian officers, but for the older ones like Wolseley, their time was over. A new generation of soldiers was advancing into the spotlight; the old guard was fading away into the wings.

Having advocated tighter ministerial control over the War Office, Lord Wolseley now found himself constrained by the reforms he had himself suggested and he never obtained another field command after leaving Egypt in 1885. Wolseley still remains one of the greatest soldiers the British army has ever produced. Much of the good work done to reform the army in the years since the Crimean War must stand to his credit. To achieve those essential changes he had fought a long and hard campaign at great personal cost, especially to his relations with the Queen. He created a modern professional army, one that would be fit to fight the large-scale European wars of the early twentieth century as well as the ceaseless colonial campaigns that occupied the British army for much of Queen Victoria's reign.

Some of these changes in the army, in recruitment, length of regular and reserve service and the introduction of the territorial system, have already been discussed. Change nonetheless continued in the years between 1885 and 1896, especially in dress and armaments.

There was once a joke in the British army that 'the Infantry wear red coats to hide the blood . . . and the Cavalry wear blue coats to hide the blood', a jibe at cavalry claims to social superiority. The red coats that British infantry had worn for centuries went out of daily use after Gennis, as did the blue tunics of the cavalry regiments.

Splendid uniforms were now reserved for ceremonial parades or walking out of barracks. Serviceable, sensible, dull-brown 'khaki', in serge or lightweight cotton now took over in the field, though the Highland regiments retained their kilts and pipers to lead their attacks, as they were to do at the Second World War Battle of El Alamein, more than fifty years later.

Rather more important to the conduct of war were the changes in armament. By 1896 the erratic Gatling and Gardner hand-crank and hopper-fed .45 calibre machine-guns had been replaced by water-cooled, belt-fed .303 calibre American Maxim guns which had a high rate of fire and were less inclined to jam. These medium machine-guns, especially the model later manufactured by Vickers, remained in service with the British army until after the Korean War of 1950–3.

The British troops who marched to rescue Gordon in 1884 carried the .45 calibre falling-block action, single-shot Martini-Henry. The Martini-Henry rifle was still carried by the Egyptian army in 1896 but the British infantry who arrived the following year were equipped with a five-round magazine rifle, the bolt-action .303 calibre Lee Metford, which carried them through the Boer War and into the early months of the First World War. This was gradually replaced by the SMLE, the Short Magazine Lee Enfield rifle and then by the much-loved No. 4 rifle that the British soldiers carried throughout the Second World War and was to remain in service with the British army until the 1960s.

The Lee-Metford was superior to the Martini-Henry in every way but one: it was considered that the smaller size of the round and the pointed head of the bullet would have less stopping power against a rush of Ansar warriors charging home in their thousands. The British battalions who crossed the Sudan frontier in 1896 had not forgotten those warrior 'Fuzzy-Wuzzies' who had broken the British square at Tamai and Abu Klea. The pointed .303 ammunition was therefore replaced with round, hollow-headed type, a forerunner of the notorious 'dum-dum' bullet that spread or broke up on impact and inflicted appalling wounds. These hollow-point rounds were soon withdrawn and later banned but they did grievous execution among the Ansar at the Atbara and at the battle of Omdurman.

*

Kitchener was very determined to make a success of the invasion. This was his chance to make a name for himself and he decided to take his time over it. His first move, in March 1896, was to call up the Egyptian army reserves. He then ordered his forces to concentrate, on or about 4 June 1896, at Akasha, a village south of Wadi Halfa, and a few miles north of the most northerly Dervish positions at Firket. Nine thousand men had assembled there by the first week of June 1896.

His army made its way south as before, by rail and route march or in Thomas Cook's Nile steamers, but Kitchener had no intention of letting his communications and supplies for the Sudan campaign be dependent on the capricious Nile or the uncertain progress of camel trains. His advance on Omdurman would be supported at every stage by a railway and construction of this would begin as soon as his troops had secured the country south of Wadi Halfa.

Until that time there was a mixture of road, rail and river transport from the Delta to Akasha. The potential for confusion and delay was considerable for the journey to Akasha required several kinds of transport. From Cairo to Akasha is around nine hundred miles, the first three hundred and fifty of which could be covered by train. Then troops and supplies must take to the river and travel by steamer as far as Aswan. The First Cataract at Aswan was then avoided on a six-mile stretch of rail track. Then the river steamers came into service again for a further two hundred and twenty miles to Wadi Halfa, and a final short stretch of narrow-gauge railway took the troops to Sarras. From there they must march or go by camel for the last fifty-five miles to Akasha . . . and only then did the campaign really begin. A railway following closely behind the advancing troops would save great quantities of time and greatly increase efficiency.

Kitchener managed to start his campaign on 7 June 1896 with a successful attack on the Dervish position at Firket, twenty miles south of Akasha. The Egyptian army made a swift night advance and stormed the Dervish zareba at dawn. In less than an hour of fighting they drove the Dervishes out with great loss and this victory, small though it was, did put Cromer and the Sirdar's minds at rest over the fighting spirit of the Egyptian army.

Over one thousand Dervishes were killed for Egyptian losses of one hundred and thirteen killed or wounded. Apart from the Maxim gun crews and most of the senior officers, the victorious army was entirely composed of Egyptian or Sudanese troops. Thanks to this success about fifty miles of river had fallen into Kitchener's hands; the next task was to bring up the railway.

Kitchener was anxious to press on and follow up his victory at Firket but he had the usual difficulties of transporting supplies to maintain his army in the field. He hurried on the construction of the railroad, bringing the *courbash* back into use to hurry the labourers to greater effort. The workers thus encouraged, the railway crept south towards Kosheh, ten miles beyond Firket.

On a recent visit to Britain, seeking money and weapons for

additional firepower and artillery support, Kitchener had ordered the construction of several screw gunboats, all with shallow draught and able to operate safely and speedily over the rapids and sandbanks of the Nile, all well-armed and armour-plated to resist Dervish rifle and shell fire. Three of these craft – named by Kitchener the 'Zafir' class – were shipped out from Britain in sections and reassembled by the Nile at Akasha. Unfortunately, the *Zafir*, the first of these gunboats to be assembled, promptly burst her boiler when she was launched on 5 September 1896.

This was not the only setback. Cholera broke out in the army camps along the Nile and over six hundred men died before it could be stamped out – a task which tested the skills of the newly formed Royal Army Medical Corps. Then a great wind and rain storm ravaged the Nile valley and flash floods swept away over twelve miles of freshly built embankment and track on the railway from Wadi Halfa.

Kitchener was not an engaging character but in this sort of situation he appeared at his best. He stopped all other work and ordered every spare man to help in rebuilding the embankment and relaying the track. He rode up and down to urge the men on, even leaping from his horse to seize a pick or shovel and show them how it should be done. His example was an inspiration and the track was relaid in a matter of days.

With Cromer always at his back, urging the contradictory merits of speed and economy, Kitchener was eager to get on with the campaign. On 16 September 1896, as the campaigning season opened, he began his advance, marching south along the east bank of the Nile towards Dongola, only to discover that the Dervish commander, the Emir Wad Bishara, a very wily soldier, had left his former defensive position, crossed to the west bank of the Nile and was preparing to contest Kitchener's advance by the rapids of Hafir. Since the new screw gunboats were not yet ready, Kitchener's men had to rely on the support of field artillery and some 1885 vintage steamers to clear a way past the rapids.

The old steamers' guns proved unable to silence the Dervish batteries around Hafir and their armour proved vulnerable to Dervish shells. It took two days of skirmishing and more artillery had to be brought up along the banks before the steamers could force the rapids on 19 September and steam south towards Dongola, thirty miles further upriver. When Kitchener came forward with his army, which now numbered some thirteen thousand men, he found that Wad Bishara had skilfully slipped away into the desert. Kitchener therefore transferred his troops to the west bank of the river and began the march on Dongola with Wad Bishara's forces falling back steadily before him. The newly repaired *Zafir* came steaming up the Nile on 23 September, and with her guns raking the banks the army entered Dongola without loss later that day. The first phase of Kitchener's advance on Omdurman had taken just over three months, the costs and casualties had been kept to a minimum and Lord Cromer was delighted.

Kitchener was still not going to be rushed. He intended to develop Dongola as a base for further operations; although he sent troops forward to seize advance posts at Korti and Merowe, all further advances were stopped until the railway could come up and his base made secure and filled with the necessary supplies.

There was another problem: money. Kitchener's success with Cromer and the support he enjoyed in Cairo was almost entirely due to his commitment to austerity. In Cromer's case this frugality was in order to fulfil his prime task, of restoring the Egyptian economy. In Kitchener's case the main aim was to ingratiate himself with his superior, even if the troops suffered.

Kitchener was notably frugal in the conduct of his campaigns, always getting two-pennyworth of value for every penny spent, but some things could not be done without money and Cromer, though eager to see the advance continue, was reluctant to fund it from the Egyptian Treasury. He had been instructed to gain a foothold further up the Nile and this he had done. Dongola lay four hundred and fifty miles south of Wadi Halfa, but if the British government wanted a further advance they must pay for it. Fortunately, the French were in the field again, making offers to the Emperor of Abyssinia, sending small parties east from Equatorial Africa towards the headwaters of the Nile. As always, such news caused tremors at the Foreign Office.

Therefore, when Cromer sent Kitchener back to England in search of funds, Kitchener was able to exploit this situation – and the success of his Dongola campaign – in order to obtain a £500,000 grant from Parliament. This money went towards the construction of more river gunboats, an extension of the existing railway to Dongola and the construction of another railway line south across the desert from Wadi Halfa to Abu Hamed. This new line would enable supplies and munitions to travel from Wadi Halfa to Abu

Hamed in a couple of days and Kitchener could then swiftly build up his supply dumps for a further advance to Berber.

The construction of this railway across the Nubian Desert, which later became known as the Sudan Military Railway – or SMR – and is still in service, was a considerable undertaking, but the British had plenty of experience in railway construction and Kitchener was, after all, an officer of the Royal Engineers. He knew what could be done and he had just the man to do it, another of his 'pets', a French-Canadian officer, also a Royal Engineer, Lieutenant Percy Girouard. Girouard assembled a task force of fellahin with Royal Engineer subalterns serving as foremen, and the work began on New Year's Day 1897.

The construction of the SMR called for a great deal of skill and ingenuity. Wells had to be found or sunk in the desert to provide water for the steam engines and the work force. Rolling stock was ordered from Britain while maintenance workshops were set up at Dongola to repair and refurbish any railway engines found in Egypt. Everyone flung themselves into the task and with Girouard and his sapper officers to spur the men on, the track was soon being laid across the wastes of the Nubian Desert at the rate of one and a half miles a day. By mid-July 1897, Girouard's railway was more than half-way across the desert towards Abu Hamed.

This work was not without risk. Dervish Baggara cavalry were scouting in the desert, sniping at the working parties and attacking small groups of workmen coming down the line; it was necessary to maintain constant guards and patrols. Therefore, at the end of July 1897, with about a hundred and twenty miles of newly laid track to protect and patrol, and before the opening of the new campaigning season, Kitchener decided to make a strike against the Dervish garrison at Abu Hamed in an attempt to deter them from making forays against the line. The striking force commanded by Major-General Archibald Hunter was drawn from the tough Sudanese brigade of the Egyptian army, the 9th, 10th and 11th Sudanese battalions, a brigade commanded by one of the most famous soldiers of his day, Colonel Hector Macdonald DSO, of the Gordon Highlanders – 'Fighting Mac' – the tragic hero of the Omdurman campaign.

Hector Archibald Macdonald was born in a croft near Dingwall in Ross-shire in 1853. The Scots have always believed in a sound education and the young Hector was given a good grounding at Dingwall School before becoming apprenticed at fifteen to a tartan draper in Inverness. Hector, however, had no real interest in the drapery trade: he wanted to be a soldier.

In 1870 he enlisted in the 92nd Highlanders. He was already a lance-corporal when he was sent with a draft to the 1st Battalion in India and by December 1873, just two and a half years after enlistment, he was a sergeant. His sights were set, however, on higher things.

It has never been easy for a private soldier to gain a commission in the British army. It was particularly difficult in the Victorian army where it was felt that any potential officer should first be a gentleman. Though difficult, however, it could be done and the surest way to such elevation was by conspicuous gallantry in the field. Sergeant Hector Macdonald continued to study his profession and often caught the eye of his superiors. In 1876 he was Sergeant of the Guard to the Prince of Wales but his big chance came in 1879 when he took part in General Frederick Roberts' famous march from Kandahar to Kabul.

The Afghan warriors barred the army at the Karatiga defile and were driven off by a mixed detachment of Highlanders and Sikhs commanded by Colour-Sergeant Macdonald and a Sikh *jemedar*, Sher Mahommad, both of whom were praised by the commanding general. A few days later, in a skirmish at Charasia, Macdonald did it again, driving an Afghan party from their ambush position. On the day after this action – or so it is said – Roberts offered the twenty-six-year-old Colour-Sergeant Macdonald the choice of the Victoria Cross or a commission. Saying he would win the VC later – though he never did – Macdonald accepted the commission, in his own regiment.

This action was remarkable on two counts. It was very rare for rankers to be commissioned into marching regiments and usually, to save problems or embarrassment with old comrades and former superiors, those rankers who *were* commissioned went to a different regiment. Macdonald, however, stayed with the 92nd where his elevation met with general approval. The soldiers of his platoon bore him on their shoulders to the Officers' Mess where the officers greeted him warmly and presented him with a claymore. His old comrades in the Sergeants' Mess completed his regalia with a ceremonial dirk.

Lieutenant Macdonald completed the march from Kabul to Kandahar and apart from his commission was twice Mentioned-in-Despatches. In 1881 he embarked with his battalion of the old

92nd, now the 2nd Battalion the Gordon Highlanders, and sailed for the First Boer War in South Africa.

The First Boer War of 1881–2 was a short-lived affair. The most significant action came at Majuba Hill on 26/27 February 1881, a week after Macdonald's battalion had arrived in Natal. The commanding general, Sir George Colley, had sent troops to Majuba Hill and Lieutenant Macdonald was commanding his platoon as part of the force of six hundred men holding the summit overlooking the main Boer encampment. Colley's force made no attempt to build stone sangars or dig trenches and were therefore totally exposed when the Boer riflemen scaled the hill in the darkness and opened fire on them at dawn.

Majuba Hill was a disaster. Expert Boer riflemen shot down the British soldiers in quantity and killed Sir George Colley. Over half Macdonald's men were also killed or wounded; Macdonald fought on until he ran out of ammunition and then he was captured, totally unscathed. The Boers took him into Natal where Piet Joubert himself returned his presentation claymore. The war petered out and after Sir Evelyn Wood signed an armistice at the end of 1881, Macdonald returned to his native Scotland, an officer and a hero.

In Scotland matters began to go awry. In 1884 he secretly contracted a form of marriage with a Miss Christina Duncan. This was a problem, for Miss Duncan was only sixteen and Lieutenant Macdonald's salary could not support a wife. For an officer without private means life in Britain was far more expensive than in India or on active service, and Macdonald was soon in debt. He therefore transferred to the 1st Battalion of the Gordons and in 1884 he sailed for Egypt to take part in the Gordon Relief Expedition. He did not see his 'wife' again for three years.

Macdonald left the Gordons in 1885 and spent the next two years in Valentine Baker's Egyptian gendarmerie. He returned to Scotland on leave in May 1887 and in March 1888 his wife Christina gave birth to a son. Since no one but the couple knew of their marriage, this caused Christina and her family considerable embarrassment and her parents insisted on a public declaration of the marriage by Macdonald in order to secure their daughter's good name.

This Macdonald declined to do. He swiftly returned to Egypt where he joined the team of officers under Sir Evelyn Wood, training the reformed Egyptian army. He now had the rank of major

– 'bimbashi' – and even though his salary was well above that paid to a major in the British service he still declined to bring his wife and son to Egypt or even acknowledge their existence.

He continued to do well as a soldier. He picked up two more Mentioned-in-Despatches and was awarded the DSO for his gallantry at the battle of Toski in 1889. One of Macdonald's fellow officers at this time was Major Herbert Kitchener. It is hard to believe that they got on. Kitchener was never interested in anyone who could not further his career. Added to that, apart from being an ex-ranker, with few social graces, Macdonald had a sound tactical sense and a glowing military reputation which Kitchener would have envied. Therefore, when Kitchener became Sirdar of the Egyptian army in 1892, Macdonald's problems multiplied.

Kitchener would not recruit or employ married officers but in the same year, tired of waiting for some public recognition of her married state, Christina Macdonald applied to the Scottish courts for a writ. The Courts found that she was indeed legally married to Macdonald, now a colonel, and a writ to that effect was served on him in 1894. He duly admitted the match and the paternity of his son and the Edinburgh Court of Sessions declared that he had been legally married to Christina for the last ten years.

Somehow none of this got to the ears of Sir Herbert Kitchener. Macdonald remained in Egypt and continued to serve with his Sudanese soldiers. He was recognized throughout the British and Egyptian armies as one of the finest soldiers of his generation and his secret marriage – perhaps just one of his secrets – was still unknown to the world at large at the end of July 1897 when he led his Sudanese infantry brigade out of Merowe on the march to Abu Hamed.

Hunter's entire force consisted of some two thousand seven hundred men, mostly infantry, with a troop of cavalry, a battery of Krupp twelve-pounder cannon and four Maxim guns as support, with all their stores and ammunition carried on thirteen hundred camels. The proposed attack was a risky venture for they were going well beyond the reach of assistance should anything go wrong, and large Dervish forces were certainly mustering somewhere to the south. The distance from Merowe to Abu Hamed is one hundred and thirty miles, and this small force, moving at night whenever possible, had got to within forty miles of Abu Hamed before their presence was detected.

Before the Dervishes could muster, Hunter and Macdonald took their men on a forced march and attacked Abu Hamed just after dawn on 7 August. They killed over three hundred Dervishes for the loss of twenty-five Sudanese soldiers and announced their success to Kitchener by throwing the dead Dervishes into the river. Two days later the Sirdar saw these bodies floating by his camp at Merowe. He then knew that the SMR was secure and another Dervish fortress had fallen on the road to Omdurman.

17

Advance to the Atbara

1897–1898

Kitchener rode along the line, the British brigades
raising their helmets on dark, smeared bayonets,
cheering him in the loud enthusiasm of successful war.

Winston S. Churchill,
The River War, 1898

THE VICTORY AT Abu Hamed brought Kitchener an unexpected
bonus. Those Dervishes who were able to reach their horses or
camels and escape the slaughter, fled south across the desert and
some miles from the town met Ansar reinforcements coming up
from Berber. Any account of a battle tends to grow in the telling
and the survivors said enough to stop these reinforcements putting
in a counter-attack on the town. They carried the reinforcements
back with them in their retreat, and this victory at Abu Hamed
then had a fatal effect on Dervish morale in positions further south.

Fearing attack, the Dervish emir at Berber sent a request for
more men to the emir commanding at Metemmeh. On 24 August,
when no reinforcements were forthcoming from Metemmeh, he
elected to abandon Berber and fall back towards Omdurman.
Hearing of this, Hunter sent troops forward from Abu Hamed and
they occupied Berber without a fight on 31 August 1887. This
completed the second phase of Kitchener's advance and the campaign season of 1887 had hardly begun. The stage was now set for
a further advance but Kitchener's army, or Kitchener himself, was
not yet ready to move.

The sudden collapse of Dervish opposition around Berber put

Kitchener in a quandary. Berber was a very important town. It was the largest port on the river below Omdurman and the junction of the Nile with the important camel route from Suakin. Whoever held Berber had a grip on the trade routes to Omdurman and a springboard for a final advance on the Kalifa's capital. Unfortunately, Kitchener had not yet begun to move his main army up as far as Abu Hamed and he remained determined that neither defeat nor victory would deflect him from his original intention: a steady, well-supplied and phased advance, stage by stage to final victory at Omdurman.

A large Dervish army from the south and a strong force of Osman Digna's formidable Hadendowa warriors were still lurking close to Berber and to occupy the town without sufficient troops to secure the stages along the way would, he felt, stretch his army dangerously thin. The fall of Berber was a bonus but a bonus that had come too soon; clearly, Berber had to be occupied, but that must be the limit of advance for the moment. The Suakin–Berber camel route was reopened and gunboats sailed up the Nile to shell Metemmeh, but the army itself stayed put.

There was another problem, but one that related more to Kitchener's ever-present ambition than to military necessity. It was generally agreed that to advance beyond Berber and overwhelm the Kalifa and his large Dervish armies before Omdurman, the Sirdar would require the assistance of British troops. Kitchener did not dispute this but he was very anxious that he alone should command all the forces that destroyed the Dervishes, reconquered the Sudan, and avenged Gordon.

Whoever commanded the army that achieved these triumphs would be marked for advancement but Kitchener, though Commander-in-Chief of the Egyptian army, had the rather less exalted rank of major-general in the British army. If the British sent a substantial force to Egypt they would certainly send a senior general to command it. This man, whoever he might be, would probably outrank Kitchener and therefore hog the lion's share of the glory, the titles, the medals and the money that would go to the man who defeated the Kalifa. Kitchener's anxiety on this point had been increased in July 1897, when the former Sirdar, Sir Francis Grenfell, returned to Egypt as commander of the British army of occupation.

Kitchener hesitated to lay this self-seeking objection to British assistance before Cromer, and fortunately he did not need to do so for the moment. There was another shortage of funds and Cromer, while agreeing to the occupation of Berber, forbade Kitchener to advance beyond that point until fresh funds were guaranteed by the British government.

Cromer was also worried about Kitchener's state of mind. From time to time, and especially in moments of crisis, the normally assertive and imposing Kitchener seemed to suffer from depression and a failure of nerve, and so it was after the fall of Berber. At one point, Kitchener even offered to resign his command, an offer that Cromer sharply refused, but even the completion of the railway up to Abu Hamed on 1 November 1897 failed to rouse Kitchener's spirits . . . and the Dervishes were now moving up to contest his advance towards Omdurman.

*

With strong Egyptian forces established at Berber and Abu Hamed matters came to a head in January 1898. Colonel Francis Reginald Wingate, Kitchener's intelligence chief, reported that the Kalifa was on the move, marching on Berber with all his power, apparently seeking a decisive engagement and, suddenly, all outstanding problems were resolved. Cromer found the funds to feed and supply the Egyptian army, British troops in large numbers began to arrive in the Delta and by virtue of his long experience in the Middle East, Kitchener was confirmed as commander of all the forces, British or Egyptian, operating south of Wadi Halfa. Thus reassured, and far more cheerful, Kitchener began the march for the Atbara river and the next phase of his campaign.

He began by moving all his men up the Nile and concentrating the Anglo-Egyptian army, as it now became, at camps in and around Berber. This move had the advantage of securing the town against a Dervish counter-attack and providing a firm base for a further advance. The first of the British battalions also began to arrive: the 1st Battalions of four marching regiments, the Lincolnshire, Cameron Highlanders and Royal Warwickshire Regiments – which had been in garrison in Egypt – and the 1st Battalion of the Seaforth Highlanders, which had just arrived from Malta. These battalions were used to the Mediterranean theatre and had no great need of acclimatization. They were brigaded under Major General W. F. Gatacre, an officer newly arrived from India where he had commanded a brigade in the Chitral expedition.

Major General Gatacre was a remarkably difficult officer and a great trial to his subordinates, who referred to him privately as 'General Backacher'. Totally unable to delegate, he interfered constantly with his battalion commanders and insisted on being consulted on the slightest measure, right down to platoon level. This proved a sore trial to his officers and men, but the arrival of these British battalions greatly comforted General Kitchener, who was becoming concerned at the large Dervish forces mustering to his front.

As soon as Gatacre's brigade arrived, Kitchener sent a Sudanese brigade forward for twenty miles to that point south of Berber where the Nile is joined by the Atbara, a major tributary, which flows in here from Abyssinia. Once on the Atbara, this brigade built a large zareba and a mud-walled fort on the point of land between the two rivers. This position was not as secure as it might have been since the Atbara ran dry during the winter months, but it was an adequate forward base. The Sudanese troops then prepared to hold this position against the Dervish forces gathering in large numbers somewhere to the south.

The Kalifa himself was not present on the Atbara. Although he sent the bulk of his forces forward, he had elected to stay in Omdurman and in his absence the Dervish emirs fell to quarrelling among themselves, unable to elect a field commander or decide what joint action they should take against Kitchener's ever-expanding army. Eventually this Dervish army retired in frustration to Omdurman.

Waiting at Omdurman was the emir of Metemmeh, Mahmud Ahmed, a pugnacious warrior who had a force of twenty thousand Ansar under his personal command. Mahmud begged the Kalifa to let him attack Kitchener at Berber in conjunction with Osman Digna, who had brought a large force of Hadendowa up from Suakin and was waiting in the desert some distance east of the Nile. Having obtained the Kalifa's permission, Mahmud's army left Khartoum on or about 14 February 1889 and joined Osman Digna's forces at Shendi a few days later.

Kitchener was well supplied with news on the Dervish moves and probable intentions. His chief intelligence officer, Colonel Wingate, was bringing in a great quantity of information because the steady advance of his army was unnerving some of the Kalifa's supporters and a steady stream of deserters and disaffected tribesmen were reaching the Anglo-Egyptian lines. After interrogation, most of these men enlisted in the Egyptian army where they fought cheerfully against their former colleagues. With the newly arrived British brigade, Kitchener's force had reached a strength of some eighteen thousand men, mustered in two brigades, the Egyptian troops under Major-General Hunter, the much smaller British force under Major-General Gatacre.

Mahmud and Osman Digna were not in agreement about their course of action. Ever wily, Osman Digna wanted to harry the Anglo-Egyptian supply lines, destroy the wells, cut off the working parties and dig up the railway. This would probably have been the wisest and most effective strategy. Mahmud, being younger, a fervent Mahdist and eager for glory, wanted to lead their forces in a frontal attack on Berber and destroy the Anglo-Egyptian army before it grew stronger. These leaders were still unable to decide on a joint course of action as the Dervish army moved steadily north.

On 13 March 1898, Kitchener's cruising gunboats spotted large Dervish forces moving down the east bank of the Nile towards the Atbara junction. Kitchener swiftly ordered his army to concentrate around the newly built fort at the Atbara-Nile confluence, but this move had hardly begun when Kitchener's cavalry scouts reported that the Dervishes had changed direction near the village of Aliab. They were now heading almost due east, away from the Nile, probably intending to cross the dry bed of the Atbara, encircle Berber or attack the town from the east, down the caravan route from Suakin.

Kitchener left the Atbara position garrisoned by one Sudanese battalion and marched the rest of his army down the east bank of the Atbara, aiming to intercept Mahmud somewhere near the village of Ras-el-Hudi. Mahmud crossed the dry bed of the Atbara on 21 March and positioned his army in a stout zareba concealed in the undergrowth on the east bank of the river near Nakheila. He was not detected there until 30 March. The advancing Anglo-Egyptian army had meanwhile halted on the defensive at Ras-el-Hudi on 20 March, as from that position they could screen Berber and the Atbara defences and block any move north by Mahmud and Osman Digna.

The Emir Mahmud had not done well so far, while Kitchener had handled his forces with considerable skill. Mahmud's every move had been observed or anticipated by Kitchener and unless Mahmud elected for a rapid retreat across the Atbara he was threatened with a battle against a well-armed Anglo-Egyptian army almost matching his own strength.

Mahmud elected to stay behind the stout mimosa-thorn zareba his warriors had built around the village of Nakheila, for the dense undergrowth along the river was well suited to the Ansars' close-quarter fighting tactics. He also had over four thousand Baggara horsemen, a force which greatly outnumbered Kitchener's available cavalry, some seven hundred and fifty Egyptian horsemen, mustered in eight squadrons and commanded by Lieutenant-Colonel R. G. Broadwood.

Though the British had detected his position, Mahmud's situation was by no means critical and it was made even easier when Kitchener was yet again smitten with an attack of indecision. He could not decide whether to attack the Dervish zareba or wait until the Dervishes came out against him. His chief subordinates, Generals Hunter and Gatacre, gave conflicting advice and, unable to decide, Kitchener took the alarming decision – alarming at least to Lord Cromer – of telegraphing Cairo to ask for instructions.

It is not usual for a commanding general, with an army at his back and in the presence of the enemy, to telegraph his political chief a thousand miles away and ask for advice on tactics. Cromer showed the telegram to Grenfell and Lord Salisbury showed it to the War Office and all the military men were amazed. Grenfell recommended that if Kitchener was in any doubt about the attack he should sit tight, while Salisbury sent back the soothing but unhelpful reply that the British government would support Kitchener's actions, whatever he decided to do.

Cromer had many good qualities but he was no general and he knew it. The consensus of opinion advised delay, and delay there was, while a considerable number of telegrams flew between Cairo and the Atbara. Then Major-General Hunter, who had previously advised delay, changed his mind and recommended attack. That tipped the balance, Kitchener became himself again, and on 4 April 1898 the advance from Ras-el-Hudi began.

Kitchener took forward an army of some sixteen thousand men with twenty-four artillery pieces, a quantity of Maxim machine-guns and a rocket detachment commanded by Lieutenant David Beatty RN. Mustered in four large squares, this force advanced some five miles on the first day before stopping for the night behind a hastily built thorn zareba. At dawn the next day, Broadwood's Egyptian cavalry, with Maxim gun and horse artillery in support, rode out to reconnoitre the Dervish position. The Ansar were dug-in and well hidden among the thorn bushes, and by holding their fire they concealed their position from Broadwood's scouts. Broadwood's force was also challenged by the Baggara horse and met some artillery fire from Dervish positions along the Atbara. There was some sporadic fighting along the riverbank, which lasted until dusk. The Baggara put in two spirited attacks against Broadwood's cavalry and were only driven off when the Egyptian troopers dismounted and engaged them with carbine and machinegun fire. This cavalry sparring continued over the next three days as Kitchener's infantry battalions came up, but by the evening of 7 April Kitchener had his forces mustered six miles from the Dervish zareba and ready for a final advance.

As soon as dusk fell that night, the Anglo-Egyptian army marched out towards the Atbara. The infantry brigades, Egyptian, Sudanese and British, were marching in square, a difficult formation to adopt at night in that close country, with the cavalry, artillery and supply columns bringing up the rear. This advance continued, with frequent stops to realign the men, until 4 a.m. By that time Kitchener's army had reached a plateau less than a thousand yards from the Dervish zareba, which was hidden from their view behind a low crest of the ridge overlooking the east bank of the Atbara river.

At the first peep of day, the army drew up in a great arc of battalions just behind the crest of the ridge, with the British brigade on the left. The 1st Camerons were deployed in line with the other British battalions drawn up in column of companies just to their rear. The Egyptian and Sudanese brigades deployed to their flank were in a similar formation, one battalion in line, the supporting battalions in column, with the artillery and Maxim guns deployed at intervals along the entire front. The cavalry were on the flanks and the supply echelons, transport, medical, ordnance and the rest, were mustered just to the rear.

At 6.20 a.m. the Egyptian artillery opened the battle by firing a shattering salvo of shells into the centre of the Dervish zareba. Within a few minutes all the guns on the ridge were raking the Dervish zareba with fire, moving their point of aim from one end of the Dervish position to the other, sweeping the ground with shells and machine-gun fire. This pitiless hail of shells, rockets and bullets went on for well over an hour. An attempt by the Baggara horse to drive the guns off was met with a blast of carbine and

Maxim fire from the Egyptian cavalry and this attempt at a counter-attack soon withered away.

There was no return fire from the zareba, either because the Dervish guns had been hit or because their crews could not leave the trenches to man their pieces. At 7.40 the Anglo-Egyptian guns fell silent and, bayonets fixed, magazines charged and 'one up the spout', the infantry moved forward to the attack.

The infantry advanced in line on a one-mile front, their bayonets glinting in the early morning sun, bagpipes ranting from the Scots battalions. Every so often the leading battalions would halt and rake the bushes ahead with a massive volley before moving forward again, but the leading troops were less than three hundred yards from the dusty, entangled branches of the zareba when the Ansar riflemen opened fire.

Men began to fall among the Sudanese and Cameron Highlanders leading the attack, but the advance continued. The men were now ordered to 'fire at will' at any target they could see in the undergrowth, and there was a sudden increase in the firing as the leading battalions reached the zareba and began to drag the thorn bushes aside. The supporting battalion columns then poured through these breaches and spread out among the maze of trenches, stockades and rifle pits inside the zareba and around the huts of Nakheila village. The extended Anglo-Egyptian line overlapped the Dervish and flowed around it as a wave sweeps round a rock, leaving little opportunity for escape.

It was now about 8 a.m. and the sun was well up. The fighting inside the zareba was now hand-to-hand in the familiar fashion of these Dervish wars, bayonet against spear, revolver and rifle against sword and dagger, dust clouds swirling, shadowy swordsmen rushing out of bushes, huts, or swirls of smoke to hack and slash at the British and Egyptian infantry before they were bayoneted or shot down. The Dervishes swarmed everywhere in the scrub along the banks of the Atbara, stabbing and slashing, screaming war cries, firing at the kilted or fezzed figures which came looming out of the dust and smoke. The noise was tremendous and the Anglo-Egyptian advance through the zareba slowed, the Ansar warriors savagely contesting every inch of ground.

Finally, after about half an hour of this close-quarter fighting, the Dervishes broke; Kitchener's panting soldiers reached the banks of the Atbara and dropped on one knee to fix wavering rifle sights on the backs of hundreds of jibbah-clad tribesmen fleeing across the dry bed of the river. By 8.30 a.m. the Battle of the Atbara was over and the Anglo-Egyptian soldiers had time to look about the zareba and see what they had achieved.

They had killed over two thousand Dervishes. Thousands more, hit by heavy Martini-Henry bullets or the expanding Lee-Metford rounds, lay in and around the zareba, many with terrible wounds. Their principal commander, the wounded Emir Mahmud, was a prisoner, and a defiant one. He had fought on until he was out of ammunition, and only then was he dragged from his trench by the Sudanese soldiers. Other Dervish prisoners were less troubled by this defeat and most of the surviving Ansar were swiftly recruited to make up the losses in Kitchener's Sudanese battalions; these had sustained three hundred and eighty casualties in that frenzied half-hour of fighting. There was no sign of Osman Digna, who had escaped from the zareba before resistance collapsed.

Anglo-Egyptian losses totalled eighty killed and four hundred and seventy-nine wounded. The 1st Battalion the Cameron Highlanders were the worst hit, losing sixty men killed or wounded. The wounded men from the Anglo-Egyptian army were swiftly sent back down the river to Dongola for treatment. Dervish wounded were not accorded such care and consideration: those who could walk were hustled off to prison camps where many died of their wounds. Those who could not walk were left to die in the undergrowth, many perishing from lack of water.

The Atbara was a useful victory. After his initial hesitation, Kitchener had handled his men well, the Anglo-Egyptian army had destroyed a large Dervish force and although Osman Digna was still at liberty, Kitchener had one of the Kalifa's chief subordinates as a living trophy. Kitchener chose to exploit his prisoner, loading the captured emir with chains and then having him run behind the Sirdar's horse in a triumphant progress through Berber. This arrogant treatment of a defeated enemy and his neglect of the Dervish wounded did Kitchener no credit, but his victory was nonetheless hailed as a triumph in Cairo and London.

Kitchener himself later came to regard this victory on the Atbara as more crucial to the eventual outcome of his campaign than the final battle at Omdurman. If this is indeed so, it made no difference to his strategy. The advance did not speed up and he made no attempt to exploit his success. Instead the army went into summer quarters along the Nile and the fellahin laboured under the sun to bring the railway forward to Fort Atbara. With it came more men,

British, Sudanese and Egyptian, raising Kitchener's command to nearly twenty-six thousand men. It was not until the middle of August 1898 that Kitchener was ready to advance again.

18

Omdurman

2 September 1898

'It was not a battle but an execution.'
G. W. Steevens, *With Kitchener to Khartoum*, 1898

THERE IS SOMETHING almost chilling about Kitchener's reconquest of the Sudan. The advance of his army towards Omdurman resembles that of some inexorable juggernaut, moving up the Nile and across the desert, grinding into dust anything or anyone that stood in its path. Kitchener would advance only when his supply lines had been secured and he refused to be rushed, even though it was now abundantly clear that any Dervish force could not stand against modern weapons manned by confident, disciplined soldiers.

Kitchener's campaign remained slow but steady, one stage at a time. After the Atbara victory he paused again, putting his army into camps, urging the railway forward, bringing his supplies and gunboats up, waiting until he was completely ready for that final two-hundred-mile thrust up the Nile to Omdurman. Only when he had all the force he wanted at hand would he advance to avenge the death of General Gordon, destroy the Kalifa and put an end to Mahdism once and for all.

Thanks to the ever-extending military railway line, Kitchener did not have to wait long. Even while his troops were celebrating their victory on the Atbara, cheering the general whenever he appeared, fresh troops and more supplies were coming upriver. The river gunboats had proved their worth again and again in scouting ahead, in harassing fire and providing artillery support for the troops ashore. Commander Keppel's little squadron now received three more screw gunboats to bring his fleet of steamers up to ten, all equipped with artillery and Maxim machine guns. More support artillery and machine-guns arrived for the Egyptian army battalions, together with two batteries of the Royal Artillery equipped with howitzers. Kitchener intended to win this war with firepower and as his firepower increased, so the odds against the Kalifa's survival lengthened.

There was also an increase in the infantry strength. Kitchener now had six infantry brigades: Lewis's, Macdonald's, Maxwell's, Wauchope's, Lyttleton's and Collinson's, plus cavalry and a camel corps. When Brigadier Lyttleton arrived with his 2nd Brigade to join Brigadier Wauchope's 1st Brigade, there were enough British units in the field to give Major-General Gatacre a full Division.

Lyttleton's men had a need to 'get their knees brown' for two of the four battalions, the 1st Battalion the Grenadier Guards and the 2nd Rifle Brigade, had only recently arrived in Egypt and the men suffered severely from sunstroke. The other two elements in this four-battalion brigade, the Lancashire Fusiliers and the Northumberland Fusiliers, had been in garrison in the Delta and were able to take care of themselves in the arid deserts of the Sudan. In all, Kitchener had a force of twenty-five thousand, eight hundred fighting men, a third of them British.

If the infantry was in splendid order, the recent British cavalry reinforcement was something of a disappointment. This consisted of the 21st Lancers, the most junior cavalry regiment in the British army, commanded by Lieutenant-Colonel R. M. Martin. In their forty years of existence the 21st had never been in action; the joke in army circles was that the motto of the 21st Lancers was 'Thou shalt not kill.' The officers and men of the 21st Lancers did not find this jest at all amusing and Colonel Martin was very anxious that his regiment should find glory in the Sudan. This desire was to get his regiment into considerable trouble in the weeks ahead.

Riding with the 21st Lancers was a young officer of the 4th Hussars, Lieutenant Winston Spencer Churchill, who should not have been in the Sudan at all. To augment his pay, Lieutenant Churchill was in the habit of submitting articles to newspapers and writing books about the various campaigns he took part in. The views expressed in these books and articles were not always favourable to the generals conducting the campaigns; in fact Kitchener had expressly forbidden Churchill to come to the

Sudan. Here he was anyway, trying to stay out of the Commander-in-Chief's way, serving not only as a supernumerary officer with the 21st Lancers but also as the war correspondent of the *Morning Post*.

Newspapermen and war correspondents were now starting to appear at the front in all military campaigns and more than a dozen rode with Kitchener's army towards Omdurman. One of them, Bennet Burleigh of the *Daily Telegraph*, had been with the Gordon Relief Expedition and had some tart comments to make about his present colleagues:

> I returned to Cairo in early July where, having paid into the Financial Secretary's hands the £50 security required of war correspondents to cover the cost of railway fares and forage, I received my permit to proceed to the front. All the restrictions on the number of correspondents allowed up during the Atbara campaign had been removed and an 'open door' policy substituted. In consequence there was a large number – sixteen in all – of so-called 'Representatives of the Press' at the front. As one old correspondent observed, some of them represented anything but journals or journalism, the name of a newspaper being used merely as a cover for notoriety or medal hunting.

The last remark was probably a thrust at Lieutenant Churchill. General Kitchener did not yet know that Churchill was with his army. Like Wolseley before him, Kitchener detested journalists; emerging from his tent one morning to find a group of correspondents waiting to interview him, he returned their cheerful greetings with 'Get out of my way, you drunken swabs.'

Newspapermen accompanying Victorian armies took their full share of risks and were by no means entirely non-combatant. Bennet Burleigh carried a revolver and shot down an attacking Dervish warrior at Omdurman. Colonel F. Rhodes, representing *The Times*, was wounded at Omdurman and Hubert Howard of the *New York Herald* was killed by shellfire shortly after the city was taken. Thanks to these people and their reports, the Omdurman campaign of 1898 is particularly easy to follow.

The Egyptian army now mustered sixteen battalions, six of them hard-fighting Sudanese infantry, so the total Anglo-Egyptian forces numbered more than twenty-five thousand men, two-thirds of them Egyptian or Sudanese. This force gradually moved upriver by route

march or steamer and by the end of August were mustered at
Wadi Hamed, just sixty miles from Omdurman. Bennet Burleigh
recalls that the Sudanese infantry marched into the camp at Wadi
Hamed behind their regimental band playing a popular ditty of
the day, 'Oh, dem Golden Slippers'.

Bands apart, this was a modern army, a very different creation
from the one Lord Wolseley had led into the Sudan in the previous
decade. This army had rifled artillery, lyddite shells, machine guns,
searchlights, magazine rifles, steam gunboats and a large quantity
of trained, battle-tested fighting men. Kitchener could not lose
and in their hearts his men knew it; Kitchener himself was still
uncertain.

The Kalifa's reaction to the impending assault is not on record
but his actions and orders indicate that he was well aware how
serious his position had become. He had numbers on his side and
warriors of unmatchable courage, but he had no answer to the
late-nineteenth-century firepower and technology that General
Kitchener was bringing against him.

The Kalifa had ordered all his emirs to arm their men and come
up to Omdurman with their entire force. His army eventually
totalled some fifty-five thousand men, about a third armed with
rifles, the rest with edged weapons. While they were mustering he
fortified the town and prayed for guidance and support at the tomb
of the Mahdi. As with Mahmud at the Atbara he considered his
choices of fighting on the defensive in the town or leading his men
out against Kitchener and fighting in the open desert, north of the
city. He did not seem to have considered the other options, to
harry Kitchener's extended supply lines and commence a guerrilla
war, or withdraw into the wastes of Kordofan and let Kitchener
waste men and energy marching about after him before risking a
battle, so repeating the tactics that had destroyed Hicks Pasha in
the first years of the Mahdi's rule.

The courses open to the Kalifa in 1898 were fewer than those
available to the Mahdi in 1881–5. The Kalifa was a ruler, not a
saint to his people, and Mahdism was not the force it had been.
Many of the tribes in Kordofan and Darfur and along the Nile
valley had become discontented with the stern rule of the Kalifa
and fear of disaffection was probably the main reason for his
decision to stand and fight at Omdurman.

Kitchener began his march on Omdurman on 28 August 1898.
The British division was in one vast square, marching along the

west bank from Wadi Hamed, with the steam gunboats keeping pace alongside or forging ahead up the river. The Egyptian brigades were deployed in the open desert with their camel corps further out covering the flank, while the British and Egyptian cavalry patrolled ahead and checked every wadi before the infantry came up. Meanwhile, a two-thousand-strong force of Sudanese and Abyssinian irregulars commanded by Major Stuart-Wortley kept pace with the army along the east bank of the river.

So for three days the advance continued. There was no sign whatsoever of Dervish scouts or the Dervish army. It was not until 31 August when the army was in sight of the Kerreri Hills, the last physical obstacle before Omdurman, that the advance patrols of the 21st Lancers saw Dervish horsemen observing their advance from the 'heights' ahead.

The Kerreri Hills are hardly hills at all. They run out into the desert at right angles to the west bank of the river for about two miles, and rise at best to only two hundred and fifty feet, but in the flat country beside the Nile they offered a good observation point and the only natural defence line before Omdurman.

Kitchener was again undergoing one of his more cautious phases. On 1 September, while his cavalry scouted the hills, he sent Commander Keppel's gunboats steaming upriver to Omdurman. They arrived opposite the city at mid-morning and opened a heavy fire on the defences, raking the city walls with machine-gun fire and deploying their guns against various points within the city, concentrating especially on the tall dome of the Mahdi's tomb, which soon displayed several large shell holes.

Meanwhile, a firing point on the east bank, within range of the city, had been seized by Major Stuart-Wortley's band of Arab irregulars. The five-inch howitzers of the Royal Artillery were then ferried across the river and joined in the gunboat bombardment of Omdurman, causing great destruction and considerable loss of life.

This bombardment may also have decided the Kalifa's course of action. Street fighting is notoriously hard on infantry and had he elected to fight in the narrow streets and alleyways of the town, his Ansar swordsmen might well have inflicted considerable damage on the Anglo-Egyptian army. The crashing shells, the smoke and noise, the whistle of shrapnel, the screams of the citizens and the crumbling of the Mahdi's tomb must have convinced the Kalifa that the city was untenable as a battleground. That night he ordered his forces out of the city and prepared his Ansar warriors for their last great fight on the flat plains to the north of the town. This move was soon detected by Kitchener's scouts.

Colonel Martin's Lancer patrols had crossed the Kerreri Hills on the morning of 1 September, and just after dawn his vedettes were drawn up on the Jebel Surgham, a solitary hill 260 feet high, some distance to the south of the Kerreri ridge. From this they had a clear view of Omdurman and Gordon's old palace above the ruins of Khartoum on the opposite bank. Looking back to the north, they had sight of the Anglo-Egyptian army now debouching through the Kerreri Hills.

The Lancers stayed in position, observing to their front until about noon. Out to their front between the Jebel Surgham and Omdurman lay what appeared to be a zareba; on closer observation and as the sun rose this 'zareba' was seen to move. The Lancers realized then that it was actually a large Dervish force, numbering some forty thousand men in five beflagged divisions, a mass which spanned the plain ahead for four full miles. This great forest of men and spear-points was now advancing fast towards the Jebel Surgham.

Colonel Martin decided to stay on the jebel as long as possible, observe the enemy and erect a signalling heliograph to report Dervish movements back to Kitchener. He also elected to employ that unwanted and unwelcome 4th Hussar officer, Lieutenant Winston Churchill, sending him back with a report to General Kitchener. Kitchener had come up with the rest of the army and was waiting by the village of El Egeiga on the west bank of the Nile, and had not yet seen the Dervish army.

Churchill, who had so far managed to avoid any contact with General Kitchener, was naturally somewhat reluctant to accept this assignment; he was far more interested in observing the Dervishes than in a confrontation with the Sirdar. Yet orders were orders and Churchill rode back across the plain to deliver Martin's report. In the event, Kitchener had more on his mind at that time than one insubordinate cavalry officer, and Lieutenant Churchill was soon back with the Lancers on the Jebel Surgham.

The Dervishes had been milling about on the plains below but were now gradually coming to a halt. Heliograph messages flashed back to the Sirdar; cavalry and camel patrols continued to scout into the desert throughout the afternoon to prevent any surprise flanking attack; and as night fell the two armies settled down within a few miles of each other, waiting for the morrow and the battle it must bring.

For most of the day Kitchener had kept his army halted around the riverside village of El Egeiga. As dusk fell his troops were ordered to occupy a wide arc around the village with their backs to the river, and build a zareba. The local people had long since scoured the country for firewood; mimosa and camel-thorn bushes were in short supply hereabouts and these were swiftly appropriated by the British. The Egyptian and Sudanese troops therefore attempted to build stone sangars or dig trenches. That done they lay down by their weapons and watched their front as the 21st Lancers came back to the zareba and the Jebel Surgham was occupied by Dervish scouts.

The main risk to Kitchener was a massive Dervish night attack. The Dervishes had no particular objection to night attacks and although searchlights on the river steamers swept the desert constantly throughout the night, the darkness would have offered them some protection from aimed rifle and artillery fire. Some reports state that Kitchener turned the villagers out of El Egeiga after telling them that he intended to put in a night attack against the Dervishes and that this intelligence kept the Dervishes on the defensive until dawn. It is more likely that the Kalifa did not know what to do and since any forward movement would have been caught in the beams of the searchlights, he elected to wait until dawn.

Few soldiers in either army got much sleep that night. The heavy rain storms which had soaked them every night for the last week had passed but sentries were changed every hour and the ceaseless throbbing of drums from the Dervish encampment kept most men awake. At half past three in the morning the twenty-two-thousand-strong Anglo-Egyptian army 'stood-to', all men watching their front as the sky grew gradually lighter.

Reveille was sounded at 3.40 a.m., the pipers pacing up and down among the Highland battalions, drums beating and bugles blowing among the English regiments and the battalions of their Egyptian and Sudanese comrades-in-arms. Shortly after 5 a.m. the cavalry jingled out towards the Jebel Surgham, while within the Anglo-Egyptian zareba the infantry made preparations either to march out or stand off a Dervish attack.

Kitchener deployed his men to meet either situation, setting them out in a wide semi-circle of battalions around the village of

El Egeiga, with the Rifle Brigade on the river bank to the south of the village and the rest of the army curving round like a bulwark to where the Egyptian battalions completed the line. The stores, transport camels and hospital tents were in the centre and the gunboats had steam up on the river, ready to join the artillery in giving support.

Thus arrayed, Kitchener's army waited for more than an hour as it grew steadily lighter. Then one of the Lancer patrols came cantering back, then another and another. Word gradually spread down the line that the Dervishes were on the move. As the last cavalry patrols came in, a great line of banners was seen far away across the desert and the sound of drums grew louder. Soon infantry and horsemen could be clearly seen, advancing towards them beneath a forest of spear-points and banners; thousands, even tens of thousands, of Dervish warriors were coming on to the attack.

What the Anglo-Egyptian army saw before them that morning was the largest native military force raised in Africa since the Crusades. Apart from a few thousand rifles, the Dervishes were armed entirely with medieval weapons, swords, spears and daggers, many carrying shields, some of the emirs in chainmail armour. The Dervish advance swept around both sides of the Jebel Surgham; first into view was an eight-thousand-strong mass of Ansar bearing white flags. This 'division' was followed at once by an even larger body of warriors, maybe twenty thousand men, topped by a line of green banners. Both these forces headed directly for the Anglo-Egyptian zareba, coming on across the open desert at a fast trot, the men on foot, their emirs on horses or camels. These divisions, large as they were, were but part of the huge force which was advancing behind them across the front of the zareba, heading for the Kerreri Hills, which some of the Egyptian cavalry, camel corps and mounted infantry were still occupying.

According to Bennet Burleigh, the order to open fire on the Dervish army was given at 5.30 a.m. precisely – the official despatch says 6.45 – but whenever the firing started, a slaughter of the Ansar soon followed. First into action were the artillery and the gunboats, pouring shells and Maxim bullets into the Dervish mass at a range of about three thousand yards. Each shell burst, leaving a circle of dead and wounded men and animals. Fountains of smoke and sand erupted in the midst of the Ansar ranks but still the warriors came on, flayed by bullets and flying metal fragments, chanting war-cries, beating drums, waving banners.

At two thousand yards the Anglo-Egyptian infantry opened fire. The Grenadier Guards, standing in two ranks on the left of the British line, began pouring platoon volleys into the mass of Ansar now milling to their front. Then, one by one, the other battalions joined in, the men harking to the orders of their NCOs and officers, 'Fire low and fire slow . . . pick out the banner wavers, the chain-mail-armoured horsemen, the obvious emirs.' Within minutes the zareba was wreathed in a thin veil of smoke and the desert in front was gradually being carpeted with fallen Ansar warriors, horses and camels. So far hardly a man of Kitchener's army had even been wounded; only a few long-range Remington rounds slapped across the top of the zareba.

Unable to face that furious rifle fire the Ansar swerved away to their left. They were at once assailed by Martini-Henry fire from the Sudanese battalions of Maxwell's and Macdonald's brigades. This was sheer slaughter; no Dervish warriors had got within a half-mile of the Anglo-Egyptian line or looked likely to do so and they were going down in swathes as the shells, machine-gun and rifle fire cut into their ranks. This slaughter of the first Dervish force went on for over half an hour before the survivors slowly drew off, leaving a few Remington-armed men lurking in the under-growth. These began to snipe at the battalions until machine-gun fire was brought to bear on their positions and cut them down.

The initial Dervish attack had failed either to penetrate the Anglo-Egyptian zareba or tempt Kitchener into following the defeated Ansar as they pulled back. Had he done so there were plenty of Dervish formations waiting in the desert to put in a counter-attack, for the bulk of the Kalifa's forces had still to engage.

The zareba position was secure but on the slopes of the Kerreri Hills the cavalry and mounted infantry of Colonel Broadwood's force were coming under pressure. Broadwood's force was there to prevent the Dervishes circling the zareba in the dead ground behind the hills and sweeping down unobserved on the right flank of Kitchener's army. Coming up now under dark green banners were no less than fifteen thousand warriors commanded by the Kalifa's son, Osman-el-Din. Broadwood swiftly signalled news of this advance to Kitchener and was ordered to leave the hills at once and withdraw to the safety of the zareba.

This proved none too easy. Broadwood elected to hold on for a while and then withdraw to the north, hoping to lure the Dervishes away from the zareba, but he left this move too late. Before his

camel corps could mount and get away, galloping Baggara horsemen were among them with sword and spear. Broadwood's horse
artillery were forced to abandon two guns and his force was then
split in two, the camel corps riding hard for the zareba, the cavalry
hastening away to the north, both bodies pursued by the Baggara
who were close behind and gaining on them.

It might have gone very hard with Broadwood's men had not
the captains on two river gunboats seen their predicament and
come to their assistance. Two ships, the *Abu Klea* and the *Melik*,
opened fire on the Baggara, pouring Maxim and 9-pounder
shellfire across the desert, but Broadwood had to gallop hard for
another three miles before he could halt, reform his men and take
them back in a charge against his scattered pursuers. That done,
he took his men back to the river bank, and protected by the
gunboats they eventually regained the shelter of the zareba.

It was now about 9 a.m. The focus of the action now shifts to
one of the most dramatic events of the Omdurman battle, the
charge of the 21st Lancers. While the young Osman-el-Din had
been chasing Broadwood, the Dervishes had put in another equally
massive and fruitless attack against the zareba. This had been
repulsed with great Ansar loss and now, as far as Kitchener could
judge, the back of the Dervish attack had been broken. It was
therefore time to leave the zareba and drive forward for Omdurman
but before doing so, the ever-cautious general decided to send the
21st Lancers beyond the Jebel Surgham to report any Dervish
forces lurking in ambush between there and the city.

Colonel Martin had had a rather disappointing morning. His
men had patrolled forward at dawn and spotted the advancing
Dervishes, but apart from that useful service the 21st Lancers had
had no opportunity to make a significant mark on the battle. This
time he took his entire regiment out, some three hundred men in
all, together with the supernumerary Lieutenant Churchill. Small
patrols were sent ahead to scout the ground while the bulk of the
Lancers trotted along in one solid column.

Beyond the Surgham ridge they found scattered parties of
Dervishes apparently withdrawing to Omdurman and reported
this information back to Kitchener. Kitchener then ordered Martin
to 'Annoy them as far as possible and head them off from Omdurman.' Martin was obeying these instructions when one of his
patrols spotted some Dervishes strung out along the edge of a khor,
a shallow valley just in front of the advancing regiment. Martin

therefore swung his column left, intending to take these Dervishes in the flank. This was not a wise move for as his troops rode across their front, the Dervishes opened fire, emptying several saddles and shooting a number of horses.

This was the moment Colonel Martin had been waiting for. There lay the enemy, about three hundred in all; here were the 21st Lancers, and between them lay two hundred yards of open desert. One trumpet call and the 21st Lancers swung into line, dropped their lance tips, dug in their spurs and began to thunder across the desert towards the Dervish line. On the way young Winston Churchill managed to sheath his sword, no easy task at full gallop, and draw a more useful weapon, his Mauser pistol. Then, as the 21st Lancers went galloping into the Dervish line, they realized they had been tricked.

The scattering of Dervishes manning the crest of the khor was only a small part of the force. More than four thousand Ansar were concealed in the khor itself and as Martin's men came galloping over the top they rose and charged to meet them, swinging swords and hurling spears. For the Lancers there was no time to stop and no room to turn; the troopers had no choice but to drive in their spurs again and crash into the Dervish line.

The force of the charge carried the Lancers deep into the Dervish ranks. Some of the troopers dropped their lances or drove them into a Dervish chest, then drew their swords and began to lay about them. Lieutenant Churchill shot his way through the enemy and then returned to the ruck to rescue a lance-corporal who had been unhorsed. According to one participant, it took less than a minute for the Lancers to hack a path through the enemy and across the khor, but in those few seconds twenty-one Lancers and more than a hundred horses were brought down. The Dervish commander, a mail-clad emir 'on a fine black Donglawi horse', was killed with a lance thrust. Those Lancers who rode or scrambled clear of the ruck then engaged the enemy with their carbines until the Ansar drew off. The 21st Lancers lost twenty-two men killed and around another fifty wounded in that charge, apart from losing more than a hundred horses, the highest regimental loss in the entire battle; Colonel Martin's search for glory had cost his regiment dear.

News of the charge of the 21st Lancers had not reached Kitchener when he elected to order the infantry to move out towards Omdurman. Colonel Martin's action had not only damaged his regiment but he had not carried out his main task, to scout the ground ahead for the rest of the Kalifa's divisions. There were still plenty of Dervishes milling about on the plain or on the slopes of the low hills, but apparently no groups of any size. The battle of Omdurman appeared to be all but over.

Kitchener's brigades and battalions therefore broke up their line in the zareba and began to march south along the river bank towards Omdurman, taking position one behind the other as they came out. This had the effect of placing the British brigades in the lead and the Egyptian brigades in the rear. Kitchener ordered the advance on Omdurman to be made 'in echelon of brigades from the left.' This order put Macdonald's 1st Sudanese Brigade well out in the desert, on the extreme right flank of the Anglo-Egyptian army.

Stepped back in echelon as ordered, the army then crossed the Surgham ridge, coming under scattered rifle fire from some Dervish riflemen on the top of the jebel. This distraction to the flank drew Kitchener's attention to the fact that something more serious was occurring over on his right where Colonel Hector Macdonald's Sudanese battalions were deploying into line and opening fire with rifles and Maxims on some as yet unseen enemy.

Macdonald's three-thousand-strong brigade was actually under attack from the entire Dervish reserve, seventeen thousand war-riors fighting under the black flag of the Kalifa. This large force was sweeping in to take Kitchener's marching army in the flank and all that stood in their way was Macdonald's three Sudanese battalions. Kitchener sent Macdonald a hurried order to withdraw to the river while the army changed front to meet this new attack, but Macdonald had wounded men to protect and was already closely beset by the Dervishes. He refused to obey Kitchener's order. 'Ah'll no do it,' he is reported as saying. 'Ah'll see them damned first. We maun' just fight it out.'

Fight it out they did. Macdonald's Sudanese troops held their fire until the Ansar were down to a thousand yards range and then began to flay the Dervishes with fire. At first the Sudanese fire was ragged, too ragged for an old Gordon Highlander like 'Fighting Mac'. With the enemy almost upon him, Macdonald ordered his men to cease fire, and then rebuked them for firing wildly. If Macdonald's Highland accent was as broad as reported, the men may not have understood his words, but they got his point. They commenced firing ordered platoon volleys and shot the advancing Dervish line to pieces. Macdonald's men held the Dervishes at bay for thirty long minutes until Wauchope's brigade came round the Jebel Surgham and took the Kalifa's force in the flank. Just as all seemed secure, however, another Dervish force swept in against Macdonald's brigade.

This time the attack came from behind, from the direction of the Kerreri Hills. Those Ansar who had been pursuing Broadwood, fifteen thousand men commanded by the Emir Osman-el-Din, had given up the pursuit and were following the remainder of the army towards Omdurman when they came upon Macdonald's three-thousand-strong brigade out in the open desert and already under attack. Quickening their pace, the Dervishes swept down to take Macdonald's battalions in the flank.

The Dervish attack had not yet been finally driven off, but Macdonald proceeded to wheel his men to face this new threat. He could not get much help from the newly arrived brigades of Maxwell, Lyttleton and Wauchope, for his men were between them and Osman-el-Din and so masked their fire. The Ansar opened a heavy fire on Macdonald's wheeling battalions and over one hundred and twenty of his men were shot down before he had the brigade arranged to his liking and began to fire back. Macdonald's men then stood fast and again fought off the advancing Dervishes. They were down to their last few rounds of ammunition when Wauchope's brigade finally got into position on Macdonald's left and brought them some relief.

Bennet Burleigh of the *Daily Telegraph* saw Macdonald's brigade in action that day and his account of the events is almost lyrical:

I then saw the Dervishes, for the first time in all these years of campaigning, turn, stoop and fairly run for their lives. Beyond all else the double honours of the day were won by Colonel Macdonald and his Brigade . . . he achieved the victory off his own bat, proving himself a tactician and a soldier as well as what he has long been known to be, the Bravest of the Brave. The Army has a hero and a thorough soldier and if the public want either they need seek no further. I know that the Sirdar and his Staff fully recognized the nature of the service he rendered.

If the last sentence is true, Kitchener's 'recognition' did Colonel Macdonald very little good.

Macdonald's stand by the Kerreri Hills was enough to tilt the balance of the battle. Slowly now the Dervishes began to pull back, and when one last charge of the Baggara horse was driven off the entire Dervish army, now scattered into groups, began to retire at speed across the desert. Firing on the corpse-littered battlefield ceased at around 11.30 a.m. and the Anglo-Egyptian army began to pour south towards Omdurman.

The Dervishes lost more than twenty-six thousand men killed and wounded at Omdurman. If the estimates of the Kalifa's forces are correct, this represents a casualty rate of around fifty per cent – a tribute to the courage of the Ansar and evidence of the terrible effect of modern weapons when used against massed formations. Kitchener's losses were minimal: just forty-eight men killed and three hundred and eighty-two wounded. The comparisons are too terrible to require further explanation, but G. W. Steevens, one of the British war correspondents, summed up the Mahdist achievement:

Our men were perfect, but the Dervishes were superb beyond perfection. It was the largest, best and bravest army that ever fought against us for Mahdism and it died worthy of the huge empire that Mahdism won and kept so long.

If Charles Gordon ever wanted vengeance – which is most unlikely – he had it here in full in the blood-soaked desert outside the city of Omdurman.

EPILOGUE

Fashoda and After

1898–1890

> The great vindication of our self-respect was the great
> treasure we won at Khartoum. We undertook to leave
> Egypt and we have redeemed that promise in an
> unforeseen way, but without us there would be no Egypt
> and what we have made we shall keep.
>
> G. W. Steevens, *With Kitchener to Khartoum*, 1899

THE BATTLE OF Omdurman was over by noon. An hour or so
later Kitchener rode into the town, surrounded by his officers and
guided by Rudolf Slatin, the former prisoner of the Kalifa who
was now serving on the Sirdar's staff. Slatin led the party directly
to the Mahdi's tomb while other parties fanned out into the streets
to find the Kalifa and shoot down any recalcitrant warriors. There
was very little further resistance for Omdurman was in chaos, the
streets full of Dervish wounded, the houses crammed with frightened women and children. All opposition had ceased but the town
was still under fire from the river gunboats; one shell killed Hubert
Howard, war correspondent for *The Times*, before the gunboats
were informed that the town had fallen.

Omdurman was a shambles of shattered houses and wounded
men. Many thousands more wounded lay on the desert outside,
but of the Kalifa Abdullah, his wives, his concubines and the
surviving emirs there was no sign. His palace in Omdurman was
empty. The Kalifa had returned to the city as his lines collapsed
and prayed briefly at the tomb of the Mahdi. Then he had taken his
family and a few thousand loyal followers and fled into Kordofan.

Kitchener ordered his army to prepare for an immediate pursuit of the Kalifa and disarm all Dervishes remaining around the city. Then he went directly to the House of Stone, where he found the Prussian prisoner Karl Neufeld, still in heavy chains. It took a couple of days and a great deal of hard work with a hammer and a cold-chisel to set Neufeld free. That night, most of the Anglo-Egyptian army slept in their blankets around the town while thousands of Dervish wounded crawled across the desert towards the Nile in search of help and water.

On the following morning, 3 September, Kitchener sent the Egyptian cavalry and camel corps to scour the desert in search of the Kalifa while the rest of the army and the Dervish prisoners set about cleaning up the town. Two days after the battle he had a band and a Guard of Honour ferried across the Nile to Khartoum and there, in the cracked and weed-covered forecourt of the governor's palace, he held a memorial service for his much-admired fellow sapper, General Charles Gordon.

It was an emotional occasion; by the time it was over almost everyone on parade was in tears. The band played Gordon's favourite hymn, 'Abide with me', before the hoisting of the Union Flag and the Khedival banner, the troops giving three rousing cheers for the Queen. Kitchener was so overcome with emotion that he was unable to dismiss the parade. He did recover in time to write a long letter to the Queen, detailing his careful treatment of the British wounded, who were even now on their way to hospitals in Egypt.

Her Majesty was always very concerned about her wounded soldiers and this despatch raised Kitchener even further in her esteem. She was also moved to tears by his account of the memorial service for Gordon in Khartoum. 'Surely now he is avenged,' she noted in her diary.

In Omdurman, Kitchener proceeded to eradicate all memories of the Mahdi. On 6 September he ordered the destruction of the Mahdi's tomb and had the work done by the local people who, on exhuming the Mahdi's body, were instructed to throw it into the Nile. This gruesome task was supervised by Major W. S. Gordon, a nephew of the late general, who decided to keep the Mahdi's skull and present it to the Sirdar.

Before this tasteless presentation could take place there were other distractions. Orders arrived from Cairo, instructing Kitchener to advance to the south, where he must find and halt the party of French troops under Major Marchand who were believed to be advancing on the Nile from Equatorial Africa.

Kitchener had enough to do in and around Omdurman, where a thousand pressing matters competed for his attention, without further problems in the south. He had a population to feed, a host of wounded enemy to attend to, a country to reorganize. However, the urgency of this extra task was suddenly reinforced by the arrival on the quayside at Khartoum of two river steamers from the south, both crammed with startled Dervishes. These warriors were unaware of the recent battle and the destruction of the Kalifa's army and had come to report an engagement with another European force further upriver, near the village of Fashoda. Kitchener's victory at Omdurman had come only just in time, for the French had indeed reached the Nile.

Major Jean-Baptiste Marchand and his small party of 120 Senegalese soldiers had taken two painful years to make their way east to Fashoda and open a route from Central Africa to the Nile. Once there, firmly on the great river, he had hoisted the tricolour and declared the Upper Nile and the Bahr-el-Gazal annexed to France. He had then been attacked twice by strong Dervish forces who, having been beaten off, retired downriver in search of reinforcements and so brought confirmation of Marchand's presence to General Kitchener.

Kitchener's actions over the next few weeks were a masterpiece of military precision, diplomacy and tact, only matched by that displayed by Major Marchand. Had these two men acted differently, the 'Fashoda Incident' of 1898 might have developed into an all-out war between France and Great Britain.

Kitchener was fortunate in having Colonel Wingate as his Chief of Intelligence. Head of the Egyptian Military Intelligence Department, Wingate was a spy-master whose eyes and ears were everywhere, in the depths of the Khedive's private apartments, and throughout Omdurman. Very little happened in Egypt or the Sudan without word of it reaching Wingate, and this, plus long experience of the country – he had first arrived in Egypt in 1883 and served on the Gordon Relief Expedition with the Sudanese infantry in 1885 – made him an invaluable aide to the Sirdar. Wingate counselled Kitchener to handle this French incursion with tact rather than force and wait to see how the French government reacted once they heard of the victory at Omdurman.

On 10 September, accompanied by Wingate and Rudolf Slatin,

Kitchener set off upriver with a battalion of Sudanese troops and a battery of artillery. At Fashoda he met Marchand who had his troops in prepared positions anticipating another Dervish attack. If the arrival of Kitchener and a battalion of the Egyptian army surprised him, Marchand recovered quickly, declaring that he had hoisted the French flag, intended to annex the Bahr-el-Gazal for France and would fight if attacked.

Kitchener, wearing the full panoply of an Egyptian general and backed by a strong force, declared mildly that he intended to hoist the Egyptian flag over what he maintained was Egyptian territory and formally protested at the presence of a French force on that territory. The Khedival flag was duly hoisted and that done, the two men and their staffs sat down to a long and enjoyable lunch.

The outcome of their discussions was that both flags would be flown for the moment and the two parties, French and Egyptian, then stayed peacefully in sight of each other, leaving any decision over the future of the Upper Nile to be settled in discussion between their respective governments in London and Paris. Leaving a strong detachment of soldiers behind, Kitchener then returned to Omdurman.

During his short absence the glow of his triumph had dimmed somewhat. His neglect of the Dervish wounded had now been reported in the British press, and the public, while hailing the victory, were less than happy with Kitchener's failure to respect the wounded survivors of the gallant Dervish army. Kitchener had already explained the arrangements he had made for the treatment of the Anglo-Egyptian wounded and their rapid evacuation to Egypt; since they had sustained less than four hundred wounded, caring for his own troops was no problem. The Dervish wounded were far more numerous and many of their wounds were appalling, the result of those soft-nosed bullets.

The battle had left some sixteen thousand Dervish wounded, many now dead or still dying out on the desert and in the town. Having seen to their own wounded, many of the army doctors did what they could for the Dervishes, but their numbers swamped the available facilities, even had the will to help really existed.

A greater public row then arose over the matter of the Mahdi's skull. When Kitchener's officers presented him with the Mahdi's skull and suggested that he should mount it on a stand and use it as an inkpot, public reaction in Britain was unfavourable. Press, Parliament and the War Office already regarded the destruction of the Mahdi's tomb and the exhumation of his body as desecration and the idea that the Mahdi's skull should sit on the conquering general's desk was seen as barbaric. Her Majesty was not amused and Cromer swiftly advised Kitchener, if he valued his reputation, to have the skull decently interred in the nearest Muslim cemetery. Kitchener then left for Cairo and home and had the skull buried as he passed through Wadi Halfa. To this day, no one knows where this relic of the Mahdi lies.

In Cairo, Kitchener received a welcome that was warm but not effusive. Cromer was well aware that defeating the Mahdist army owed more to Girouard's railway and the crushing fire-power of the Anglo-Egyptian army than any strategic or tactical talent deployed by the Sirdar.

'It is a fact,' wrote Cromer later, 'that no occasion arose for the display of any great skill in these tracts of the military art. When once the British and Egyptian troops were brought face to face with the enemy, there could be little doubt of the result.'

In London, however, like Gordon before him, Kitchener was the man of the hour. He was raised to the peerage as 'Kitchener of Khartoum' – 'K of K' to his contemporaries – voted a grant of £30,000 towards an estate, given an honorary degree by Cambridge University and the freedom of a large number of towns and cities. After accepting a few of these he let it be known that instead of the usual swords and scrolls presented on such occasions, he would welcome more practical gifts – plate, bone china, paintings – for his new mansion in the countryside of Kent.

Kitchener also raised £100,000 to build a college in Omdurman, Gordon College, in memory of General Gordon. With great public support, including a donation from the Queen, the money was raised in a few weeks; Gordon College still stands, though it no longer bears his name and is now a part of the University of Khartoum. In the 1940s, long after Kitchener's death, the Mahdi's tomb was rebuilt. It still dominates the skyline over the city of Omdurman; many pilgrims visit it and the local people are convinced that the Mahdi's body still lies inside.

While Kitchener was being fêted about Britain, the French Ambassador called on the Prime Minister and informed him that in view of the new situation, Major Marchand had been ordered to leave Fashoda. An accord was signed a few weeks later and Marchand came out via Khartoum and Cairo, where he was warmly greeted by Cromer before boarding a French warship for

Marseilles. Credit for the happy ending of the 'Fashoda Incident' also went to Kitchener's account.

With his position in Britain secure, Kitchener returned to the Sudan where he took up the post of Governor-General, the role once predicted for him by Gordon. There he began to rebuild Khartoum, laying out the streets in the pattern of the Union Flag and throwing off the tutelage of Lord Cromer who was tackling the knotty problem of what to do with the newly re-conquered Sudan.

In theory at least the Sudan had been re-occupied in the name of the Khedive of Egypt, but the British had no interest in handing this hard-won territory back for further ruinous exploitation by the Egyptians. On the other hand, they could hardly take it for themselves, partly because the still-simmering French would raise an outcry, partly because the Sudan was worthless, and the Kalifa was still at large with a great number of followers.

In the end, Cromer came up with an unusual solution: a condominium. The Sudan would be ruled by Britain in the name of the Khedive of Egypt, but the Egyptians would have no say in how it was ruled. This new and curious entity, the Anglo-Egyptian Sudan, came into existence in January 1899, four months after the Battle of Omdurman. It endured until 1956 when it was replaced by the independent Republic of Sudan. The Mahdist Party, now a religious and political grouping, has played a major part in the affairs of the republic but the more recent history of the Sudan has not been happy. A military government took over in 1958 and a vicious civil war between north and south has been devastating large parts of the country since the 1970s.

The first Governor-General of the Anglo-Egyptian Sudan was, inevitably, Lord Kitchener of Khartoum. He rebuilt Khartoum, completed the building of Gordon College, and bickered constantly with Lord Cromer, in overall charge of the condominium. Flushed with success and his newly won honours, Kitchener no longer saw any need to defer to Lord Cromer. He also hunted down and eventually killed the Kalifa Abdulla.

More than a year after his defeat at Omdurman, the Kalifa was still at large. Then, in November 1899, a messenger arrived in Khartoum with news that the Kalifa was approaching the Nile some two hundred miles to the south, and a brigade of Sudanese infantry, accompanied by artillery and commanded by Colonel Wingate, was sent to intercept him. On 24 November 1899, the

Kalifa and some five thousand Dervishes were found and attacked near Kosti.

Wingate sent his men in at dawn and what followed was the usual slaughter. Once roused, the ever-gallant Ansar swarmed forward to the attack and were cut down by machine-gun and massed rifle fire. When the Sudanese overran the Dervish camp they found the bullet-riddled bodies of the Kalifa and his principal emirs lying dead on their prayer rugs, their faces turned towards Mecca.

Only Osman Digna escaped from this massacre and his freedom did not last long. He made his way east to the Hadendowa country and in January 1900 he was captured in a cave near Tokar. By then, old Osman Digna, the last of the Dervishes, was a hero even to the British, and his captivity – which lasted another twenty-six years – was spent in ever easier situations. He died in Wadi Halfa in 1926 aged ninety, honoured alike by his fellow countrymen and his former foes.

Kitchener left the Sudan in 1899 to take command of the British armies mustering against the Boers in South Africa and though the South African War was to become a graveyard of British military reputations and Kitchener's old indecisiveness returned, he survived with his reputation more or less intact. Others were less fortunate. Sir Redvers Buller led his men to defeat after defeat against entrenched Boer riflemen. When Kitchener replaced General Roberts – 'Bobs' – at the apparent end of the war, the fighting flared up again, with Boer commandos roaming at will across the veld for another two years.

Kitchener then spent seven years as Commander-in-Chief in India, but failed in his bid to become Viceroy. He became a Field Marshal in 1907 and Secretary of State for War in 1914. He still held that position when the cruiser HMS *Hampshire*, in which he was travelling to Russia, hit a mine off the Orkney islands in June 1916. Lord Kitchener, with most of his staff, was drowned.

Reginald Wingate became the second Governor-General of the Anglo-Egyptian Sudan and stayed there for the next seventeen years, suppressing various Dervish risings and army revolts, recruiting the cream of Britain's universities to serve as District Officers. The Sudan became known as 'the country of Blacks ruled by Blues' and enjoyed more prosperity and peace during that time than it had known before, or has known since.

Wingate was assisted in his task by Rudolf Slatin, who became his chief subordinate and firm friend. Slatin died in 1932 as Major-

General Baron Von Slatin Pasha KCMG, CB, his name surrounded by titles from three countries. Sir Reginald Wingate retired from public life in 1918 and lived until 1953. He was outlived by another Omdurman veteran, Winston Churchill, who died laden with honours in 1965. Sir Evelyn Baring, Lord Cromer, who became Earl of Cromer in 1902, left Egypt in 1907 and died in London ten years later.

The fate of the other players in this twenty-year drama may be quickly told. Father Ohrwalder returned to the Sudan after Omdurman and stayed there working as a simple priest until his death in 1912. Karl Neufeld, who had endured so much, and stoutly refused to abandon his faith, returned to civilization to find himself an outcast. He was accused of manufacturing arms and ammunition for the Kalifa and of actively fighting on the Dervish side at Omdurman. The German government declared that he had forfeited German nationality by staying away so long, ignoring the fact that a prisoner incarcerated in the House of Stone had little choice in the matter. Neufeld stayed in Egypt and opened a travel agency in Aswan but was expelled on the outbreak of the Great War. He returned to Germany and died there in 1918.

The saddest fate of all befell the heroic Hector Macdonald. After the battle it was widely expected by the British public that a great deal of glory and some generous reward would fall on his shoulders. None of this happened. His contribution to the victory, though lauded to the skies in the press, was dismissed in a few lines of Kitchener's report.

Macdonald was promoted to full colonel and appointed ADC to the Queen, a doubtful honour as the Queen already had scores of ADCs. The only practical effect of this appointment was to cost Macdonald money he could not easily spare for a new uniform. There was widespread resentment at this treatment and a Scottish newspaper asked tartly if the government was really interested in recruiting Scottish soldiers.

Macdonald returned to Britain in 1899 and his fellow countrymen tried to make up for these slights. He was fêted and given banquets, at one of which he was presented with a sword of honour by the Duke of Atholl; Kitchener, though invited, declined to attend. He met the Prince of Wales, reminding him that he had been Sergeant of the Guard when the Prince visited India in 1877. He visited his home town of Dingwall, where there are still many memorials to his life and fame, and he may even have seen his wife and son. By 1900 he was in Cape Town as a local Major-General, and he commanded the Highland Brigade in the South African War.

The Highland Brigade had already been shot up badly at Magersfontein and then again at the Modder River, just before Macdonald took command. He was wounded in the attack on Cronje's laager, and after that nothing went right for him. In July of 1900 he requested a posting to India and Kitchener, who was now in command, sent him there on the first troopship. In 1901 he went to Ceylon as Commander-in-Chief and his problems came to a head.

During his time in South Africa a story had gone about that Macdonald was homosexual and had had an affair with a Boer prisoner. Nothing came of this but such stories would not go away. There were comments in Ceylon society about the General's bachelor habits and in 1902 a snide and unpleasant letter appeared in *The Times* of Ceylon intimating that Macdonald did not like ladies.

A year later two schoolmasters complained to the Governor of Ceylon that Macdonald had made homosexual advances to their pupils. After that the end came swiftly. The Governor sent Macdonald home to consult his superiors and the Secretary of State for War sent him back to Ceylon to face a court martial. On the journey back, Macdonald shot himself through the head in the bedroom of a Paris hotel.

One by one, and in their various ways, the actors in the twenty-year drama of the Mahdiya faded from the scene. Less than a hundred years after Omdurman, all signs of the British occupation have vanished from the Sudan and Egypt. The statue of de Lesseps is gone from Port Said, and the statue of Gordon, which stood for many years in Khartoum, now stands in the grounds of the Gordon Boys' School in Surrey.

The Suez Canal, which was a prime cause of Britain's involvement in Egypt and hence the Sudan in the 1880s, functions still as an international waterway. It has survived two World Wars and countless local Arab-Israeli incursions and in 1956 it provided the British government and people with a forceful reminder that the days of empire were over.

Early in 1956, the Egyptian government broke their treaty with Britain and France, nationalized the Canal Company and seized the Suez Canal. The ghost of Colonel Arabi must have smiled. That act led to the Suez landings of 6 November 1956, and though the British and French troops got ashore and took their objectives the world had had enough of imperial adventures. After a few days the United Nations moved in, the Anglo-French forces were obliged to withdraw and any imperial pretensions left to the British were fatally exposed as false.

Britain's takeover of Egypt was the last adventure of the Victorian age. Prime Minister Gladstone always maintained that entering Egypt, let alone the Sudan, would prove a terrible mistake and did all he could to prevent it. The story of how and why he failed in that sensible ambition has been the major theme of this book and history proved, as history so often does, that the peace-loving man is usually right.

Select Bibliography

Sir Samuel Baker, *The Albert N'yanza*, 2 vols., Macmillan, 1874
Michael Barthorp, *War on the Nile*, Blandford Press, 1986
Charles Beatty, *Ferdinand de Lesseps*, Eyre and Spottiswoode, 1956
Bennet Burleigh, *Khartoum Campaign 1898*, Chapman and Hall, 1899
Winston Spencer Churchill, *The River War*, Longmans, Green, 1899
The Earl of Cromer, *Modern Egypt*, 2 vols., Macmillan, 1908
Lord Elton, *General Gordon*, Collins, 1954
Byron Farwell, *Queen Victoria's Little Wars*, W. W. Norton, 1972
——*Mr Kipling's Army*, W. W. Norton, 1981
——*Eminent Victorian Soldiers*, W. W. Norton, 1985
——*Prisoners of the Mahdi*, V. W. Norton, 1989
Donald Featherstone, *Khartoum 1885*, Osprey, 1993
——*Omdurman 1898*, Osprey, 1993
General C. G. Gordon, *The Journals at Khartoum*, Kegan Paul, 1885
Philip Guedalla, *The Queen and Mr Gladstone*, Doubleday, Doran 1933
P. M. Holt, *A Modern History of the Sudan*, Weidenfeld and Nicolson, 1961
John Hyslop, *Sudan Story*, Naldrett Press, 1952
Joseph H. Lehmann, *All Sir Garnet*, Jonathan Cape, 1964
Elizabeth Longford, *Victoria R. I.*, Weidenfeld and Nicolson, 1964
Philip Magus, *Kitchener: Portrait of an Imperialist*, John Murray, 1958
John Marlowe, *The Making of the Suez Canal*, Cresset Press, 1964
Alan Moorehead, *The White Nile*, Hamish Hamilton, 1962
——*The Blue Nile*, Hamish Hamilton, 1962
Father Joseph Ohrwalder, *Ten Years in the Mahdi's Camp*, Sampson Low, 1893
Rudolf Slatin, *Fire and Sword in the Sudan*, Edward Arnold, 1896

George W. Steevens, *With Kitchener to Khartoum*, Blackwoods, 1898

A. B. Theobald, *The Mahdiya*, Longmans, Green, 1951

University Press of Africa, *Sudan Today*, UPA, 1971

Philip Warner, *Dervish*, Macdonald, 1973

Scott Wayne, *Egypt and the Sudan*, Lonely Planet, 1994

Robert Wilkinson-Latham, *The Sudan Campaigns 1881–1898*, Osprey, 1976

F. R. Wingate, *Mahdism and the Egyptian Sudan*, Macmillan, 1891

Index